Not My Worst Day

*A personal journey through violence
in the Great Lakes Region of Africa*

Alex Mvuka Ntung

with Chris Sanderson

Published by EARS press

Not My Worst Day

*A personal journey through violence
in the Great Lakes Region of Africa*

By Alex Mvuka Ntung

with Chris Sanderson

Published by EARS press

ISBN: 978-0-9575559-0-7

Little Lamb had lost his mother.
All alone in the forest, he felt afraid but he tried his
very best to look strong and fearless as he trotted on.
When he met Snake, he stood firmly and looked him
in the eye. Snake laughed, "Just go! Today is not your
worst day; you will die by someone else's hands, not
mine, and the route ahead is even harder."
So Little Lamb continued on his way,
trying to be brave.

Next he met Lion. Hiding his fear, he looked
Lion in the eye and the same thing happened:
"Just go!" said Lion, "Today is not your worst day.
You will die by someone else's hands, not mine,
and the route ahead is even harder."

Then he met Crocodile and other fearsome beasts
but always the same thing happened.

Finally, after many terrifying encounters,
he was safely back, by luck as much as by
his own bravery, with his mother.

From an old African story

This book is dedicated to the characters in
this book who did meet their worst day

Contents

	Acknowledgments	vi
	Foreword	viii
CHAPTER 1:	Who am I?	1
CHAPTER 2:	My early years	11
CHAPTER 3:	Danger	25
CHAPTER 4:	The love of herding	41
CHAPTER 5:	Lost in the jungle	50
CHAPTER 6:	Having fun with AK-47 Bullets	58
CHAPTER 7:	Hostage in a war zone	62
CHAPTER 8:	Lower secondary school	71
CHAPTER 9:	My first glimpse of the wider world	78
CHAPTER 10:	The search for a new life in the city	84
CHAPTER 11:	Starting Azahuri Institute	90
CHAPTER 12:	Malaria and worse	96
CHAPTER 13:	Tension rises	106
CHAPTER 14:	Jimmy is born	116
CHAPTER 15:	Tutsi "crimes"	122
CHAPTER 16:	Ambush	130
CHAPTER 17:	Another perilous journey	137
CHAPTER 18:	Homeless	145
CHAPTER 19:	Hardship	154

CHAPTER 20: Things get better 161

CHAPTER 21: Catastrophe 167

CHAPTER 22: Escaping from Uvira 178

CHAPTER 23: Arriving in Rwanda after genocide 183

CHAPTER 24: Reunions and losses 192

CHAPTER 25: Rushashi – an opportunity 198

CHAPTER 26: A new challenge 206

CHAPTER 27: Expulsions 215

CHAPTER 28: Escalation in the Congo 225

CHAPTER 29: Uganda 232

CHAPTER 30: Back to Rwanda, "the country of 240
a thousand hills"

CHAPTER 31: Becoming a humanitarian worker 249

CHAPTER 32: Genocide in the Congo 253

CHAPTER 33: My family experiences "Africa's 263
World War"

CHAPTER 34: Child victims 270

CHAPTER 35: Child Soldiers 274

CHAPTER 36: Inside NGO Work 282

Epilogue 290
Further reading 294
Timeline 296
About the author 304

Acknowledgments

THIS BOOK WOULD NOT HAVE BEEN POSSIBLE without the invaluable commitment of wonderful people with great skills and intelligence. They are: Chris Sanderson, Gillian Brookes, James Kerr and Tim Lay. I am especially indebted to Chris Sanderson for her countless hours in shaping the drafts of this book. Her creative skills helped to arrange a well-told story and led me to focus on facts as they happened.

The inspiration for writing the book came from a number of sources: firstly, my friend George Budagu, who tirelessly encouraged me to document my personal experiences. His courage and commitment in promoting justice and fairness has been the basis of my strength to complete this book. His friendship has taught me to actively contribute towards leading change, as a mechanism for healing myself and others. Using this approach, I later realised that being in the position of helping others meant hiding my own vulnerabilities. Writing this book has been the first time I have re-connected with some of my most painful memories and experiences of tragic events. It has been emotionally draining and has sometimes caused horrific nightmares.

Coming from the Great Lakes Region of Africa to Britain, I chose to close down my past so that I could move into the future. Culturally, it was extremely challenging to detach my community experience from my personal experience. The four hour visit from my friend Richard Wilson in 2008 was a defining moment in considering the 'I' experienced rather than 'we' experienced.

My involvement in the BBC 'My Story' competition which aimed to find the most remarkable true life stories in Britain, in which thousands people sent in their stories was another motivational opportunity. I was amazed to see my story being short listed from the thousands, and to become part of the fifteen winning stories broadcast on BBC 1 in October 2010. Through this, I met amazing people, including Frank Gardner whose story of survival and remarkable journey shows that there is indeed 'light' at the end of the tunnel.

I am very grateful to Kay Green and Erica Smith for their professional help and support, to Elias Ntuyahaga for your assistance in conveying the historical backgrounds of some of the events referred to in this book. To a wonderful charity, Children In Crisis, for their help in accessing some of the photographic images from the High Plateaux and your tireless commitment in promoting education for wars affected children in one of the most inaccessible places in the world. I am grateful to friends Myriam Schelling, Carmen Nibigira, Eliane Baumgartner, Zephir Grayland, Tim Miller and Pablo Mcfee for their advice, encouragement and backing to take a decisive action.

I am particularly thankful to my wife Esther, daughters Abigail and Keziah for their patience, constant encouragement and support, both practical and emotional, throughout preparation and during the time I worked on this book. I am thankful for the peaceful life I enjoy in Great Britain, which has provided a space to write and an opportunity to reflect upon the amazing safety that my daughters Abigail and Keziah will always enjoy, I am grateful that their lives will be completely different from my childhood, none of them will have to look up at their shoulders, fearing to see the Worst Day like I did. Their aspirations are unlimited and of greatest potential. This is my wish to all the children of the world.

Foreword

Chris Sanderson

ALEX FEELS THAT HIS ARRIVAL IN EUROPE AS A REFUGEE in 2000 brought him not only to another place but also to another historical era, as if he had taken a trip through time itself. This is not to say that he escaped a "primitive" life of suffering. The book, especially in its early chapters, gives a fascinating insight into the traditional life of his people, showing a rich and valuable culture that commands respect. His people are still struggling to preserve those positive aspects of their lifestyle whilst facing the double threat of modernisation and on-going violence. Readers born in the "developed" world will sympathise with this dilemma and consider how many of our traditional values – for example the strength of family and community bonds – have been eroded by our modern way of life. Through these pages we can experience, perhaps, a journey back into history when we read of the traditional life of people who live in small villages far from modern amenities. Sadly, we may also see similar causes of conflict.

Alex almost called the book "Between Two Worlds" to convey his personal feelings of dramatic contrast; how, even when he takes a plane to attend an international conference on human rights or when he sits working at the computer, he is able to sense within himself another person, a man who would enjoy herding cattle in the high plateaus of South Kivu, far from any modern housing or amenities. However, the book is far more than a personal story of experiencing two completely different lifestyles: his journey takes him through extraordinary experiences which will make the reader aware of many hybrid worlds between those two extremes: places where traditional and "modern" clash and erupt into confusion and conflict. The events that form the background to his journey are modern African history and the people he meets on the way are ordinary people whose lives have been torn apart by it. For me personally, the wealth of this book is in the variety of characters and how they are affected by the horrific events that have ripped through their part of the world. What previously I had only heard about through the news is made personal in these pages. I now have names of individuals to give faces to some of those grim statistics of violence and genocide. For me, Alex's story is not just his personal account: it is a testimony to the people he met on the way, many of whom did not survive the upheavals. It is a story that records the paradox of human nature – that people can be unbelievably cruel or unbelievably kind.

Alex found writing his autobiography extremely challenging. Not only did he need to struggle to remember in detail events he would prefer to put out of his mind, but also the whole concept of writing about himself was culturally strange. In Banyamulenge society, the community matters so much more than the individual that expressing important events using the first person pronoun (I, me, my, mine) is almost unnatural. Added to this, English is his fifth language, after Kinyamulenge (his first language which is mutually intelligible with Kinyarwanda, Kirundi and other "Rwandaphone" dialects), Lingala, Swahili and French. We worked mainly with drafts sent by email, meeting or speaking on the telephone sometimes to clarify points. After a while, we realised that it was easier for both of us if he wrote in French, the language of his secondary education in the Congo and University in Rwanda. Much of what he had to write was emotionally draining and, occasionally, we needed to talk about it rather than work from a written document.

It was difficult to know how much historical/political explanation we could give without interrupting the flow of his story. Alex now has an in-depth understanding of the upheavals in Central Africa but, as a boy, he was simply hurt and confused. We felt that this autobiography should express the pain and confusion of his boyhood experiences rather than give a retrospective, educated view of what happened. It is hoped that the time line will give more depth to events for those readers who would like to understand his life in its historical perspective and, of course, more factual information is available on-line and in other books. Alex's story as told here holds the reader's attention because it is seen through the eyes of an ordinary person: it brings humanity to the bare facts and statistics that we hear on the news.

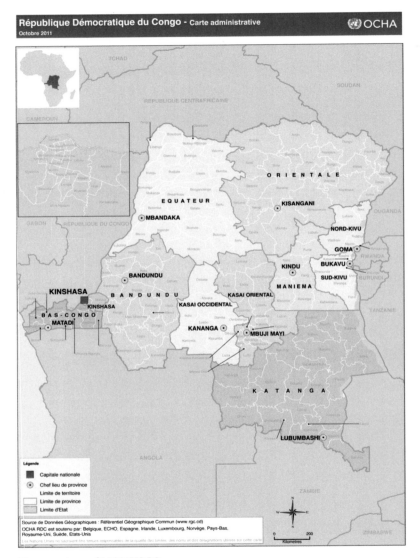

Map, courtesy of MONUSCO

CHAPTER 1
Who am I?

I HESITATE TO WRITE EVEN THE FIRST LINE OF MY STORY. I would like to begin with "My name is so and so and I was born in such and such a time at such and such a place" but these three basic things are not easy to say. The date of birth on my passport is an educated guess and my name on it is not the one I was given at birth; as for the place, I know the name of my village and area but my country has changed name several times even within the space of my lifetime. My story is one where history, geography and politics combine to complicate what should be the simplest statements about when and where I was born.

Where was I born? A map of Africa still shows quite plainly by its straight lines how bizarrely Africa was carved up between the colonial powers in 1884. A huge area (as big as the whole of Western Europe) was allocated to King Leopold of Belgium and called the Congo Free State. Its borders did not take into account the hundreds of different languages and dialects representing varying ethnicities and cultural groups and some cultures and languages straddled over them. In 1908, King Leopold's control having become notorious for its exploitation and brutality, the country was taken over by the Belgian government and renamed the Belgian Congo. After Independence in 1960 (for which the country was not well prepared, having very few Congolese educated beyond primary school level or trained in administration) it became the Congo; then in 1971 under President Mobutu it changed to Zaire, and now it is the Democratic Republic of Congo (DRC). These changes were not peaceful – this is a part of the world that has been torn by conflict for decades. Throughout all its changes of name, Congo/Zaire/DRC has been diverse in its cultures. It has as many as four hundred different ethnic groups speaking hundreds of different languages and dialects so divisions run deep, with its various peoples finding difficulty in identifying themselves as fellow citizens.

My ancestors were one of the tribal groups whose traditional land did not fit into the borders created by the colonialists; they were the Banyarwanda or people of Itombwe, Tutsi moving across an area that overlapped the colonial borders. It was a beautiful land watered by many rivers and streams with large, open, green spaces nestling between breathtakingly majestic mountains – a land perfect for herding cattle. Needing to move the cattle according to the availability of pasture, they were nomadic and therefore never completely accepted by other ethnic groups in the region but they lived peacefully enough alongside them, trading their cattle for items the other groups produced. Tension with other tribes grew after colonisation when they were expected to respect the new borders and settle in one place.

My people know of this recent history as well as more distant events because of our very strong oral tradition: still today the elders can recite the names not only of close relatives but also of their forefathers for several generations back. My father told me in great detail the story of his great grandfather, Kayira Sagitwe, a traditional king of great influence and vision. During a devastating famine in the area that is now Rwanda in early 1800, he provided refuge and protection to families that fled the starvation. He himself had great wealth in the traditional form of thousands of cattle (the king's cattle), and many servants. Before the Bazungu (white people) came, Kayira's kingdom was highly respected by all the surrounding communities and tribes. The Bazungu, however, were so impressed by his organisation and influence in the area that they were afraid it would threaten their own. So, his people were not among the tribal groups that were favoured under colonial rule. Using a complex system of "divide and rule" that the British had first introduced to Africa, they manipulated concepts of ethnicity to organise and change existing chiefdoms and then decided which groups had a "native authority". The colonial citizenship law stated that to be Congolese a person had to belong both to the state (the Belgian Congo as it was then) and to a native authority. Our people were one of about four groups in the Kivu region who were not given their own native authority. (Nowadays they are the only one to remain excluded on this

2

basis.) This constituted a threat to Kayira's leadership because other chiefs were recognized while he was not. It also sharpened divisions between various tribes by highlighting tribal differences and making a contrived distinction between those who were "indigenous" and those who were not. Historically, our people were nomadic and had crossed areas that were now suddenly seen to be different countries divided by official borders. This encouraged the perception that they were outsiders, foreigners in their own land. Racial exclusion, with persecution based on cultural background and perceived differences in physical features, followed. With no "native right" there was little that could be done to refute these injustices: my people were simply denied the right to be a distinct ethnic group living lawfully within the borders of the new state. The violent problems that continue right until the present day can all be said to be a result of the "cross-border identities" that resulted from the way that Africa was parcelled into different countries by the colonial powers so long ago.

When my great great grandfather died, his son Kayira Bigimba took over. Like his father, he is held in great respect amongst our people because he opposed the Belgians' refusal to recognise our right to move from place to place, seeing it as an attempt to enslave his people. The colonial government, claiming to be trying to prevent conflict between our tribe and the Bafulero tribe, forcibly "relocated" our clan and some other clans from our tribe to another area. This was to reduce what they saw as a threat to the colonial authorities and to prevent conflict with King Mahina of the Bafulero. Known as Lulenge, the new homeland was terribly inhospitable. Set in the middle of tropical forest at low altitude, it was plagued with tsetse mosquitoes that are responsible for spreading such diseases as tropical elephantiasis as well as with microscopic trypanosomes, which cause sleeping sickness in humans and trypanosomiasis in animals. Life in this place was tragic. Thousands of cattle were lost and many people died of sleeping sickness.

My great grandfather, King Kayira Bigimba continued to fight against being forced to live in Lulenge. My father's generation was born in this place of exile, which even today is still called Kwa Bigimba (Bigimba's place) after my ancestor, and after one of his wives Nyiranzogeye. At one point, the whole clan made a determined attempt to leave Lulenge but were stopped by the Belgian authorities when they reached a place called Mumihanga. They were forced to go back to that inhospitable land they hated so much.

My father was quite literally born into the middle of this dispute and because his mother went into the final stages of labour as the group was being driven back by force, shot at by the colonial police. Unable to keep up with the rest in the confusion of the flight, she was left behind and had to deliver her baby, my father, alone. Under normal circumstances she would have had the support of friends and relatives experienced in childbirth to support her. They would have encouraged her and held her by the arms as she squatted in the traditional way, feet on birthing stones to give space beneath. As it was, she gave birth alone. Terrified of the pursuing soldiers, she could not rest for long. As soon as she could walk again, she took off her *urubega* (animal skin used to cover the middle part of the body), wrapped her new baby in it and carried him all the way to Kuwinzonvu to join the rest of the family. Eventually they were allowed to leave the place they hated so much but the new land allocated was in a remote area isolated from recent developments.

Our tribe is still located in that area, Minembwe, in South Kivu in the north-eastern part of DRC and it has become our homeland. The Banyamulenge attitude towards "home" and land is shaped by the needs of our animals. Our philosophy of *Iwacu*, meaning where we belong, has a spiritual and traditional significance. Iwacu includes an intricate and personal relationship with the wide area of land where our cattle have multiplied. Here we have raised children, grown crops and buried our dead. In this wide-spread place, we have worshipped Imana, the supreme God, and celebrated births and deaths. While we may not necessarily live for a relatively long period in one specific place, family land is identified by an umuvumu tree grown to symbolize how long the community has lived in a particular land (*Itongo*); this tree stands as a memorial to all our relatives who lived and died there.

Minembwe is a spectacularly beautiful area but has not been developed and still has practically no basic services such as roads,

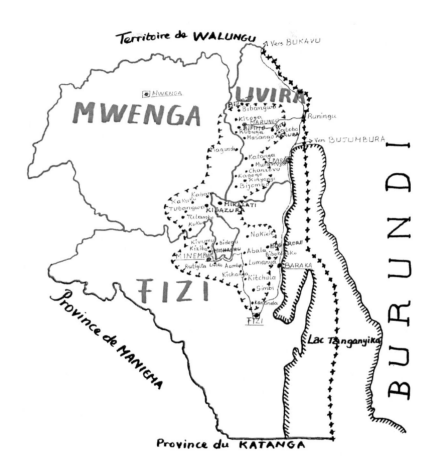

South Kivu Region, includes city of Uvira, Lake Tanganika,
villages of High Plateaux of Itombwe and Fizi areas
Map courtesy of Children in Crisis

Courtesy of Children in Crisis

Typical Minembwe village huts
Courtesy of Children in Crisis

electricity or healthcare. Most people live in small hamlets, clusters of four or five traditionally built houses, with some living in larger villages of as many as fifty or so houses with perhaps other facilities such as a school and church. We are known now as the Banyamulenge which means 'people who live in hamlets in the Mulenge mountains'; this is a name that became popular in the 1970s in an attempt to make other people nearby accept us as fellow Congolese rather than accuse us of being foreigners, Tutsi who should be sent back to where they come from. This mistrust of our origins dates back to the old colonial laws about settling but has been exacerbated by the other political upheavals and our reluctance to take part in political movements, most notably the Mulelist rebellion (*see timeline*). Other ethnic groups came to view us with even more mistrust and repression gradually increased with government attacks in the area commonplace.

It was hard for my people to identify with "the State" when our only real sense of belonging to it was through government taxes and from attacks we couldn't understand. Largely these attacks were caused by unpaid soldiers who stole instead of earning a wage and who viewed us as Tutsi foreigners. Some of them were simply gratuitous.

One of my childhood memories is of seeing a neighbour, Eremiya, being stabbed by soldiers from a paracommando unit trained by Belgian Mercenaries. He had been trying to defend a woman called Leya who was being beaten for no apparent reason. With childhood innocence, we gathered around to see what was happening and to get a closer look at their guns, the first modern instruments we had ever seen. Suddenly, it changed to complete horror as the soldiers started beating everyone including us. They continued stabbing Eremiya in the head and neck and we recoiled as his blood spurted all over us. We were terrified and started screaming. Eremiya was helpless because the other men had gone to look after cattle.

When government or rebel troops were in the area our people would warn each other through our traditional methods of communication – whistling or shouting from one hamlet to another '*mube maso mube maso twatewe*' which means 'be alert we have been attacked!' Where the weather or distance made oral communication impossible, strong runners would go off to other places to warn people there; then fresh runners would take over and transfer the message to the next hamlets in a complex relay. So, in a matter of about thirty minutes, everyone living in a very large geographical area would have been forewarned.

Through measures such as this, my people have survived years of insecurity but they have been left with a mistrust of authority and "development". Many of the older generation, such as my father, tried hard to keep to their traditional lifestyle rather than become embroiled in the new way of life. As head of our family my father tried to keep us safe by keeping out of any new developments and continuing as much as possible with life as it had always been. He knew that we were not safe to do as we pleased and could not easily move into "modern" society so he never encouraged his children to go to school. He let his daughters marry very young in the traditional way and he encouraged us all to steer clear of politics and the new ways that seemed to bring so much disruption and violence with them. So this is the place and people I was born into – people with a strong sense of community but surrounded by a world that was often antagonistic.

And when was I born? Amongst my people no written records were kept of births though, in accordance with our custom, my family remember the season and important events that were happening at that time. I was born in the rainy season a few years after the Mulelist rebellion and two or three years after our dictator, President Mobutu, renamed the country Zaire. Like my brother Oreni, who was a year or so older than me, I was not allowed a "Christian" name. This means I was born after Mobutu's *retour a l'authenticité* which was introduced in 1972. '*Olinga olinga te*', meaning 'everything or nothing' in Lingala (a language widely understood in the region), was Mobutu's main slogan and whether you wanted it or not, you were born a member of his political party and followed his laws. The "return to authenticity" was, for him, about returning to African cultural values and making these values a part of our everyday lives. He introduced various measures such as banning religious symbols and tightening the dress code so that, for example, ties were not allowed because they were too European. Titles and names were also affected. Nobody was to be called Monsieur or Madame or the like; everyone was called Citoyen or Citoyenne, meaning "citizen". Also we could have African names only and those Christian names that had become popular since the missionaries had converted us were banned. In this way people who were born before me, including my older siblings, were forced to change the names they commonly used.

These remembered events gave me a way of providing an official birth date for my passport, placing my birth in November 1974. Strange though it may seem, my parents remember this time as happy and peaceful, not because it was peaceful in the true sense of the word but because it was less violent than it had been previously or has been since. Violence can become a way of life where instability is measured by how severe one event is in comparison to another.

What is my real name then? My people do not traditionally take on their father's name as a surname, though often they take their grandfather's or the clan leader's name. This did not happen in my case: I was just called Mvuka Ntungane. In 1990, Mobutu gave a speech which repealed much of his authenticity law and gave people the right to dress as they wished and use whatever names they wanted. Many people reverted then to Christian names they had used before the law and many, like me, took pleasure in choosing a new "modern" name, that was when I became Alexis, or Alex as I prefer to be called, though this never meant much to my family who saw it simply as my "town name". By 1993, discrimination and exclusion of my people had become so strong that it was embedded within the corrupt system and I was afraid that my name, which other Congolese recognise as belonging to my language, would mark me out for failure in examinations. It was at this point, before taking my important *examen d'Etat* (National Examination – the equivalent of the baccalaureate) that I became Alex Mvuka Ntung. There was no legal procedure involved, I simply chose that name. It may sound rather odd to many people but it gave me, I hoped, some anonymity. Discrimination against my people, who were clearly Tutsi both by their physical appearance and their language, had grown and I hoped this name would at least hide my background on paper. The name has stayed with me officially though my friends and family do not use it.

On the one hand, I was born into a world where I had the security of being loved and cared for by a proud people with strong traditions. Long before the missionaries came we had strong beliefs, even a belief in a Supreme Being, and a strict moral code. To a large extent our beliefs and values were transmitted through the traditional stories we told in social gatherings by the fire in the evening or under a shady tree in the heat of the afternoon. Embedded within the narrative of these traditional stories handed down from one generation to another were our religious beliefs, philosophy and much of the wisdom of our forefathers. From them we learnt how to survive as a group and adhere to strict codes of conduct. Within our group we are almost one large extended family with a strict hierarchy that gives everyone a place that we do not question. Children are loved and cared for not only by their close family but by any older person and I was lucky to be given the self confidence that comes from being born into this supportive environment. On the other hand, as I grew up I came to realise more and more that I was surrounded by a wider society that rejected me and my people. I travelled away from home to find a new world where everyone would be treated fairly but then I frequently found myself alone and rejected, even at times in mortal danger. I have witnessed many horrors. Through it all I have believed that a fairer, safer world is possible and I have travelled a long way to find it. Now I am a British citizen with work, family and other strong ties in England but in my heart I am not only that. I am British, African, Rwandan and Congolese.

CHAPTER 2
My early years

*Note: the traditional practices described
in this chapter continue to this day*

I WAS BORN IN A PLACE CALLED ILUNDU, one of the many little hamlets of *les Hauts Plateaux* (the High Plateaus) of the Itombwe area, beautiful rolling hills accessible only after climbing 2000 metres or more through rainforest. Still today there are no roads either into or within this area and it has always been extremely remote. Partly savannah and partly forested, it is scenically spectacular but with no towns or modern facilities of any sort. Largely because of this isolation, the Banyamulenge were the last people in the Congo to be converted to Christianity. They had always had their own strong spiritual values: faith is important in helping us to understand what happens and in revealing predictions about the future, as well as in giving fortitude to live through violence and extreme problems.

The earliest convert shocked the community by breaking traditions, such as by eating meat, fish and eggs and wearing shorts. As a result he was cast out but the movement continued to grow until it became so powerful that it influenced almost everyone in the community. Very quickly Christianity was established and greeted with enthusiasm, many of our traditional songs and dances being adapted to it. So when I was born, the *gusohora umubyeyi*, the official name-giving ceremony after the mother's customary seven day confinement, was traditional but then a few weeks later there was also the *kubarika*, the christening. Both ceremonies were important and loud with music, dancing and singing, notably the atmospheric Swahili song, '*Tunawatiya mikononi mwako watoto hawa uwalinde sana*', meaning 'We place these little children in your hands. God, please protect them'.

When they called me "Mvuka", many people laughed in surprise because this name does not have any relevant meaning within my clan as names normally do. It simply means "destined to be born" and I have often been teased about it. Really, it was only given to me as a sort of joke, because it was the same name as an unusual man who lived a strange life independent from the rest of the community. He did things beyond society's norms, the strangest being that he used to cut his own hair – a sure symbol of rebelling from his own people.

Like all the other children, I grew up regarding practically all adults as parents, grandparents, uncles or aunts and had implicit trust in them as well as great respect. Our traditional way of life is firmly fixed in the extended family and community. The immediate family is of very special importance though, and my father's brothers' families are regarded equal to my own family, their sons and sisters being my direct brothers and sisters. My cousin Ndoli was like a twin brother to me. When he was a baby of a few weeks old, his mother fell ill and so he was breastfed by mine, even though I was only a month or two older and she was still feeding me. This meant we were *abonse rimwe*, an expression that means we shared the same breast milk, like twins. Later, when his mother had recovered, we spent a lot of time with her together too. Ndoli and I remain close though thousands of miles now separate us.

From my actual parents I had two sisters and three brothers when I was born; two more brothers and a sister were born later. When I was very small, my sisters cared for me while my mother worked, though the eldest, Dina, married when I was only about two or three years old so I hardly knew her. My brothers were an important influence on me also. The eldest was a father or uncle figure to me while Oreni, who was only about a year older than me, became something of a role model – the handsome, talented big brother I always looked up to. My mother was closer to us than our father because traditionally fathers stay distant and women care for the little ones. I was very close to her and can still remember many of the songs she used to sing to me; there were many different ones to entertain, to comfort, to send to sleep and so on.

While the women stay in the village area looking after the children and growing crops such as beans and maize, the men spend a lot of time away with the cattle; they see their role as fathers to encourage their sons to be strong and tough. In my case though, I spent more time with my father than anyone else in my family and so became closer to him than is usual in our society. This was because I had a medical condition that meant when I cried a lot I would lose consciousness so my family spoilt me a little to avoid making me cry. Thus I had an opportunity to be closer to both my mother and my father than most children were.

I believe now that being rather "indulged" in this way helped me to develop a sense of pride, freedom of expression and opinions. It seems I was always more confident and forceful than most of the other children.

When he was young, my uncle, Zakaria Semagagara, had been one of first five men from our tribe to convert to Christianity. At first this was seen as a disgrace but later, when the whole community converted, he became one of our most important religious leaders. When I was still very small, he was appointed to lead the newly established church in a larger village of about fifty homes called Runundu and, when he moved there, we went too.

Though this village was larger with its own church and school, the buildings were of the same type, made of bush materials. Our nomadic origins had meant that houses needed to be easy to build as we were constantly moving. Built using skills passed from father to son through the generations, they were simple huts relatively easy to build and this style of building was retained even when, due to laws introduced in the colonial period, our lifestyle changed from nomadic to semi-nomadic and our villages became more permanent. Bamboo or other wood was used for the posts and long grass for the roofs, the walls being made of small sticks sealed with muddy soil.

Being semi-nomadic rather than fully nomadic meant we had our base village but most of the men and boys moved livestock around larger areas of land according to the season and availability of water and pasturage. Every dry season (in Western terms, between May and October) they moved from one place to another to search for good pasture so the men and older boys were away from the village for long stretches of time. Whether away or in the village, it was the men and boys who looked after the cattle, including milking them. For me, this meant I began to work with cows at the age of about four.

Women never worked directly with the cows but they were responsible for collecting milk and making butter. Though men would do the physically heavier work, cutting down trees and burning wood to make the gardens, women do most of the farming, largely beans and maize. In the fully nomadic days they would also have found food through gathering and by exchange of goods with other tribes. My sisters, like all the other girls, began these tasks as soon as they were able to: carrying water from the nearby streams, fetching firewood from the forest, cleaning the house and collecting and preparing food. They learnt not only how to cultivate beans, sweet potato, cassava and other farmed produce but also which wild herbs to recognise as useful. They helped our mother to cook, using the traditional pots that we made ourselves or bamboo containers. The girls also had to look after all the necessary equipment to milk cows, though it was a man's job to actually milk them.

Herding and milking were the most important tasks in our society and milk was the most important part of our diet. In traditional times, when we were still fully nomadic, there had been very little farming so people relied on milk. Generally speaking, we didn't drink water. If we had seen someone drinking water, we would offer milk, thinking they must have insufficient. In the evening we would usually eat *umutsima* (made from maize flour) embellished with *imboga* (any vegetable dish to accompany it) along with plenty of *amata* (milk). In fact, milk was always considered the most important part of our diet and, when they were away herding, the men and boys lived on nothing else. Though we kept animals, they were for prestige and trade with other tribes rather than for eating.

We had two main meals each day: one prepared very early in the morning and the other at night. Very young children were also given a drink of milk at midday. "Very young" children would mean those who were not yet considered strong enough to look after cattle on their own, which probably would mean less than about six years old. As well as having no calendars and no officially recorded dates of birth and so on, there were, of course, no clocks or watches. We read the sky and the small children had their milk when the sun was vertical above. My father taught me how to estimate the time from the sun. For example, our home had a hole in the wall for light and air but that also served as a clock – when the morning sunlight came through it, this would indicate that it was time to wake up to help my older brothers and father to milk cows. When the sun was vertical above, it was time to take the baby cows to the river or streams; just after it started to slant I should return home.

Water was kept in a pot inside our hut so the morning began with a quick wash of our faces and mouths, cleaning our teeth using coals or fingers as a toothbrush. Then the men, with the support of the whole family, milked cows before the first meal of the day. This early morning was the busiest time for the whole family as we prepared for a new day, milking cows, clearing cow dung and collecting cows' urine, which was used as disinfectant for the pots that stored milk. Drinking vessels were also washed in cows' urine – it made the drink taste a little bitter but kept the milk cleaner and fresher.

As soon as they were old enough, children had to take part in useful activities but we still found time to play. Generally speaking, girls and boys had completely different interests and games. I remember that girls spent a lot of time with *mukange* – a game involving two girls jumping, while looking into each other's eyes and clapping hands. One of the two girls would make sure that her feet remained oblique while the other kept hers straight. Each had to watch the other's foot movement carefully and the winner is the one who can mimic her partner's movements perfectly. Like girls the world over perhaps, making and playing with dolls was important. They used the flower of the *ibisage*, a beautiful and soft plant that flourishes close to streams at different seasons, to make the doll. Its large, soft, round, multi-coloured flowers made a pretty head to peep out of any cloth they found to wrap round the stem. They then carried their "baby" tied on to their backs, just as adult women carried their young children. At meal times, they would mix dust with water on a leaf "plate" to feed the child or hold it to their chests to suckle. Knowing that when they were adults they would be in charge of milk and making butter, they made their own little *inkongoro* (milk vases) from ibishasha sticks or hollowed out bamboo. They also sometimes played at being grown women doing household tasks.

A time when boys and girls would be together was for storytelling – a very important part of our way of life. Embedded within the narrative of these traditional stories handed down from one generation to another were our religious beliefs, philosophy and much of the wisdom of our forefathers. From them we learnt how to survive as a group and adhere to strict codes of conduct. In the heat of the afternoon, a time when there was not a lot of work to be done, we would gather round an uncle or grandfather in the shade of a tree and share jokes and stories. It was through our traditional stories that we learnt our cultural and moral values because they would be tales of bravery, courage, herding, people who behaved well and so on. Often they were told in the form of poetry that had been handed down through the generations and sometimes they would even be accompanied by music, especially the beautiful, soft tone of the *inanga* (a traditional instrument similar to a zither). It was good to gather together like this and sometimes we would nod off to sleep, which was good because we didn't have early bed times.

Some of the stories were actual oral history and my own grandfather and father were recognised in our community as experts in this. One terrible story I heard more than once from them was about umwani w'umuzungu, a white king, whose *ababeresh* (Belgian officials) committed extreme atrocities, killing people and forcing many others into exile. This *umuzungu* (white man) was very cruel but extremely powerful. He conquered our "world" and enslaved many tribes. Those who opposed him or did not accept his instructions had their hands chopped off. His *ingoma* (regime) fed itself on the blood of innocent people including children: under him, our world was like a killing field with many families destroyed. '*Twarabagwanyije baratunanira,*' my grandfather said, meaning that we (our tribe) opposed and resisted him but his ababeresh had smoke guns and were too powerful for us. He was incredibly rich and owned thousands of herds of cattle. His soldiers used to dig big holes on the tops of hills, including Runundu (the biggest hill near our village), to hide precious materials such as money, gold and diamonds. This story stuck in my mind throughout my childhood: I wondered what my grandfather meant by an Umuzungu, a white King who fed himself the blood of children. It was only much later that I realised he was not speaking literally but meant this regime (of King Leopold) caused the death of many children.

In the evenings we would gather at a grandmother's place for more stories. This was a safe place where even our parents wouldn't dare to intervene, grandmother being older and therefore a figure of respect. These traditional stories could go on for two or three hours, depending on how much the storyteller embroidered them. No one will ever know who first invented these stories but over the centuries they have enchanted many children and become a part of our culture. Some of them helped sustain me through bad experiences later in life, particularly the story of Little Lamb who encountered so many dangers but lived through them all. Little Lamb had lost his mother. All alone in the forest, he felt afraid but he tried his very best to look strong and fearless as he trotted on. When he met Snake, he stood firmly and looked him in the eye. Snake laughed, "Just go! Today is not your worst day; you will die by someone else's hands, not mine, and the route ahead is even harder." So Little Lamb continued on his way, trying to be brave. Next he met Lion. Hiding his fear, he looked Lion in the eye and the same thing happened: 'Just go!' said Lion, 'Today is not your worst day. You will die by someone else's hands, not mine, and the route ahead is even harder.' Then he met Crocodile and other fearsome beasts but always the same thing happened. Finally, after many terrifying encounters, he was safely back with his mother, by luck as much as by his own bravery. In my future experiences I would often recall this story, saying to myself, 'Today is not your worst day!'

Boys' games were chiefly climbing trees and whistling communication with other children on the other side of the village. We used this method to insult and flatter each other because we shared a language of whistles. For any insult it would be some sort of melody referring to the other person's mother, which it is not polite to do. To flatter each other we would whistle a cattle song as a sign of respect for someone manly enough to look after cattle. Boys' toys were mainly carved wooden cows: we talked to them, pretending to make them drink water and so on. Of course we also initiated fights at the risk of many serious accidents and injuries to ourselves.

Around our village there are two large rivers, the Minembwe and the Lwiko, both running through very fertile land used for farming in both the dry and the rainy season. The Lwiko is more dangerous because it has many strong-flowing currents; over the years many people have been killed there in the rainy season when they were trying to cross to the other side of the river to get to or from the maize fields. The Minembwe is wider and calmer. Often it was used for baptisms and people from nearby villagers would gather around the main crossing to watch this significant ceremony.

All the children taught themselves to swim in the sparklingly clear water of the Minembwe River and we loved to splash around there. It was always magical to go swimming in the heat of the day in that lovely place with its spectacular backdrop of mountain scenery. Either side of the river, in addition to gardens, there were slopes covered with beautiful flowers and inyovu, naturally short grass unlike the coarse tall grass of the savannah. There was a spiritual belief connected to the Minembwe River: as children we were told about a small goat-shaped animal called Nyagahene and we were warned that wherever it appears it is a sign of deeper and dangerous water. Older children used to take younger ones by force into the deepest water as a test; they would laugh as the little ones struggled and only save them when they were very tired and about to drown. One day it happened to me and a friend: we were terrified and thrashed around in the water for our lives, but luckily my brother Oreni rushed to our rescue and pulled us out.

Other activities boys enjoyed were catching birds and locating honeybees. Like most children, we loved sweet things but our only source was honey and natural fruits. We did not know of soft drinks and confectionery. My older brother Oreni was very good at searching for honeybees; I would follow him and, once we had located a nest, we always made sure that we kept the location a secret. We would go every week to check on it but wait for the dry season to ensure getting as much honey as possible. The day of extracting the honey would be a secret known only to the children who planned together to get it. Our only equipment for this dangerous operation was black cloths to cover our faces and we set fire to leaves to make smoke. We would travel in the evening to arrive in the night at the tree where the bees had their nest. One child would climb and the others would stay down to keep distracting the bees. It was a time of exhilaration and excitement and we would scream with laughter before we finally settled with a delicious dripping honeycomb. We would divide it equally between us to take home. It was wonderful to experience such a rare treat and know it was the result of our own efforts. We felt blessed by what nature had provided for us.

A boy's job was mainly looking after young calves. I had my own stick for tapping the cows. It had been made especially for me and was just like those belonging to the men but larger. On Sundays we were allowed to look after older cows by ourselves because the adults had gone to church. I loved doing this work because it was an adult activity and it was an opportunity to meet with other children from other bigger villages. The naughtiest thing I used to do in the absence of my father or other adults was to mix our cows with those of other people so that our bull could fight with someone else's bull; this often resulted in serious injuries. My father knew very well his cattle's physical wellbeing. In fact he would probably notice more about them than he would notice about his children. Cows were practically equal to humans and he had cared for them since their birth. He had trained them to behave in a certain way so this meant he would be able to tell if I had forced our bull to fight. For me it was a fun activity as long as our bull did not lose the battle. When it lost, I was not so happy: I would be teased by the other children and feel terribly sorry for the bull, which was part of our family. More worryingly, I was afraid my father would notice the signs.

Most of my activities as a child were tied up one way or another with family work. During the rainy season I had to wake up before daylight to guard the maize fields, which were often attacked by birds, monkeys and other wild animals. It was very cold in the early morning and we did not have warm clothes. In traditional times, our people wore clothes made from animal skins but by my time people were aware of the dress code in the outside world and tried to follow it. We would have liked to buy more clothes but we had very little money. Wealth was measured traditionally by the number of cows a family owned and in this sense we were quite wealthy but with the recent changes that made money important, this wealth did not mean a lot because we could not sell the cattle. Culturally it was considered a bad thing to sell cattle, converting a living thing to money or material possessions. Each of these animals was a part of the family so selling one would be a tragic thing and there would need to be extreme reason. We also had a large stretch of land but making money from land depended on whether or not the owner could afford to hire someone to cultivate it. My parents for the most part only had their own labour. With our land and cattle we had quite a high status but this did not convert into money. We sold a few chickens and goats, as we never ate this meat ourselves, but this could not bring in enough money to dress the whole family well. I only had one pair of shorts and one top and always went barefoot whether in forest or savannah. I used to dream of having a pair of shoes one day.

Even if my parents had been able to earn money it would have been difficult to find goods in the area. The nearest and safest market was only on a Wednesday and was about a half-day walk away, which I would estimate now to be about twenty kilometres. Going to any market always presented a high risk of being attacked by soldiers and women were in danger of being raped. In fact I once witnessed this myself when I was very young but I never told anyone about it because I knew even then that the girl concerned would be rejected by society if it became known. She was a young girl in her early teens attacked by a tall, strong military man. She screamed for help but I was little and helpless and afraid that the soldier would shoot us. I felt terribly sorry for her and I cried uncontrollably afterwards but she advised me to wipe away my tears so that no-one would find out what had happened. Until today I have never said anything of that experience because there was no hope of justice for the girl. Had I said anything, she would have suffered more pain in the community; she would have been rejected and would not get married, so becoming a victim twice over. Even as a child I could see that it would be better for her to deal alone with the one issue she had faced. However, the experience has remained vivid in my memory because I could see that she felt so humiliated fighting for her dignity in front of a little boy.

Our diet was mainly vegetarian. Though there were wild animals all around us, we did not hunt them and our cows were hardly ever slaughtered. We ate beef only once a year at the New Year celebration and the only other time we had meat was when we had been lucky enough to trap partridges. My brother and I were busy most Saturdays preparing traps for these birds. We did this in the traditional way, using bush materials to construct snares which would catch a bird in a noose if it followed the little trail of corn we put down. Sometimes this work required staying in the fields until very late in the evening but we were not afraid, even though we had no torches. On dark evenings we followed each other by our sense of smell or by shouting. We ate perhaps one partridge every month; it was tasty and the only meat we had as children. Widespread farming and cultivation of the land was encroaching on the forests and endangering the animals that lived in them but there were still many wild animals. When I think back to those times now, I tremble when I remember some of the places or experiences I went through with the naivety of a child, ignoring all the dangers. There were many different kinds of snakes and sometimes they came close to our homes. It has even been known to find a snake lying around a baby, enjoying the warmth. If a poisonous snake bit us, we could not take an antidote because we did not have access to any medical facilities: there was no clinic or hospital or any modern medical help for illness. When it was time to give birth, women looked after themselves.

Our society has a very high respect for and expectation of women. They are mothers and, as such, the heart of the community and the source of our continuing family genealogy. Coping with the pain of childbirth is a part of this responsibility and what gives a woman her self-pride. Men are not allowed to help in childbirth: a husband may not intervene either physically or emotionally. There were some women who were experienced in helping others in childbirth and my mother was one of these women who helped when there were complications. In extreme circumstances a woman in a difficult labour might be carried to the nearest clinic but, as this would involve a walk of one or two days, this was not usually possible. Then they would call for a "midwife" like my mother. Sometimes they were forced to use razors to operate. In some cases when the child could not be delivered, they would take the only option left to them: to try to save the mother by inserting razors and small knives inside her womb and cutting the baby into pieces.

Banyamulenge women, photographs courtesy Children in Crisis

Usually in those circumstances the mother would die also but occasionally one survived. At emotional times like this, people would express their feeling is song and prayer. Most of my community had converted suddenly from traditional religious beliefs to Christianity so, at times like this, they would sing a song of *Wokuvu* (salvation) called *muponyi apitaye yote in Yesu*, meaning, "The biggest healer is you Jesus". This approach to healing had just replaced the traditional witch doctors.

The first time I ever saw a nurse was when I went with two friends to get circumcised. We were probably under six years old and we went by ourselves to get this operation. I stole my neighbour's chicken to pay for it as my mother's chicken had disappeared into the bush and I could not tell her why I needed it: this was a male business and it would have been too embarrassing to talk about it with her. The nurse operated in a small bush hut in the Valley of the Minembwe River. Although he had some modern equipment such as bandages to prevent heavy bleeding, he could not provide local anaesthetic to deaden the pain. I was the first of the three children to be treated. It was painful but I was so happy to be growing up into a man that I could bear it; I knew that it would allow me to swim with other children without being teased about not having undergone circumcision, an operation which is done for reasons of hygiene but also perceived as a rite of passage.

It took me about a week to heal and, although my mother must have known about it when she saw me in pain or walking differently, she would never ask me about it, because that would not be in keeping with our culture. My older brother, Oreni, who was only my senior by about a year but who always took special care of me, looked after me and taught me about the rituals associated with it; for example he explained to me that I shouldn't cross over a place where women urinated as this would mean that the wound would stay unhealed. One of my brother's friends had a serious problem after his circumcision: instead of healing, his penis kept bleeding. Though he was unable to walk properly, he would try hard to hide this by pretending to be normal. After about a month, we decided to help him without letting any adult know. We took him by force and cleaned him. We found that an old piece of bandage was embedded in the flesh so we pulled it out and then made a new bandage from a piece of cloth that we stole from a woman in the village and cut into pieces. The only medication we had was chalk powder and paint powder. These were not medications of course but to us they looked like penicillin so we used them and he healed soon after.

Shortly after, I had good reason to be pleased that I had been circumcised when a violent man threatened to perform the "operation" on me and my brother Oreni with a machete. Oreni and I had been on our way to join our mother as she worked in the fields, which were situated at some distance from the village. We had just crossed the river Minembwe when we saw a man sheltering from the rain under an Umuko tree by the bank. Suddenly he blocked our path, stole from us the things we had been taking to our mother and threatened to cut our throats. We had no idea who he was or where he was from and it seemed to us that he might not even be a man at all but a *kanyonya* – a blood sucking creature of traditional belief who, it was thought, might be implicated in the murder of two women whose bodies had been found in the Nyarubira forest in a place called Mikenke. Whoever he was, he spoke sometimes in Swahili and sometimes in Lingala – a language that instilled fear in our people because it was President Mobutu's language. He terrorised us for several hours and, at one point, forced us both to the ground and pulled down our shorts to see if we were circumcised. If not, he told us, he would do it himself with his machete. It was very unusual for my strong-minded brother to cry but he cried constantly on this occasion, begging the man to kill him if he must but to spare his little brother. Eventually we were freed and ran off to find our mother but we did not feel safe until we heard the voices of the women singing *akangiringiri* as they worked together. The incident affected me deeply and served as a constant reminder that, though our lives might seem happy and content, terror could threaten us at any time.

CHAPTER 3

Danger

THERE HAD BEEN DECADES OF VIOLENCE from different rebel groups or government soldiers against my people though the Banyamulenge were not the instigators of any fighting. In fact, it could be argued that we were punished for not having taken part in the Mulelist rebellion of 1965 to 1968 (*see timeline*). For one thing, our area continued to be under-developed with no modern facilities or services such as clinics and roads but there was also direct aggression. The most serious was "Dark Thursday" in 1966 when all the men of two villages were beheaded. Other atrocities followed and it seemed to us that the rebellion, which had officially ended so many years before, continued. Because of the huge size of the Congo (Zaire as it was at the time I am writing about) and the fact that there is little infrastructure or communication, our area remains dangerous right to the present time. Communities live for the most part in little hamlets scattered throughout an area bordered by vast areas of wild country on the one side and equatorial forest on the other. Much of it remains inaccessible to government authorities and other organisations so, when I was a boy, it seemed as if the rebellion still hadn't really ended. Though the violence no longer had any obvious political motivation, it highlighted resentment against the Banyamulenge people, still considered "foreigners" and was a good excuse to steal cattle and other goods.

Cattle are the foundation of our lifestyle and are almost as important as people. They are the source of pride, power and influence and are the symbol of wealth and success. We depend on them and they depend on us. Until the 1970s, we still made *ikerenve*, food made from blood taken painlessly from the living animal and still today they provide us with the main element of our diet: milk. Socially, cattle are used as gifts to strengthen family ties, *Guhana* or *gushumbusha*, and are used to build friendship with other tribes. If people are affected by a disaster or epidemic that affects their herds, a collection of donations in cattle will be made to help them; sometimes such gifts are given to those who just do not have enough cattle. Building friendship with other tribes in this way is known as *umwira*. Dry horns are used as water containers and musical instruments. *Ingunga*, leather from the hides, used to play a significant role as a source of clothing before modern textiles were introduced and it is still used for musical instruments such as drums as well as for bedding. Cow-dung plays an important role in building our huts: mixed with watered soil, it is used to support sticks on the ground and for roughcasting huts.

Another major role of cattle is in religious rituals such as engagement and marriage. They are an important part of the engagement ceremony. After a bride has been requested through a small ceremony called *kubaza*, and if the girl's family agree, the man's family come with a few selected beautiful cows as a symbol of *gufata irembo* – 'a word has been spoken and promise made'. Following this, several months later they come for the official dowry negotiations which again involve cattle. The debate is not about the value of the bride in terms of material possessions: the more cattle given to the girl's family, the more the girl will be able to give to the future married couple, *kurongoranya*, so the groom-to-be has an interest in his family giving more cattle. Depending on the family, the "bride price" can be as many as twenty cows. In fact this is one of the main reasons other tribes or communities find it difficult to marry within the Banyamulenge community as they are unlikely to have cattle.

The importance of cattle, therefore, goes far beyond their value in terms of a source of food. In a similar way to human beings, they have individuality and may acquire flattering names. We communicate to them through various traditional songs, poems or whistling, telling them when to move to water when to come for milking and so on. For them to have enough food and water, continued access to a nomadic lifestyle is absolutely essential: the men take them to better pastures during the dry season and have no choice but to take risks in entering dangerous areas. To find pastures they are obliged to go to the great open areas that have not been "liberated" by the government despite extensive use of foreign mercenaries.

I was only about six years old when I had my first experience of an attack by militias. I was with my father, some other men from the village and one other boy about my age, Janson. We had just passed a month in a spectacularly beautiful area – the wide valleys of Rebera and Lungulungu. The wonderful environment had elated everyone: little streams ran through the forests and open spaces and the area was rich in colourful birds of many different species and interesting wild animals. The cows seemed as happy as we were; drinking from the clear, fresh streams that ran down from the mountains through their pasture, they were able to combine their food and drink. Unfortunately, this idyllic setting was known to be occupied by violent "nationalist" militias, that we referred to as *abajenesi* or former Mulelist militias, to the extent that it had become a common insult in our language to say '*Urakaja Ilungulungu*', meaning 'Go and get yourself killed in Ilungulungu!' Knowing the danger, the men got together and decided we must leave this ideal setting and go to the mountains of Mubonyoni, a totally different environment, stony underfoot with steep inclines. It was a matter of compromise, weighing the danger of that lovely large valley against the inhospitable conditions of alternative places. So we moved to the hilly area where several cows died. Janson and I watched helplessly as one we were looking after slipped and tumbled down, breaking her horns and bones as she went. We ran as quickly as we could to help her, leaping down the cliff-like incline, but could do nothing when we reached her. We simply tried to comfort her as she battled for breath. There was no way even of calling an adult to help us.

Around midnight one day, my father woke everyone by whispering in a low voice 'Get up! We are being attacked!' Born to a life of danger and having grown up with conflict always around him, his experiences had given him the ability to half sleep and somehow be aware of danger even when he was asleep; he knew how to half sleep so that he could pick up warnings and he had become aware of a warning voice calling towards the mountains in the traditional way my people use in emergencies. When he told the others they wanted to confirm the message first by sending someone off to shout back. A man called Mazinda was sent to do this and after a few minutes he was indeed able to confirm that the message '*muhunge muhunge twatewe*', (go immediately as we are under attack) had indeed been sent. He had verified not only the message but the person who had sent it, Ruramirwa, someone from our village. Ruramirwa had himself just received the message from someone further away on the other side of him and then relayed it on to us. Now it was up to us to send it on further and Mazinda went to do this. With both messenger and message confirmed, we had to be ready to leave within minutes.

We prepared the cattle and checked they were all there. Janson and I were trembling with fear. It was dark and we were very worried that more cows would fall down the vertical sides of our route. My father assured us that he would come and look for lost cows when peace was restored but insisted that for now we must simply accept that some animals might be lost. Then we heard a rifle shot. One of our men, Semuhanuka, was a *guerrier* – someone experienced in military matters and expected to defend the community – and he reassured us that the gun was at a considerable distance but said we would lose cows if the shooting continued. Our greatest problem was that we didn't know from which direction the militias would approach and we were wary of falling into an ambush. We had to climb the mountains of Mwibumba in the dark. By the early morning, I was starting to nod off as I walked but my father pulled me back on the track. Hearing the continuing gunshots, I completely lost my need to sleep. Without shoes, I was in real pain with my feet; there was no light and the rough path was littered with stones, wood and roots. Finally, we arrived at the summit, the flat plane on the top of the Mwibumba Mountains, as the sun was rising. We weren't the only ones to have fled here for safety; there were other herders there too and it was a great relief to feel safe at last.

Suddenly my sense of relief was shattered as I heard my father calling for help. This time the danger was not from militias but from a snake that had attacked one of our cows and was firmly attached to its lower leg. It was a kind we call *igihoma*, not long but as thick as a man's arm. It does not bite like other snakes but sucks the blood of a person or animal. My father could not throw his spear to kill it because the cow was moving and he could accidentally hurt her instead. Finally he cut it off with a machete and the cow did not seem to be badly hurt. By this time, my respect for my father was even greater than it had been before we left the village. He was my hero and I loved the way he seemed to be the leader amongst the men.

He called them all together to evaluate the situation and count their losses, to see if anyone had been hurt and how many cattle were lost. It seemed that no-one had been injured but a number of cattle had perished, having fallen on the difficult terrain. In addition, the militias had managed to pillage cattle belonging to a man called Barita. Luckily, none of the men had been killed or injured because our way of warning each other had resulted in us avoiding ambush and the aggressors had found it difficult to continue attacking once we had reached this mountainous area. Consequently, it was decided to stay on this high plateau for a while, even though the conditions were not good for grazing.

For Janson and me the whole experience felt like a nightmare so we got together and made our plans for leaving the men and looking for a way back to our mothers and the safety of the village. Janson pointed out that, if we left, life would be even harder for the men because there would be no-one to do the jobs at base camp while the men were out taking the cattle to pasture. Still, we decided to do *gutoroka*, a term used to mean children leaving the herders without permission. As soon as the adults had left for the herding in the morning we started our journey, knowing that they would not find out until they got back in the evening; then they would immediately realise that we had decided to escape that hard life and return to the village. We knew they would not worry about us or question whether or not we would be able to find our way to any villages or if we might encounter danger in this deserted and wild area. For them, being a child meant having time to learn through experience how to be hard and survive so, though they knew this land was harsh and there were no paths and that there were wild animals as well as the possibility of dangerous people, they would not really worry about us. Besides, if there were any rebel troops around, children stood a better chance alone than if they were with adults. At some point a message would be sent back to see if we had arrived but that was all; then there would be no anger at our disobedience either because they would be proud that we had managed to survive alone.

Janson and I travelled for a whole day, running more than we walked. We were terrified the whole way and had an agreement never to look behind us even if we heard someone call to us. I kept thinking of the incident about a year before when Oreni and I had been attacked by the man but I didn't tell Janson about that as I didn't want to make him even more afraid. I can still recall the great relief I felt when I was finally with my mother. She massaged my aching legs with warm water and cheered me up with good news of things that had happened in the village and her recent good harvest. I had only been away for about three months but this seemed like a very long time because of all the things that had happened to me and the various things that had happened in the village while I was away.

THIS FRIGHTENING EXPERIENCE impressed on me that, though I loved herding cattle, I did not want to spend my life doing it. I began dreaming of another life in one of the more "civilised" places I had heard about. Such a life seemed very remote though. In our village of Runundu, the only facilities were a Church and school in a rudimentary state. Villagers had campaigned long and hard to get this school and, government funding being scarce, still needed to contribute to its upkeep and the teachers' salaries. Our village had only one qualified teacher and he ran the school, supported by three other men who had accessed a year or two of secondary education. From time to time there was an inspection-type visit for the official headmaster, who was responsible for all the schools of the area. The building was made of traditional materials, open at the sides and vulnerable to the rain in the wet season or to wind in dry season. As our much-loved cows were allowed to roam freely, the sides were often damaged and needed constant attention. Class sizes were very large because children walked in from all the surrounding hamlets if they could pay the fees. These fees were a small sum but they were a stiff challenge for families who lived by subsistence farming and hardly saw any cash.

I longed for the day I could go to that school and join the other children as they learnt their lessons. I knew it would not be straightforward though because my three older brothers had needed to overcome opposition from our father. (Eventually the eldest, supported by a family friend from another tribe even went on to college. The next one, Samuel, dropped out after primary school. Oreni, always more physical than studious, gave up after a year at the closest secondary school.) With little support from home, it was difficult to be motivated to succeed. Though I understood that education was out of the question for my sisters, girls being expected to marry early and then take on responsibilities within a new family, I had no idea at the time why my father opposed it for us boys; later I came to understand that it was largely because of his own experience as a young man. When my father's family was finally allowed to return from exile, the colonial style of education for boys had just started. However, going to school was perceived as a way of breaking down our traditional tribal values and customs and also as a kind of forced military recruitment so none of my father's generation ever went to school if they could avoid it. In his case he was forced to go as a young man in his twenties but he escaped as soon as he had learnt to read and write. It was only towards the beginning of the 1950s that a few of our people voluntarily attended and this resulted in his scepticism being confirmed: in the late 1970s, a number of Banyamulenge, including my cousin Samson Muzuri, managed to study up to University level but were still barred from any posts of responsibility because of their ethnicity. Samson was known to be a very gifted and capable man who had accessed Western-style education at the highest level and yet he had still been unable to find employment at the right level in the Congo. My father could not believe that we might fare any better if we followed the same path. In addition, he knew that if we went on to secondary education we might need to travel far away from the village thus risking further danger in those troubled times. Finding the fees for all of us would be a terrific burden on our family but that was by no means his major concern. So, for my brothers and me, my father's only ambition was that we should live a peaceful traditional life looking after cattle.

Without realising it, my mother inspired me to crave an education. In our "hut' house were four books that we considered very precious: *Bibiliya yera* (bible), *Indirimbo Zogushimsihsa* (hymn book in Kinyarwanda language), *Wokovu* (hymn book in Swahili language) and *Igitabo cy'Umungenzi*, a Kinyarwanda translation of John Bunyan's *The Pilgrim's Progress*. We identified so strongly with Bunyan's story that we referred to him as "Yohana Bunyana" – a name that suggests he could be Munyamulenge like us. Because she wanted to know what was in these books, my mother learned to read from her cousin who went to school. I was fascinated when I saw her reading and asked her to show me how to do it. So she taught me and told me that I didn't really need to go to school as she hadn't been either.

Of course this did not stop me from wanting to go to the village school and I waited impatiently to be old enough. As there were no records of a child's birth date, readiness for school was determined not by asking the age but by whether or not the child could stretch his arm behind his head and touch the opposite ear with his fingers. Every day I would try to do this, hoping that my arm had grown long enough. Finally I succeeded and I took myself, my heart beating fast with excitement, to the school to speak to the teacher and register. My disappointment was bitter when he simply told me to go back home. When I asked him why, he replied that it was because I was helping my mother to look after my younger brother. Socially and culturally, this was a responsible decision he made; consideration of whether a child has any duties or obligations at home was part of school admission requirements and unfortunately in my case I had an important responsibility. Although I understood his reasons in a general sort of way, I was still puzzled about being refused by this particular man because he had just allowed his own son, Micho, to start and I was his son's close friend.

It was indeed very painful for me to see my friend doing what we had both been looking forward. He did really well, always getting the top marks. I admired him for this and also looked on him as the luckiest person I knew because his family was more liberal and understanding than mine. He stayed a very good friend for that whole year and told me about his experiences at school. This way I received some education indirectly and imagined myself at school by going through things he explained to me. He taught me basic arithmetic – addition, subtraction and so on – and various other things. Of course, in the late afternoon my mother continued to teach me to read as we sang hymns and read the Bible together.

I also learnt something else interesting that year while looking after my young brother. Missionaries had sent two guitars to the village, strange objects that amazed us because we had never seen musical instruments quite like them. Our people had many musical instruments made in the traditional way using natural materials or any discarded items that we could utilize. For example, empty metal containers brought back from the towns could be converted into *ipendo* by making holes in the sides and putting dry seeds around. The sound of a rattled ipendo harmonized well the *igondera* – a drum-shaped instrument that produced an amazing sound when a stick wrapped in damp cloth was pulled through its hole. Of course, we also had drums of all types, the *umwirongi* (a kind of flute) and the beautiful-sounding *inanga* (zither). These guitars, though, fascinated us because they were something from that distant, "advanced" world we had only heard about. Children were not allowed to touch them and they were very carefully guarded by a man called Nyamusomwa. I often hid outside his door to listen to him giving his guitar lessons.

Because I was so enthralled by this new kind of music, I dreamt of one day touching a guitar myself. One day I went into the bush with Oreni to try to make our own guitar. We cut an *umushaki* tree and made our instrument as best we could. For the strings we found some old trousers that had been thrown away and carefully unpicked the thread that had been used to sew in the zip. We even made holes to insert sticks to act as the pegs that turn the strings for tuning. These self-taught traditional guitar lessons occupied my time at home without my friend Micho.

The following year I succeeded in registering for school by promising the teacher that I would do all my jobs at home as well as my school work. Not having told my parents what I had arranged meant that I had to continue as normally as possible in the village whilst secretly going to school without telling them. Of course it didn't take long for my mother to find out but she did not tell my father so I continued going. I had no books or writing materials but just shared a slate with another child. None of the children were much better off than I was and the school itself had very few resources – often there would be only one book per class. Our lessons were taught in Swahili until the fifth year when French was introduced also, though of course we spoke our own language, Kinyamulenge, out of class. I loved being with all the other children and sharing their activities. One of my most vivid early memories is of being in a large group of children singing enthusiastic songs praising Mobutu. Schools were obliged to enforce this – no one would go against such requirements because the president had created a network of terrorists watching people and how they obeyed his leadership. So even at this early stage politics affected our lives but we made progress anyway. In fact I was doing very well and getting top marks in my class, even though I had to do all my homework just after school before reaching home so my father would not find out what was happening. Finally he did find out because people in the village were talking about it and saying that I was doing exceptionally well. One of my teachers, Yosefu, kept praising me and said I was a role model to the other children even though I was one of the poorest with the least encouragement from home. So, by the time I had finished my six years of primary school, my father had changed his mind slightly; he started to show more interest in education but still would not commit money towards it.

As I progressed towards the end of my primary school studies, I made friends who inspired me in many ways and I learnt from them as well as from my teachers. One of these friends was an older boy who had already started secondary school. He was called Tokos and had an uncle who lived in a place called Sange, quite far from our area and considered to be in contact with "modern" places. Tokos was a naturally gifted person but his gifts were artistic and, as such, not widely respected. My people valued certain things that seemed useful to their life style; they would respect subjects that led, for example, towards agriculture, veterinary medicine and teaching but would see things such as drawing or designing as foolishness.

Above: recent photographs taken of a primary school in my region. My primary school was in a very similar condition when I studied there.
Photographs courtesy Children in Crisis

Above: recent photograph of children and villagers from Kundondo village, near where I grew up.
Photographs courtesy Children in Crisis

Because of this, many in the Minembwe area saw Tokos as a rather eccentric young person behaving outside the traditional norms. He had wide general knowledge and taught me about other African countries. As I grew older and more aware myself, he told me about the apartheid in South Africa and how it was similar to our tribe's exclusion in our country. I became passionate about some world leaders such as Thomas Sankara, the former President of Burkina Faso (who was later assassinated because of his modest leadership and political ideology), Nelson Mandela and Patrice Lumumba. Tokos encouraged me to read books. This was almost impossible as the only accessible ones in the area were the Bible and hymn books but I respected Tokos so much that I started pursuing his advice; I would walk as far as 20 kilometres to search for a book, usually to no avail. Tokos would often let me know if he had obtained something new to read and, through his incredible creativity and passion to read, he miraculously used to get copies of a French magazine called *Jeune Afrique*. Although it might be a year or so out of date, for me it was about reading rather than knowing what was going on. I knew only a little French (we were taught mainly in Swahili and our own language) but Tokos helped me with it and my grasp of the language improved this way. Tokos was passionate about the struggle of the Israelis to create their state and told many stories about Israeli issues with Palestine and their war with Egypt. He encouraged me to read a book called *Raid on Entebbe*, about the mission to rescue Israelis who were hijacked by terrorists and forced to land in Uganda. This story was quite well-known in our country. Looking back, I realise these informal times with Tokos were practically as much a part of my education as the time I spent in school.

Amongst my people there were many stories of the marvels that existed beyond our homeland. We had heard of motor cars, planes and trains for example and at school I learnt about bicycles. It was Tokos, though, who first made me aware of a miraculous device that showed moving, talking pictures of real live people who were not actually there. He had heard about television but had never actually seen a TV set. He told us about images of people moving on a screen but, in my limited understanding, I could only imagine a TV as a sort of mirror where people could pass by and have their image captured. To entertain his young brother and me, Tokos made his own television and created stories based on cartoon images for us. He attached these images to a string hung in the dark and then pulled the string to show one image at a time as the light shone on them. By the time all the images had passed, we would have followed a story as if we had seen a film. The light he used was at first natural light through a small hole in the wall focused on to the right place but later he made his own torch with a bulb, wire and batteries that he had found at the market. Our "cinema" was an abandoned hut where adults would not catch us: not only would they think we were wasting our time on foolishness but they might be angry about the batteries as these were suspected as sorcery. I was fascinated by the idea of television and asked adults about it. From them I came to think that it must be some sort of transparent object that people passed behind because I heard it was used for official military and presidential parades. I was amazed to hear that someone from our village who had gone to the city and been educated to a high level had been seen on TV – we simply couldn't understand how such a thing could be. Hearing about this marvel was perhaps one of many small incidents that made me want to go further than our own villages.

From the point of view of my family, school was always the last priority, far behind my duties at home, and there was the constant problem of finding the fees. Small though they were, they could be an almost insurmountable problem for a subsistence farming family. Often I would be late starting a new term or absent altogether because I could not pay the fees. Though we never ate chickens, we raised them to sell and my mother would tell me to wait until one was big enough for me to sell. Unfortunately the village chickens grew very slowly, which meant having to wait for a few months. One particular incident when I tried to sell a chicken for school fees remains vivid in my memory. That day I had joined people going to Manunga market so that I could sell my chicken when, half way there, we were warned that there were soldiers coming towards us. Soldiers were not paid and so they survived by harassing and torturing people until they gave them things and looting everything they could see. I feared that they would take my chicken so I left the path to walk through the forest to Manunga. When I reached the market, I was told that soldiers were still nearby so I spent the whole day hiding instead of trying to find a buyer. By the evening it was raining heavily which was bad because once the chicken was wet it would look smaller and I might be offered less than I needed. I tried to hide the poor bird in my jumper but I was also soaking wet and I feared that it might die. On my journey home, desperate and disappointed, I came across the soldiers; they stole the chicken but forced me carry it for them as an unpaid porter. They had too much to carry themselves because of all that they had stolen from people at various villages or markets so I was made to help carry that too. I was devastated and couldn't bear to think that I would not be able to go to school the next day because I had lost my school fees in this way. So I formed a plan: when we reached the Lwiko River, I asked them to let me go into the bush for a toilet break.

'Well go if you need to but we have to see where you are,' one of the soldiers said.

'Hold some of the luggage for me but I don't mind keeping the chicken with me,' I said. A few seconds later, having left the path and pretended to relieve myself, I ran off with my chicken. They started shouting '*Tutakupiga masasi*', Swahili for 'We'll shoot you'. I was terrified and wondered if I should stop running and give myself up. They knew that I would be forced to stop at the river Lwiko as it is one of the largest and most dangerous rivers in the area, where people were often drowned in the rainy season. Also, although I knew how to swim, I couldn't swim holding the chicken. So I found somewhere to hide and waited, my heart beating fast, for what seemed like an age but was probably just a short time. Eventually their noise stopped – they had given up the search for me. I waited until they had gone and then came back to use the main bridge. It had continued to rain so my chicken was very tired and shivering with cold. After about half an hour I reached the next village; a man there took pity on me and invited me to come to his home for a rest and to look after the chicken. I sat with his family by the fire and they gave me and the chicken food before I continued home.

I didn't tell my mother how close I had come to being shot but I did explain to her that it was too dangerous to sell chickens at the market. I told her I would see a friend, Sebatware, in a place called Kuwabanyarusuku because he needed to make money for his fees also and had an idea what we could do. He knew a lot of people and found out how we could make bricks. I went to see him the day after my adventure with the chicken and we started work straight away, using a rectangular shaped wooden frame, *foroma*, made by a local carpenter. It was hard work for a week and I would come back home late in the evening extremely tired. Then we started searching for people who would buy our bricks. There was not much need for them as almost everybody built their houses with wood thatched with long grass. Churches were built with bricks but there were no plans to build a new church at that time in the area. We never sold our bricks and cattle damaged them a few weeks later. Finally my mother promised to sell beans for my fees as soon as she had harvested them; again it was my mother who supported me through her hard work but that year I missed a whole term because of not having the fees on time.

My school life was dominated by the pressure to raise the fees and this far outweighed any worries I had about my school work or examinations or doing my household tasks. At the end of each academic year I would spend the rest of the dry season with my father searching for good pastures for the cattle but this was something I looked forward to. Whether in the village or off with the herders, though, at the back of my mind was the constant worry about whether or not I would have the money to pay for my schooling; I hoped one day to go on to secondary school and that would cost even more.

CHAPTER 4

The love of herding

OFFICIALLY THE SCHOOL YEAR WAS FROM September to July but, in our small village in this remote part of the Congo, no-one minded too much if the dates changed a little. By about the end of May, boys would be longing to join the men cattle herding. Having spent much of the year learning about the new way of life, now they could go and live very much as their forefathers had done. For us it was like looking forward to a holiday and we loved this adventurous life far from the village.

Our camp for sleeping was always at the edge of a forest because this position has many benefits. We would build a rectangular hut but the side that faced the trees would be left open as the forest itself acted as a wall and provided good protection when soldiers or rebels attacked. I have memories of hiding behind various *inganzamarungu* (tall rain forest trees of differing species) from where I could see soldiers searching for us but not being able to see us. Trees also protected us from heavy rain and when we were not at the huts we would choose one that offered good shelter. Sometimes in the forest there would be a half-fallen tree that offered a shelter in the cavities its fall had created between its massive roots. The rich diversity of the rainforest fascinated me, particularly the massive trees stretched towards the sky, supporting many other life forms. Each tree would be entangled by creepers with ferns of all types and other plants such as orchids growing in its branches. It seemed to me that trees could be as individual as people are – each one unique in its shape. I used to like to imagine they had a personality, recognising shapes of animals or humans in them. For example, I once discovered a pair of trees that seemed to me to be an elderly couple in a fond embrace.

Whilst away from the village we lived exclusively on milk, milking the cows twice a day – very early in the morning and late in the evening. At daybreak, my father would wake up and, while the other men still slept, he would play his *umwirongi*, a kind of flute. The music he

41

played was mostly linked to traditional poems praising cattle, heroes, herders and great men of integrity and wisdom. I loved waking to this music because it put me in a good mood, giving me a positive feeling about the new day we were going to face. It is interesting that he often ended his session of traditional music with a Christian song called '*Yesu aruta abandi bose kudukunda*' meaning that Jesus loves us more than anyone. This combination of traditional religious belief and Christianity reflects how God has always occupied a central role in everyday life among the Banyamulenge, both before and after the arrival of Christianity. The name given to the Christian God is *Imana*, a name that had always been used to refer to the Supreme Being we believed in – one that is unreachable, beyond other gods.

In each hut there were about three or four men from different families and sometimes one or two young boys. These boys would be woken up early in the morning and given the *Umubanji*, the leftover milk from the night before. This tasted a bit sour but was considered to be healthy. It was forbidden to throw away unused milk, which is why the young people were forced to drink all the leftovers to empty the pots before the morning milking. I hated Umubanji because we had to have it even if we weren't thirsty in order not to waste it; so I had a way of getting rid of mine – I dug a big hole nearby so that I could sneak off, pour away my milk and then ensure the hole was safely covered. My father would check to see that I had finished it and would often tell me that I should remember there may be other children less fortunate than me who were hungry so we should never waste any. Discarding milk was believed to bring misfortune to cows. The worst thing of all would be pouring milk in a fire, as it was believed that would cause disease of the cows' udders. Although Umubanji was unpleasant, it was the only breakfast available to us. Then people would wake up a few cows so that they would urinate and we could use this urine to wash the pottery vessels that were used for milking and storing the fresh milk afterwards.

After we had sterilised the pots in this way we would be ready for the milking. First we had to allow the calves to suckle for a length of time because cows will not give milk to us before their calves. It is quite a slow process getting all the calves to feed and, depending on how many animals there were, we probably spent up to two hours milking. Following this we would separate the cows from the calves. Sometimes we did this by singing the appropriate song; our way of communicating with the cattle was through various songs which they recognised. Then the men, after drinking some milk, would take the cows to the pasture while the boys stayed near the huts and looked after the calves. We had to clean up all the dung, bring water, look after the huts where the young animals sheltered and prepare the grass that was used to build them.

We loved being left on our own to look after the calves while the men were away with the cattle, especially when our jobs were finished and we could play. Our favourite activity was climbing trees and swinging from vines but we also liked to search the forest floor for the delicious red *amachocho*, fighting off the baboons who also love this fruit. In some more humid areas, we would look for special flexible sticks called *ingumbyo*, a kind of wood that lasts for many years and so is used to make many artistic objects. Occasionally a hunter would appear, often from the Bashikalangwa people who were so different in their customs to us. Unlike our tribe, they hunt wild game and prefer sleeping deep in the forest. Walking very slowly as hunters do, they would suddenly appear, half naked, dirty and wearing nothing but a few rags or leaves. They looked fierce, armed with long, sharp knives, spears, bows and arrows. They had so many scars that their faces looked as if they were tattooed. On their backs they carried traditional bags for their catch. We couldn't speak their language and found them very frightening but they never hurt us.

Some years I would go off herding with just my father and not with the other boys and I loved spending time with him alone. As darkness approached we would light our fire, using sticks in the customary way – the "male" threaded through the "female" and the two vibrated together for about fifteen minutes. When it grew dark we slept on animal skins or just soft grass with either a cloth material used as a blanket or an animal skin over us in case it rained. As we lay beside each other, my father helped me to count the stars, especially those closest to the moon, and this made me fall asleep despite the fact that I felt afraid. Another way he used to make me fall asleep was to ask me to imagine an endless queue of sheep crossing a river one by one. I had to make sure it was a continuous crossing and that none were knocked over by the current. Sheep and cows are the most valued animals traditionally, but sheep can resist the dry season so always stayed near the villages. Because they are very slow, it was considered unsafe to take them together with cows. My reason for being afraid of sleeping was that I thought lions might find us unprotected. This was very naive because even if lions found us awake we would still be attacked. On one occasion we were attacked by a buffalo and, on another, by a large python but I had complete trust in my father; I knew that whatever attack we might face, he would be able to defend me though he had no strong weapons – just two spears, a knife and a traditional machete.

My father loved my trust in him. One day he had no choice but to leave me with more than fifty cattle while he went to find other good pastures. He did not tell me that he was going far as he knew that I would be scared; he just said that he was finding me something in the nearby forest. I waited from morning to evening time and did not cry though I was only about nine years old. My only concern was to make sure I looked after our cows properly while he was not there. He only told me about where he had gone a year later and then I was so shocked that I trembled thinking what would have happened to me if wild animals had found me. I remembered vividly the time, about a month before, when my brother and I and a younger child had been attacked by *uduhizi* (wild pigs). We had been warned how dangerous these are so we knew what to do – we climbed a nearby tree and waited until they went. But there are more dangerous animals than wild pigs and I would not like to face them alone.

I was not always a great asset to my father and, one particular occasion I was a real hindrance. We had moved the cattle to a very mountainous and stony place, Kuwakagano, where there was not enough water. My father was so anxious about finding water that he did not sleep well at night and, noticing this, I made up my mind to help him. Very early one morning, when my father had gone to look after the cows, I ran off to a forest about a kilometre away to search there. After a couple of hours of searching, I succeeded in finding a little spring deep in that forest. Excited but remaining calm,

I returned to our camp where I told first my father and then the other adults that I had found a big stream. My father reprimanded me for having gone off without telling anyone, reminding me it was naughty and dangerous for a child to go alone into the jungle. Knowing me so well, he also found my good news difficult to believe but another man persuaded him to take my word for it. Finally, at around midday, my father told me to lead the way. I set off into the forest followed by the cows, which were desperately thirsty, not having drunk for more than twenty four hours. By the time we arrived at the place, the cows were mooing pitifully and most of them began to disappear in various directions desperately looking for water. My "stream" was nothing more than a trickle, completely inadequate, and my father was furious with me. Because he was angry, I ran away too, so then his problems were greater than ever: as well as having no water and a hundred cows to find, he had lost his son. Later on, of course, my family laughed about this incident and it did not stop me from loving the adventure-filled life of a herdsman.

ONE YEAR, WHEN THE ACADEMIC YEAR was finished, it was arranged for a man called Elisha to take me to join my father. We walked for a day and I was feeling happy and confident, especially as I was wearing my first ever shoes, bought to give me protection from snakes and thorns when walking in the bush or jungle. Then, sometime in the evening when he got tired, he changed his mind and decided that I should find my own way. As we were crossing a river called Nzovu, he simply pointed me in the right direction, told me how long it should take to reach my father and then went off on his own. The direction he told me to go was a huge wild area with no proper path. All I knew was that I had to go through a forest and reach the other side. As soon as he left, I cried non-stop and was wondering what I should do. What if the night fell on me before I reached where my father was? I was little more than ten years old and had never been in that area before. As I crossed a stream, I slid on a stone in the water and the current took my left shoe away. I managed to keep the other one but I was terrified as well as sad at losing my precious shoe. Here I was completely alone, walking with only one shoe on my right foot. I kept walking and crying; I knew I couldn't go back to the village because it would take me at least a day to get there. I crossed a few other small rivers and forests. I was shaking and listening to every movement of grass and leaves. I went to the top of the hill to see whether I could see anything, either human beings or cattle. I kept going because it was starting to get dark and I was very afraid that the darkness would prevent me from locating people who might be in the area.

Finally I reached a place that I knew must be my father's camp because I saw a hut and feeding place for cattle. Imagine how I felt to find it all deserted! The tracks of cattle could be seen but their enclosure was destroyed. Evidently, my father and the others had relocated to another area as usual to search for good pasture. My father had taught me how to track people by looking at the direction of footprints and checking whether the remains of the fire were still warm. I checked where the fire had been: it was cold, which meant that they had left a few days ago so I set off following the tracks though rain had made all the footprints less visible. I decided to keep going though I did not have a torch and my left foot was hurting terribly. I was alone in the middle of the jungle late in the evening. I was so upset that gradually I became numb and did not much care what would happen to me. Sometimes I saw antelopes and often baboons. Though I lost my way in the woods and forest several times, I kept going, crying as I hurried along. I felt dizzy and disoriented, especially as the clouds had moved in. Nothing looked familiar. I paused and tried to look for my tracks, which wasn't easy in the half-light of evening. Eventually I followed fresh footprints up to another side of the mountain.

As I got higher up the mountain and above the clouds, I felt some warmth of cattle around and, looking down, saw many cows with one herder. I was relieved and full of joy because I was confident that, even if I couldn't find my father, I would be able to stay with that man for a night. He was tall and strongly built and looked relaxed even though he was the only one looking after hundreds of cattle. He had a very small radio with him, a modern object that was very unusual to have in that part of the world. This indicated that he must be an educated man, listening to the news in Swahili. As I approached he stared at me but did not say a word. I was expecting him to ask me who I was, where I was going and how I had got there in the middle of the jungle but, amazingly, he didn't even say hello. I went closer and asked him in Kinyamulenge, our language, whether he knew my father and if he knew where he and the others had relocated. He answered me in an aggressive way, saying that he did not know my father and was not responsible for knowing where he had gone. I begged to stay with him but he refused. This shocked me because I had never heard such a response to a child in my entire life. According to our culture, all adults play the role of parents and have a moral obligation to protect children. It is something very basic in our community. Children are all highly valued members of the community; they are hope for the future and the continuation of the clan. Life for is never just based on the individual but always collective. Any adult is a parent of any child and any adult can punish any child without the child's parents' consent. So this was the strangest reaction I had ever experienced, he completely rejected me and did not care that it was becoming dark and I was a child alone. Traditionally it was his duty to protect me even if he did not know me. His rejection made me feel desperate and made me wonder why an adult would behave in such a way towards a child. I did not want to start crying again in front of him: I was proud and decided not to give him the satisfaction of seeing me upset because of him.

I walked for about two hours until I reached another mountain. Nothing was moving and there was not even a sound of birds. I sat down. I was hungry and thirsty and decided to sleep somewhere there. As I looked at the stars and moon, I remembered my father's words, 'Mvuka, my son, there is only one moon and one sun. Wherever I am on the earth, the moon I will be watching is the same moon you are watching.' I was comforted by that, knowing both my mother and my father were watching the same moon; looking at the sky I felt that we were together. I knew there was no other way I would reach them that night and I thought of my mother innocently believing that I was being well protected by Elisha and looking at the same moon as the one I could see. Knowing that to avoid attacks from wild animals I must not make a noise, I didn't cry and I was still almost expecting that the big man would change his mind and come back to rescue me. Outwardly I was quiet and peaceful but I felt a change inside myself: perhaps this was the first time in my life that I really questioned things. I began to wonder whether there was any part of the world that was different. I was not complaining but it made me think how hard our lifestyle was. Gradually, I was taken by sleep, but I had nightmares about animals I had seen that day. I woke up and started thinking of all the tactics and hints that my father had taught me in order to survive in the jungle, such as making a fire to deter attacks by wild animals.

Suddenly I heard someone shouting from far away. Drowsy and half asleep, I wondered whether it was real or a dream. I pulled myself together and started calling, 'Is someone there? I am the son of Lameke and I am looking for him!' Listening more carefully, I could hear noise from far away and felt relieved. I continued to shout but I was very afraid that if I kept shouting without any people hearing me, I would just attract wild animals. Luckily there was soon the sound of a man approaching and then a tall silhouette appeared. As he approached I could see a herder in a black hat and ragged clothes walking slowly and suspiciously toward me. Smelling of fresh milk and calves, he introduced himself as Ruhemba. He was from my clan and he knew my father. He was obviously shocked to see me in that place alone; he hugged me and tried to reassure me that I would be fine and he would take me to my father. It was very lucky for me that he had heard me. It is customary for my people to communicate by shouting in this way but it is unusual for it to be done by a child and he would not have been expecting anything like that while he was in the middle of milking cows late in the evening. He asked me where my other shoe was but I was too tearful to talk about what had happened. He took me to where he and his friends were camped. They had not built a hut but simply slept in the open. When it rained they would cover themselves with cattle skins. When he introduced me to the other men, they felt sorry for me and promised that I could stay with them until I found my father. They gave me milk (which is the only food they had of course) and kept walking with me for nearly a week until I found my father.

For me it was a miracle to be reunited with my father. As soon as I saw him I completely forgot the terror of what had happened to me. When I asked him whether he had known that I was on my way to him, he said, 'How could I know and who would have told me?' This reminded me that no-one would have looked for me if I had remained lost. In those remote areas without telephones or radios there is very little contact or communication with other people. I looked at him and told him about my shoe, asking him what he was going to do about it. He tried to reassure me but had to say, 'You know there is no way I can get another pair like that but I will make you something that will protect you for a whole season.' This meant he planned to make my shoes from the leather of cattle skin sewn and tied together with any threads he could use from his trousers. I was reassured and nodded. Parents did not really make strong emotional gestures towards their children but I knew he would look after me although he never expressed any sorrow or regret for what I had gone through.

Having grown up to trust adults and expect them to care for me, my experience with those two men – both our friend Elisha who left me at the river and the big man who had refused help – had left me feeling confused. When I told my father about them he expressed no annoyance with Elisha: he understood that to him it was about making me strong by overcoming dangers. Having told me the way and not knowing that the herders had moved on, Elisha thought it was a chance for me to grow up so that I would be able to make my own way in life. I could sense, though, that he was very upset to hear about how the second man had treated me. It was obvious that he recognised the man from my description but he didn't want to admit to me that he knew him and made no comment about him to me. However, a few days later I heard him saying to a relative called Raphael, 'People who are in contact with so-called civilisation are losing our society's values', referring to the man who did not protect me. I was surprised by that comment as, apart from the little radio he was listening to, the man was a herder in the jungle like anyone else there. I had no idea of that "civilisation" he was referring too. Puzzled, I began to wonder how that outside world I didn't know about could make people cruel.

CHAPTER 5
Lost in the jungle

WHAT I LEARNT FROM THIS EXPERIENCE served me well a year later when a similar situation happened. This time was even harder. We had been hit by one of the driest seasons ever known and so, with the usual pasture exhausted, men decided to take their cattle further away than they had ever done previously. This meant walking for about two and a half days from our small village to get to a huge hot area called Lumbwe. Finding people in this direction was very difficult because the landscape is camouflaged by high trees. The areas we used traditionally were generally flat with open land for grazing near to mountains and forests. Lumbwe was completely different and there was the additional danger of many armed militias in the area. My father sent a message from Lumbwe via someone who was returning from there to say that, if I was hoping to join him after I had finished school for the year, there was a man called Lameke in a nearby hamlet who was preparing to travel and he would take me with him. Lameke came from one of the Banyamulenge clans with a reputation for being strong, tall and fearless. My father assured me in his message that he was a good man who would bring me safely. My mother was reluctant to let me go because Lumbwe was dangerous for several reasons, including being a malaria zone, but I insisted, saying that I had to go and there was no way I would stay in the village for the whole dry season. Life in the village was relatively hard in a different kind of way to cattle herding: if I had to stay there I would only help my mother on non-manly activities all day whereas being with my father meant doing men's work with the men. Seeing how determined I was, she finally agreed to let me go.

So it was arranged and the day arrived. My mother had prepared my only little t-shirt and shorts, making sure they were newly washed to begin my adventure. She had confidence in Lameke and knew I could trust him. Very early before the sunrise I went to see him in his village of Kabingo and found he was ready and had packed his food for the journey. He asked me whether I had packed food so I said I had; what I did not say is that I did not like the cold food that men took with them on these journeys, *umutsima n'ibishimbo* – unappetising bundles of compressed cooked maize meal with beans – and preferred to drink only milk on my journey. My mother had given me some milk and assumed I would get more on the way because it was the custom in our society to offer it to anyone who had none. My mother didn't know that I would not pass any huts with the customary *inkongoro*, pots of milk for passers-by, nor that I would not meet anyone who could help me in this way.

Being the dry season, it was of course a fine day as we set off and I was feeling excited and happy even when Lameke warned me that the journey was going to be very tough: 'Forget about strolling!' he said.

'Well, be easy on the child – don't go too fast!' said his wife as she gave me a sympathetic look and said goodbye.

We began at a fast walk but as soon as we had left the village we walked even faster. Lameke was a very strong, tall, long-legged man and he strode off at his usual pace so I had to break into a run to keep up with him. Our men have a distinctive way of walking, adapted to their herding lifestyle. Brandishing a stick to ward off snakes, they move quickly and seemingly effortlessly, never getting out of breath. We did not stop until late in the afternoon when we reached the jungle area. After a few hours my feet were uncomfortably hot in their home made shoes, made from many pieces of plastic joined together to give some protection from sharp stones and grass. I was tired too and felt desperate to lie down. I begged him to stop but he told me that he was worried about the distance we still had to cover and said I should be strong like a man. We continued to run or walk fast until late in the evening. As it was starting to get dark, we slowed down to look for a place to sleep near to trees in the customary way. It was only then that I realised the full extent of an accident that had happened earlier. Previously, when we were moving fast, I did not want to stop to see what had happened to me but now I could see a sharp stick of bamboo had hit me and pierced through the flesh of my calf behind the shinbone. The stick remained horizontally in my leg and it was becoming very uncomfortable to walk. As soon as I realised I was terrified. When I showed my problem to Lameke he looked but said that we needed to find a place to stay first before we could sort it out. He reassured me that it would not be long. It was not bleeding because the stick was embedded in the flesh but he knew that it would bleed a lot if we tried to pull it out.

By a strange coincidence, just at that time we started smelling fire and smoke and then suddenly we saw three men appear out of the darkness near the forest. One introduced himself as Mugeyo. Our tribe maintains a very strong kinship system whereby somehow all adults know each other, not necessarily each individual by facial features but by which family or clan they are part of, which genealogy they belong to, where they customarily live, their relatives and so on. So, although I had never met Mugeyo, I knew he would recognise me or would know my family. He looked about the same age as my father and it turned out that he was his close friend and lived in a nearby village called Kuwabanyarusuku. He looked at me and said, 'Who's this child?' I told him my father's name and he was delighted to be able to help his friend's son. He complimented me, "You are a man now!" meaning that I had made a tough journey that is generally done only by adults. In our tribe manhood is recognised not by age but by manly achievements: wisdom, integrity and sense of social responsibility.

These three men had already selected the usual kind of place to sleep – near the forest so they could be under trees but relatively safe from snakes. They had made a huge fire so we all settled down there and attention turned to the stick in my leg. I could see the surprise in their faces when they looked at it closely. Mugeyo said that the only thing to do was to operate in order to remove the stick and he took out his pocketknife. He said, though, that he used it for carving wood and other home activities and it was not very sharp. He started cutting my skin and making the hole bigger to allow the stick to come out. It seemed to take an age and I was screaming with pain. 'Ah I have something else we can use!' he exclaimed in excitement. This was his traditional shaving instrument called *akanyabganwa* – a small piece of metal that is made by a specialist blacksmith in a shape that can take out one hair at a time. He used this to ensure no pieces of stick remained in the flesh. When they finally managed to get it all out, I started bleeding profusely. Mugeyo tore off some of the inside part of his old black coat and used that as a bandage but it did not help much. They told me to press it hard against the wound and stay away from the fire.

Later that night my leg started to feel much better so I started to regain my appetite but, when I went to drink my milk, I found it had gone off. I was wondering what I could eat as they only had a little of that food I really dislike, the cold maize and beans herders use when they are travelling and cannot milk cows. Apparently they had all assumed that they would find a place where they could get milk left by other people in our customary way but this had not happened. They offered me some of their *umutsima n'ibishimbo* but I said I was not hungry because I disliked that food so much. They tried to persuade me, saying that I had a long journey the next day and must eat to be strong, but I could not bring myself to eat it.

Before sunrise we said goodbye to Mugeyo and his friends and started the journey at the same speed as previously even though I had the injury. We crossed rivers and climbed up and down the hilly land without meeting anyone else; the only other living creatures we could see were wild animals such as buffalo, antelopes, impala, monkeys, topi and baboons. Although I had already seen many wild animals, for me this was a new experience and I was so excited to see some of these beautiful animals. I particularly loved the graceful topi who seemed to leap effortlessly when they bounded away. They reminded me of how, in a previous dry season, my father had helped to capture a steenbok baby, which I took home and built a tiny hut for. I had tried to look after it, feeding it with cow's milk, but a few nights later it disappeared into the nearby forest.

As we walked past these wild animals, I felt afraid because in that same year a lion was killed in a place called Mirimba, not far from this route we were taking to Lumbwe. I was also terrified by the thought that we were going to cross the long valley of Urufunzo and the area near the river Kami where there were so many rhinos. I was wary too of some of the peaceful animals as some of them could have escaped from various hunting or traps, which could make them dangerous too. The previous year, a male eland had killed a man after it had spent days on the run being hunted. My people did not hunt wild game but nearby tribes did.

By midday I had still not eaten. I was hungry and had walked for nearly two days. We started descending towards the Lumbwe area, a place covered in mist so that we could hardly see it. Being at low altitude, it was very hot and we were being bitten by *ibibugu*, large mosquitoes that can carry sleeping sickness. There was a cooling breeze though and trees covered the whole landscape. Late in the evening we approached a huge open area that looked like good pasture so we assumed that we would find our cattle and my father. At this point I was desperate to reach a river because I was very thirsty but at the same time I felt happy, as I was confident I would reach my father very soon. We had covered a distance that should have taken two and a half days in only two days and I was longing to rest and satisfy my thirst and hunger.

Eventually we found an encampment near to a forest but nobody was there. The fireplace was still hot so they had probably moved to another place only the day before. With this disappointment I really became aware of my hunger: there was a feeling of emptiness, I was weak in my body, my saliva had dried up and I felt sick. Lameke did not have any food left and obviously realised that I was getting too weak, so he was getting worried too. He did not say this but I could see he was wondering what would happen next. We decided to overnight there, but it was already quite dark so there was no hope of lighting a fire because we could not search for the right kind of wood.

I slept deeply after my two exhausting days. At first light we started our journey to continue our search. Towards midday I saw a big waterfall a long way away and asked Lameke to take me there as I could not last any longer without a drink. Since we didn't know the right direction anyway but were only randomly searching, we might just as well search the waterfall area, I suggested. He agreed and we went there. Part of the River Lumbwe, the waterfall was huge and very noisy. I had never seen anything quite like it before and we were both overjoyed at the opportunity to swim in the cool river to refresh ourselves. It was fresh water that had run through forests and large valleys. 'Be careful of crocodiles', Lameke warned me.

'I have never seen a crocodile', I said, rather nervously. He told me he did not think there were many in the area, which reassured me a little but then he added that I should be even more careful about snakes as they would be searching for water too. Earlier he had frightened me by warning me about the buffalo, telling me they can be extremely dangerous. I did not worry too much about these stories because I had started to believe that we would die of hunger anyway; it seemed unlikely we would be rescued as the chance of seeing another human in that place was very remote. I asked him whether he had salt with him. He had and he gave me a portion to mix with water. The salt made me drink more water until I felt full in my stomach.

After a swim we were sufficiently refreshed to start more walking and searching. We spent the day going around one hill after another, crossing many valleys, shouting to check whether anyone could hear us. It was the hottest place I had ever been. We were now both extremely hungry and Lameke was losing his way. He told me that we might never find my father and it would be impossible to return to our village in three days in our condition. In the evening we mixed salt and water again. It helped. 'We will have to find the same place we slept last night,' said Lameke.

'Why can't we sleep where we are as there is no difference?' I asked. He did not reply but I guess he was worried about dangerous animals in the area where we were or some militias who might be hunting or operating in the area. By evening we found the same place we had slept in previously though it was a long distance away. As we went, I almost lost sight of him because I was dizzy. I just felt like lying down to die, no longer caring about anything. We reached the old camp and slept there. Although in Lumbwe there are so many forests and rivers, it seemed like a desert because we were unable to find fruit. On other occasions when I had been away from the village without food, I had satisfied my hunger by eating *machocho* fruit. In this area, though, I could not find any – there was just nothing to eat.

On the fourth day I was unable to walk fast and begged Lameke to slow down but he could not as he was worried about the daylight finishing before we had found people to help us. We continued at this painful pace until, towards midday, we spotted tiny shapes which looked like cattle far away; it was still misty and we could not tell whether they were buffalo or domesticated cattle. This new hope gave me enthusiasm to walk because I did not want to die before seeing my father. I wanted him to witness what I had done. We walked hopefully the whole afternoon towards the animals we had seen. When we reached a hill, we climbed it with our hearts hopeful but unsure, waiting to get a good view from the summit. Suddenly and much to our surprise we saw a man! It was Rudoviko the son of Budamu the brother of Mbiringi from my clan.

After much excitement and explanation, he looked into my face, my eyes and my mouth and said, 'You will not die today!' I think he meant to reassure me but, in my child's mind, I was wondering whether he meant that we would die tomorrow. He looked at my face again with worry. Rudoviko was herding his cattle, the animals we had glimpsed, but this place was quite far from his encampment where we would be able to get milk. Cows can only provide milk once their calves have started suckling, so we could not milk any of the cows he was looking after. He told us that we either had to wait for him or we could start the journey alone to his encampment. We chose to go. He tried to persuade me to stay or let him carry me on his back but he was lame and had a lot of cattle to look after so I insisted on walking. He gave us very complicated directions. In our tribe giving a direction is always summarised even if it is a long distance walk. Rudoviko pointed to a distant hill; he said that from there we would cross a small stream to reach a large flat area from where we should be able to smell their encampment. What Rudoviko did not say is that between where we were standing with him and the hill to which he pointed, there were a few valleys and other small hills and that there was no very obvious place to cross the stream he told us about. We set off on our journey but only reached our destination at the same time as he did about four hours later because we lost our way a few times.

When we arrived, we were greeted by other children who crowded round laughing at me as I staggered in almost collapsing; they had no idea what I had been through in the previous three days. Rudoviko told them off and instructed them to get me something to eat as quickly as possible, explaining why I was in such a bad way.

The next day, Lameke decided to go back to our village. I was embarrassed to face my mother without having achieved my purpose, especially after having faced so many issues, and I was also afraid we might lose our way again so I told him I couldn't go back. He tried to persuade me, saying 'I am a grown man but even I am giving up this search. Why should you, a child, feel embarrassed to go back?' Rudoviko supported me though and said I should stay with his children and gain my strength. So I stayed and I soon made very good friends with one of the children and we had a lot of fun together. He took me to forests around there and I experienced some different activities, such as collecting sap from the *umuvumu* tree. This liquid is stored to be used as glue in bird traps. It was a custom I had never heard of; he had learnt it, along with other useful things, from children of another tribal group who lived near to the village he came from. In their tribes, the Banyindu and Bafulero who are socially and culturally close to our tribe, children often collect this useful liquid.

I stayed there for a week until finally Rudoviko found my father about a six hour walk away. He then invited me to spend a day with him when he went to search for good pasture because he was hoping that my father would be looking after his cattle in the same area. We set off together with his cattle and towards midday we heard herders' whistles, a sure sign that men were taking cattle to water. When planning good pasture for cattle, herders would consider how likely it was that the place would have water. Although they could judge that there was high probability of a stream or a small river, it was not necessarily the case. Men would spend most of the day just walking in the forest to search for water and then if they found any they would start preparing a pathway for the cattle. Rudoviko and I followed the herders' whistles. We kept going until we found it was my father together with another man. They had spent hours searching for fresh water and had just found a stream in this large valley. My father did not even greet me as he was still preoccupied with the problems he had finding water for the cattle.

Rudeviko's job being finished, he returned to his village but he encouraged me to stay with my father. I stayed with him until the dry season was over and then we returned home together when the rainy season started.

CHAPTER 6

Having fun with AK-47 bullets

MY FATHER NEVER SPOKE TO ME ABOUT MY JOURNEY, but I kept hearing from other men that he had made comments like, 'He will become a responsible man' or 'He has endured so many challenges and passed so many tests' or 'He is a real hero' and 'I trust him and I am proud of him'. These compliments meant a great deal to me and I would ask whether they were sure that he had said those things, just to be definite it was true. His praise encouraged me and I felt motivated to do men's jobs. Sometimes this led me to do things I shouldn't and one evening I naively decided to take our cattle to an old colonial dipping tank that was abandoned, not having been used for some time.

I had heard grown men talking about how cattle might have skin bacteria and need to swim through the tank but I had not considered the complications. In the first place, it was generally considered that one man was needed for each ten cattle so, as I had forty, it was ridiculous to try this alone. There was also a danger that the cattle might not swim directly to the exit and would spend too long in the chemicals which by now were so old that they could be dangerous to the animals' health. When this happened a man was supposed to go in and pull the cow by a rope attached to its horns but I could not do this on my own. Furthermore, I planned to do this in the evening. I was not supposed to be out by myself so late and it was also the wrong time of day for the cattle. At this time they should be going back to the sheds to feed the calves. If dipping were to happen it should be in the morning sunshine after milking. I ignored all of this and took the cattle to the tank, hitting them gently to make them enter the enclosure that led to the tank one at a time. Pandemonium began among the animals as they ran here and there but I did not give up until I heard a man's voice yelling at me to stop. News travels fast amongst my people and soon many men were running up to stop me. I simply couldn't understand why. Afterwards my father was so angry that he didn't speak to me for days but he didn't hit me. I suppose he realised that I thought I was doing a good thing and he was just relieved that I had been stopped in time.

Another time I overestimated my level of maturity was when I tried to convince people that I could swim as well as my older brother, Oreni. He was able to help like a man when flooding made it difficult for the women to bring their maize crops back to the village from the other side of the river where they farmed. One day when I was out looking after calves, I acted in what I thought was a very grown up way. I called over to some women to ask if they would like me to help bring their bags over. When I told them I was now as strong a swimmer as my brother, they agreed so I took off my clothes and swam over. Wanting to impress, I took the heaviest bag and set off on the return trip. Suddenly the current washed me downstream. I had to abandon the bag and swim as strongly as I could, going with the current but at an angle so I could eventually reach dry land. When I arrived, naked, breathless and with all the maize lost, I was extremely embarrassed.

Looking back now, I realise that many of the games we played as boys were actually quite dangerous. One of our most exciting activities was climbing huge trees and sliding down or swinging from tree to tree by holding on to creepers. All of this was probably excellent exercise and a way of developing good balance but it was also dangerous as the trees were very high. We often hurt ourselves by bumping our heads or falling from a height onto sharp sticks, stones or branches. One reason we loved spending time in the forests was that there was less danger there from snakes because snakes tend to be in the savanna or around the edge of the forest. Another reason we loved the forest was because we could eat many different sorts of fruits, though we had to be careful because some of them were poisonous. We often forgot to come home as we had everything there we wanted – fruit and water as well as fun activities. Every morning we could hear gorillas and chimpanzees screaming. Though we often saw baboons and chimpanzees we never actually saw any gorillas. My father had warned me against them, saying they are shy but can be dangerous if confronted. We ignored those warnings and sometimes followed the streams deep into the forest searching for them. Though the forest appeared to be a wild place where man has never set foot, it was familiar in many ways to my father; he had stories, remembered from his childhood, about each area, river and animal.

Mulelist rebel troops had used these forests so we often discovered military equipment such as grenades and bullet cartridge cases. We knew these could be dangerous because we were warned by a relative called Raphael Ruturutsa who used to be a soldier and had fought for many years to protect the village against rebels. He knew we used to look for big bomb cases that we could use as water carriers and that we often found unexploded grenades, so he told us to stay away from military objects. He was particularly afraid we could come across landmines. Raphael demonstrated to us how bullets are built: he opened the top of a bullet and poured its powder on the ground, explaining how much damage each particle of powder would do. He also explained how a gun is made and what made a bullet fire and kill. He told us that bullets have more force when shot from a weapon because of the velocity but they can still be dangerous without the gun. In a fire, ammunition explodes due to the combustible powder inside the cartridge so when "cooked off" a round could easily wound or kill.

My older brother, Oreni, learnt all he could from Raphael but he did not listen to his warnings about keeping away from this ammunition. To him, seeing how weapons worked was just like having a lesson in physics and, being a self-confident and enquiring person by nature, he wanted to carry out experiments. He knew which of the things we found weren't active and dangerous and which ones were, and he wanted to listen to how they sound when exploded. So he made a plan to explode a few bullets we had collected.

Obviously we would need to make sure that the men were not nearby but it was not difficult to find a time when they were away because their custom was to take the cattle away in the morning to graze and then bring them back later in the evening. This left us boys alone at the cattle shelters by the edge of the forest near our hut built of leaves. We had a meeting and made our plan: we would wait for a day when all the men were on a long journey to find good pasture. The day arrived and we were full of excitement as we met at the edge of the forest a good distance from the calves but close to the hut where we sheltered. Oreni told us to stay behind him while he placed two bullets pointing towards the forest and then put fire by them. Then we waited for the explosion but we had no idea how dangerous it was going to be for us.

He had told us that we must lie down and cover our faces but we were still shocked when, a few seconds later, there was a terrific bang as both bullets exploded. Burning wood was strewn through the air, we were covered in dust and the hut was starting to burn. We were all safe but the explosion was much more frightening than we had expected. Oreni panicked because the area where the bullets had been was burning and he feared it could escalate into a larger fire. We did not have enough water to put the fire out but we used the little water we had and then decided to use milk from the pots as we had plenty. We knew that, according to our people's traditional beliefs, pouring milk on a fire can cause the cows' milk to dry up but we were facing a disaster even bigger so we had no choice. I personally found it fun but it was not fun for the older boys who knew that we were going to be in serious trouble when the men came back.

Eventually the fire was extinguished apart from a few things still smouldering. Then we all screamed, jumped and praised Oreni as our hero. The next task was to clear away all evidence of what had happened. We had to rebuild the little grass hut, making sure that the replacement grass we found was dry because fresh grass would be noticed. We also hid other things that had caught fire. The adults never found out what had happened.

The following season we were to experience the reality of bombs and other heavy weapons used deliberately to attack us. Explosions wouldn't be considered fun from then on and it was unfortunate for me that I would be one of only two children to witness it.

CHAPTER 7

Hostage in a war zone

I ENJOYED SCHOOL AND WAS VERY MOTIVATED to become an educated person who understood the modern world but I never stopped looking forward to herding with the men after the academic year had finished. Herding always had its dangers but one year towards the end of my primary schooling, was absolutely terrifying. This particular dry season my father was not there with the cattle because he had returned to the village, but I was happy to stay with the other herders. There was a younger boy, Gisaro, about twelve other men from our village, and my grandfather's cousin, Stephen Muhindanyi, who was to me "grandfather" of course. Grandfather Muhindanyi was the one in charge of our cattle. He was a highly respected elder and considered a hero by our tribe. He had fought many wars and was a very well-spoken traditional leader. He was known to be of high integrity though he could be quite arrogant too. He was one of men who resisted and fought against the Belgian colonialists and later he had worked as a judge in Nyamyanda (which later changed its name to Uvira).

We were all worried because it was the driest season we had ever experienced and the cattle had started to die of hunger. Under normal circumstances in this situation we would simply move around until we found a place that had not been so severely hit by the drought. However, we had moved everywhere in that vast area of Lulenge and there was no hope. Only one region was possible for pasturage but this was part of an area that we could not access because the government believed Mulelist rebels were still active there. Since the first days of Independence in 1960 the region had remained sealed and patrolled by government forces. The main localities were Gakambya, Maji Mbili and Hewa Bora, the latter being considered as the Mulelist rebel stronghold and headquarters. So this vast region remained inaccessible for many years and Mobutu's government had issued an order to kill anyone entering it. To enforce his orders, there were two military camps at the top of the Gakambya hills to patrol the area, and twice a week a surveillance warplane patrolled the area too to drop bombs as a way of terrorising any rebels and destroying their base. It was an absolutely impenetrable space.

However, with our cattle facing the danger of starvation due to the drought and the lack of good pasture, something had to be done. One evening when the men were all back at the camp, my grandfather called a meeting and announced that we must access the forbidden region; before we did that we would send men to check how good it was and speak to the commandants of the military camps in Gakambya. Everyone was speechless at this suggestion, feeling it was impossible to enter a restricted zone without being noticed and killed at once.

It was getting late at night but I stayed awake to listen to all the discussions carefully, holding my grandfather tightly. I trusted so much in his thinking and opinions that I was disappointed at all the replies he was getting. It was very rare for people to contradict him as he was so respected. He tried to persuade them by saying they must choose between living safely to watch all the cattle destroyed or trying this dangerous option. This was a forceful thing to say because of the way my people have always viewed their cattle. The animals we were herding were almost like people to us and though we drank their milk we hardly ever killed any. We couldn't simply watch them die without doing anything.

After a heated argument, my grandfather made a surprising suggestion. He explained how, five years previously, he had wanted to go to sell nine cows in a place called Kilembwe even though it meant passing through the restricted area that we were talking about. He had managed to get an official letter authorising him to cross the region for that purpose but then he never actually used this authorisation because he changed his plan. His idea was to use it now to take our herds into the dangerous region. We would politely explain to the commandants of the military camps that if they got into trouble for letting us in they could use the letter to avoid a life sentence from Mobutu. We would approach the commandants with red and white cloths on a stick as flags of truce so that surveillance planes would think we were surrendering rebels and not bomb us.

Drawing with a stick on the ground to show a map of his plan, he suggested that messengers should go early in the morning before daylight when the guards at the barrier might still be sleeping; they should avoid the barriers by going through the forest. At first all the men insisted the plan was suicidal but finally they reached a consensus and the idea was accepted: within the next few hours, before daybreak, three men including my grandfather would go to Gakambya to speak to the military commandants.

The adults had virtually no sleep that night as they made the preparations. They prepared their red and white "flags" to declare their peaceful intent to warplanes, guards and soldiers at the military camps and discussed how they must act. As dawn approached, the three messengers asked us all to pray for them and said goodbye. It was uncertain and concerning moment because we all knew there was a high chance we would never see them again. Shortly after, the rest of the men went about their work with the cattle as usual, leaving Gisaro and me at the camp.

While they were away, Gisaro and I tried to carry on with our tasks as normal, but suddenly we felt a thunderous boom pass through our bodies. This was followed by ear-splitting noise. To us, war planes were mysterious, modern things we had often seen high above us but couldn't understand. We had always been told they were on security patrol but had no idea how they operated. Now one was close and dropping bombs. Terrified and in a panic, we ran into the forest to hide. I injured my leg quite seriously when I plunged under a thick bush so I could not be seen between the trees. Gisaro hid fairly close to me.

It was an unfortunate coincidence that this war plane was in operation on the same day that the men had taken such a dangerous risk and it made us fear for the worse for my grandfather and the others. We had recently heard a story of a war plane bombing other places – Kwa Gitongo and Hewabora – and this had led to a massive bush fire. We were really afraid this could happen here, as well as worrying that our camp could be destroyed. However, when the planes had gone, we went back to the camp and were relieved to see that nothing was damaged. The bombs had missed their target. Still, we were unnerved by the whole incident and very glad to see the adults return.

Late in the evening of that same day the messengers returned with the good news that, having offered seven cows as a bribe and saying they could keep the letter, the commandants had said they would allow us into the area for two weeks.

So, early in the morning, we prepared all our cattle and calves for travel; we packed our things and left all the remaining milk in special pots to be used at meal times. I was excited about the new move that would rescue our cattle. My feelings differed from those of the men, who were anxious about this unusual and dangerous decision. My grandfather kept encouraging them with the words: 'If we have to die, no-one will die for us and we can only die once. Besides, no man has ever died and come back to say that being dead is painful.'

We started the journey at about 8am and by about 4pm we had entered into the restricted zone. We had prepared flags to show our peaceful intent to the surveillance planes and we waved them at the guards, who had been alerted that we were coming. As we approached them, I was shocked by their appearance. Their faces scarred and their eyes red, they looked wild: their uniforms were dirty and very old and they seemed to be tired from many years of living in the forest without pay. Some had nicknames that were words expressing how fierce and dangerous they were. I was most terrified by the look of one called Cobra: he was short but very strongly built and he looked as if he wanted to kill someone. He kept pushing some of our calves with his gun, making them move. All these hard-looking men spoke to us in the Lingala language which, being Mobutu's language, was not the local language but one used to terrorise people. They were happy to come and taste milk, and some of them had never seen or drunk it before.

We continued the journey until Gakambya near the military camps. We started building shelters made of branches and leaves. The cattle were exhausted from the journey but they were happy to find green spaces full of good grass and had started producing a lot of milk. By about 7pm the commandants had already panicked: they knew that they would be in serious trouble from the high military commandment for letting us in. They had lied to our messengers and they started pretending that they had never had any conversation allowing us into the restricted zones. They started firing and shot some cattle. Obviously this was becoming serious.

Sure enough, all the men were asked to report to the camps that same evening and when they arrived they were immediately put into prison cells and tortured. My grandfather was amongst those arrested but he tried to assert himself telling them that they must stop otherwise they would be in serious trouble. He intimated that he knew a lot of influential people in the government and that he used to work as a traditional judge for the Belgian colonial administration. It was chaos; we had spent only a few hours in this area but now we were already in trouble. Our men were stripped, tortured, and beaten with long plastic cords called *kiboko*.

While all the men were at the military camp, I and the other child, Gisaro, were forced to stay alone at the huts by the forest. I was a little older than Gisaro and understood better what was happening. As I loved pretending to be an adult, it suited me in a way to look after him and our cattle by myself but the soldiers allowed one of our men, Zakayo, to come back and stay with us all night. I realised how serious things were when he told me that my grandfather had told him I must do all the checking of cattle. This is quite challenging even for a very experienced man: he has to go through all the cattle belonging to one or two families, making sure that none has wandered away or got lost and making sure that they all look well and show no sign of being sick. My father and grandfather had around eighty cows so it was very difficult for me to do this at my age. Gisaro could not help as he was not familiar with our cattle and he had his own work to do checking the cattle of a man called Rabani who was one of the hostages and had been seriously beaten and locked in cell. I woke at first light to start the checks. My father had taught me that the easiest way to complete this process is by grouping cows by their ages or categories: starting with young females, then young males, then young mothers, then older cattle. He told me doing this would help me to notice if any were not there. According to traditional beliefs, we should not actually count cattle. Having grouped all the animals,

I realised that there was a young female missing and that one older cow did not seem well. I recognised the disease from the symptoms. She was shivering, dripping saliva and walking in a slow, tired way with no interest at all in eating. This was obviously trypanosomiasis. If the cow wasn't treated, she was likely to die after weight loss and diarrhoea. We had medication but could not inject the cow without more men to hold her and I was worried that, with all the men arrested, that would be impossible.

Then at midday the warplanes started dropping bombs. Zakayo shouted to me and Gisaro that we must hide ourselves under the trees or cover ourselves with branches and lie without moving so that the plane would not see us. We stayed in the forest most of the day while the cows were getting distressed as they were uncomfortable with no-one to milk them. Later the calves developed diarrhoea from drinking too much milk because, in normal circumstances, men would have taken some of the milk before the calves suckled so much.

My grandfather was released for one evening and told me that he was very proud of what I had done. When I reported to him that a cow was missing, I could see by the expression on his face that he was thinking we had bigger problems. He tried to milk as many cows as he could and warned me that I should be careful with that milk because it could cause an upset stomach having been too long inside the cow. He asked me to help him to inject the sick animal. Usually at least four men would do this but we managed to do it while the animal was sleeping.

After he went back to the military camp, Zakayo, Gisaro and I slept but we were woken up by the noise of gunfire. Soldiers were firing and starting to use bombs, making the cattle scatter in different directions. Later, in the morning, soldiers came again, taking milk and asking for an animal to kill for meat. We had to give them one.

In the middle of the morning the plane came back and this time it flew close to us, dropping bombs. Our men were still held and being tortured but later that day one man was released. He tried to hide his injuries but I saw he had blood all over his body, his eyes were red and his nose was bleeding too. Some soldiers came back and started beating Zakayo in front of us. For Gisaro to see an adult man beaten was something incomprehensible because in our tribe men are considered capable of anything and are fully respected by both children and other adults. He shouted encouragement at our clansman because he had never known such a thing, soldiers beating a man as if he were a child. It was a huge humiliation for Zakayo to be treated this way in front of children. I tried to help by begging the soldiers to stop but they just said in Lingala that they would kill us all. One of the soldiers, from a tribe called Babuyu, took Zakayo to one side and whispered to him that he felt sorry for us but he was only doing what he had been told to do. In the evening Zakayo stayed with us but was unable to do much due to his extensive injuries.

The following day nothing had improved but I had now become used to checking cattle, struggling to milk them though they just walked away. The day after that, things were even harder for us when we were told that we must prepare to go back with our cattle while the hostages would be taken as prisoners to Kilembwe, about 300 kilometres away. We explained that it would be impossible to take all the cattle back with just a few men, so they released three but this was still not enough for all the work involved with that huge herd. Finally the commandants compromised with my grandfather: they would keep just four of the men to hand over to higher authorities and also take nine cows, along with the authorisation letter, to justify their actions. All the other cows and people would have to go back as soon as possible or be killed. There was no time to negotiate; they simply took the four men including my grandfather and the nine cattle and ordered soldiers to chase the rest of us from the area.

As quickly as we could, we gathered our things together and prepared to get the cattle moving. Though many families herd their cattle together, individual families are responsible for their own cows. In this case I was the only one from my family in a position to look after our cattle, a job that is usually done by grown men. We were rushing because soldiers were shooting in the air to hurry us. Having got all the cattle together, we started the journey. Soldiers escorted us, still shooting in the air, which alarmed the cattle and made them run in the wrong direction. Then, just as we were about to set off again, the plane came back so we had to run into the forest, leaving our belongings behind. I was crying at leaving my grandfather. The last time I had seen him, he had hugged me and said he knew I could do what I had to do for my family. Those words meant so much to me, and I was angry and frustrated that the soldiers were not allowing me to do the work my grandfather wanted me to do in his place. I had become used to guns shooting and bombs falling but I was saddened at the idea of letting my family down.

We travelled for half a day until towards late evening when we settled somewhere to rest. The bombing had stopped and we were exhausted. I had many injuries from running through the bush and some of our group were missing. We slept at a hilly place with trees just outside the prohibited zone. Many animals were missing including Gitare, one of my favourite cows. She had been left behind because she had been shot and could not move properly.

Late in the night, people from our village, including my brother Noah, arrived to help us, having been alerted by Zakayo who had left the previous day to seek their help; he had been briefed to take unusual directions to avoid the guards on the main route. They all had spears and machetes to protect themselves from animals or even from soldiers. In the morning I showed Noah the cattle and advised him which ones needed a lot of attention. I also told him I wouldn't move from there without the injured cow, Gitare. We heard more shooting that morning and needed to move as soon as possible but I went back to find Gitare. All the men shouted that they must take me back to the village and warned me that I would be punished if I didn't go with them. Still, as soon as the shooting stopped, I disappeared again and went back to find my cow.

Noah realised that there was no way he could face me for the rest of our lives if he did not help me to bring this Gitare back with us. So, though he was worried that the danger was not over and the animal might not be able to walk anyway, we went back together to bring her. I kept worrying about how my grandfather was being treated in prison and I simply could not accept losing Gitare as well as him. We rescued her and she came with us slowly.

After being looked after carefully for a long time she recovered and healed completely. My grandfather was taken with the other hostages to Kilembwe, where he was imprisoned for many months. All the hostages were continually beaten and interrogated but were not killed so, in the end, the deal was successful: our herds survived that drought because of what they had eaten in the prohibited area and all the men survived also.

A few months later I was reunited with my grandfather. He was so proud of me and introduced me to many men by saying that he and the cattle would not have survived without me. As a reward, he gave me some money to buy shorts and shirts. This was the biggest amount of money I had ever had, but in reality it was probably the equivalent to less than a dollar.

During this terrifying adventure, I came to feel very close to Gisaro. He was younger than I was but we had supported each other as lone children in these difficult circumstances. Unfortunately, the shock of the bombs and the other traumatic events caused him many problems afterwards. He also contracted malaria on the trip and his weakened mental condition seemed to lower his resistance to that disease. He died shortly afterwards. It saddens me to remember that the name Gisaro was given to him to signify that he might one day achieve success, leadership and heroism because another Gisaro, Gisaro Muhoza is the name of the most successful Banyamulenge man at that time. He was the first person from our tribe to become a member of parliament and to advocate on our tribal issues. Tragically, my young friend Gisaro never had the chance to achieve success.

CHAPTER 8

Lower secondary school

THERE WERE ONLY TWO SECONDARY SCHOOLS in the whole of the Minembwe area and children walked to them from various villages and hamlets within an area of 1200 square kilometers. Though it was not the closest and my village was not Catholic, I had decided I wanted to go to the Catholic Secondary School, Mwangaza in Mubaturika; I had heard this was the best. Without telling my family, I went to see the headmaster, Kapule Abwe, a Babembe man who spoke his native language Kibembe as well as Swahili and French. Kapule was considered to be a strict headmaster but this was understandable because he had a tough job as the head of a school in a tribal area that was not his own. He lived by himself at the school, near the village of Abaturika but sometimes his family joined him for a few days. When I told him I would like to join his school, he laughed. 'You must be dreaming,' he said. 'This is a Catholic school. Why would a boy from an evangelical church in Runundu village choose to come here?' I explained to him that I knew it was going to be controversial, as I had not known any other child that would leave the evangelical church school to go to a catholic school. I also explained to him my family's situation and why I preferred his school. I think this very intelligent, discerning man was surprised that I had been brave enough to talk to him outside school time. He was considered as a high authority and most children would not approach him for a serious discussion. Finally he said he would give me a place as long as that didn't get him into trouble with my family.

I was absolutely thrilled and thanked him warmly. This is how I came to attend the Mwangaza School – a brick built, imposing building with real classrooms that had blackboards and desks. In a society where exact birthdates were not recorded, age limits were not strict but most of us would have been around eleven years old when we started. Because men generally had a higher status in our society, most pupils were boys though there were a few girls.

There were so many challenges in joining the Catholic school: convincing my parents, accepting tougher discipline, studying harder, paying higher fees and wearing smarter clothes. None of these things were easy for me. My mother was more sympathetic than my father was likely to be, but even she asked many questions: 'Why should you be different to the other kids in our village? Well go and start there if you must but I don't know how your father will take it,' she said. One person who really helped and supported me was my sister-in-law, Anna. In our society, daughters-in-law are very much respected and their opinions are listened to. Anna had always helped me and the rest of the family. She had kept my secrets and supported me when I had gone to school without my parents knowing. Now, in her quiet and calm way, she spoke up for me and prepared the ground so I could tell my father. He was not really surprised as he had suspected something but he was certainly not pleased. It wasn't the fact that it was a Catholic school that worried him: he was worried that my going to a school far from our village would allow me to spend more time playing, neglecting the jobs I was supposed to do for the family – milking the cows and so on. He didn't forbid me to go though – he just said that it was my business to find school fees. I knew that I would manage those with support from Anna and my mother so I reassured him that I would do my jobs at home.

So I had my way and it was agreed that I could go to Mwangaza School. By the end of the long dry season before I started my new school, I was really excited. As usual at that time of year, I was in the Lulenge area herding with my father but he knew that, to start school, I had to return to the village before the men left. Akim, a friend from the village who had already started another secondary school, went with me. It was an adventure for us to travel alone without the men and we knew the route to take. There were no footpaths because any that had formed were always washed away in the rainy season but we recognised particular landmarks.

Our long, two-day journey took us through some of the most remote and unspoilt landscape in the world, much of it breathtakingly beautiful. All of this area is at an altitude of more than two thousand metres. Some is forested but much of it is open bush, kept clear by the herders who set fire to the grass each year so that young shoots will grow for the cattle. This open land is more dangerous to walk in than the forest because of the abundance of snakes but we had our sticks ready and knew that if we saw a snake we should try to tread on the head rather than the body. Also, on long journeys like this, we would be wearing our *ubumara* on a cord round our necks. These herbal cures are not simply superstition: they really do extract venom if applied immediately to a bite. Still we were happy to reach the Lulenge Jungle, a lush tropical rainforest where we had plenty to eat because of the variety of fruit such as *amacoco*. The tranquility and harmony of this environment, so far from human influence, is beyond description. We had made this journey many times before but still we couldn't help feeling afraid, knowing that were dangerous animals around and remembering also that it had been used as a guerilla hideout in the 1960s and '70s.

To take our minds off our fears, Akim and I played out imaginary roles as we went along. While my friend became an important and influential president, I took on the responsibility of the Secretary General of the United Nations (UN), an organisation I had heard of through my friend Tokos. Akim and I had both grown up in such a remote area that we really knew very little about the wide world but we had picked up enough to know that our people were oppressed and in constant fear of undeserved violence. Though we were naïve, we knew even then that we should spend our lives trying to gain basic rights for our people.

I HAD A FEW DAYS IN THE VILLAGE and then it was time to start my new school. I coped well with getting there on time and obeying the strict rules but my main challenge was that, being one of the poorest pupils, I had only one pair of shorts and one shirt. Most of the other pupils were better off and so I was teased about my one shirt. They used to say that my mother had used it to cover cassava and then gave it to me afterwards for a school uniform. Though I suffered inwardly, I tried not to show it and I took satisfaction in knowing that my appearance did not stop me coming first or second in class or prevent other pupils from asking me the answers to questions.

Walking so far every day was no problem. I liked setting off early after doing my jobs. Looking behind me I could see the village nestling in the hills, the thatched roofs "smoking" as the smoke from fires filtered through. The scenery was beautiful the whole way and the climate in this area is always healthy and pleasant with fresh mountain air. Because I was so young, life was still relatively carefree and I had many happy moments after school too with my friends, especially playing in the stream. This was a stream that had to be crossed and in the rainy season it was often flooded. The teachers always understood if our homework was damp and didn't complain about it.

I had some really good friends in the school too. One I remember clearly was Rumanzi, a boy from a village close to mine. He taught me to recite the names of all the African countries long before I had any idea where they were or even what a "country" actually is. Rumanzi was very good at both geography and history and it was through him that I was able to put into historical context the stories I had heard from my grandfather and father. It was from him that I learned about the famous "scramble for Africa" and how King Leopold had claimed his share at the Colonial Conference of 1884 in Berlin. He claimed he would establish a fair and just state, protecting the natives and bringing Christianity to the heart of Africa by encouraging European missionaries. Instead he exploited the country for his own gains and started a spiral of brutality. Rumanzi also told me about Roger Casement who, shocked by the King's atrocities in the Congo, reported them. He was not taken seriously and was hanged by other white people as a traitor to the colonial ideal.

Another classmate who influenced me was Hagai Mugabe. He often beat me to first place and he was an inspiration to me. Perhaps some of his success was due to strong support from his family, particularly his father, but I could see that his results came from his own efforts: he was hard-working, clean, punctual and well-organised. When the school day was finished, I was still interested in learning but I was keener on general knowledge than the set school homework, mainly because I did not have much space or time to do the homework. The curriculum was quite broad and we studied about twelve subjects to provide a general background in almost everything. The children were mostly Banyamulenge but our lessons were in Swahili.

It was the official requirement for secondary schools that, after two years, every pupil should sit a national selective examination called the *Examen Selectif*, French being the official national language. Whether or not we could continue with education depended on the results of this and we all had to fill in a form before we took it to say what career we would like to follow and which school we would like to attend if we stayed in the education system. I wanted to stay at school to get a good education but I had dreams of going to another area to escape some of the insecurity and harassment from soldiers in our area. Also I wanted to be in a large town rather than a rural area. Studying in a remote area is like trying to breathe when the air is thin; I had never seen any modern technology apart from a gun and the warplanes that flew over. I felt I needed to see the modern world for myself. For example, the idea of bicycles, which a teacher had tried to explain to us, really fascinated me. I remember how an examination question asked us to work out the distance travelled by a man on a bike. I knew I had to use the formula of Distance = Speed x Time but was too absorbed by thinking about how the bike actually worked and wondering whether the chain mechanism affected my calculations. I spent so much time thinking about this that I ran out of time before I had worked out the answer. I was upset about this.

The compulsion to see modernisation for myself was the main reason why, without telling anyone, I chose a school in Uvira and put it on the form. Uvira is a town very far from our area and for many it was almost unimaginable. The headmaster called me in his office and said, 'You won your case to join my school but I don't understand how you expect to win that case and that choice!' What he didn't want to tell me was that he feared I might not pass the exam and if I did pass the exam it was unlikely that the school in Uvira would accept a child from my tribe. My name, Mvuka Ntungane, would make it obvious which tribe I came from. Although the system allowed children to choose which school they wanted to go to, there was no legal requirement for schools to accept particular children.

The day of the exam was a tense moment for the pupils sitting it. Important education officials from towns far away came to supervise it and they all remained aloof: if they were seen speaking to people they might be accused of taking bribes. There was then an anxious two weeks while we waited for results. It was during this time of waiting that I heard some devastating news: Rumanzi and another close friend had both suddenly died. To raise money for their school fees, they had travelled to an area where the Babembe live – an antagonistic tribe who always viewed my people as enemies and foreigners, a stereotype my people detested. On the way back they became very ill and this was rather suspicious. Everyone believed they were poisoned because they had taken a meal while in that hostile area. Their deaths not only upset me but also made me even more determined to escape the whole conflict-torn area. Tokos had inspired me to dream about change and searching for peace through knowledge. Going to Uvira seemed to me the best way forward towards this dream.

To my joy, when the results came through, I found I had passed with 68%. A month later the list of school allocations arrived and relatives were invited to come with their child to hear it. As my parents were very little interested or supportive in education, neither came with me to this big event. I listened apprehensively as the list was read and then learnt to my surprise that I had been accepted by Azahuri Institute in Uvira, just as I had requested. Then all the gossip started – how stupid I had been to choose that school, how would I get there and so on. Many others would also have loved to escape our troubled area but simply had not believed it possible.

The *Complexe Scholaire Azahuri* comprised two main schools within one campus, with different specialities. I had chosen the school that I thought my father was more likely to approve of. It concentrated on subjects that were obviously useful to our people: environmental sciences, agronomy (agriculture and veterinary science) and rural development. At the same time I knew there would be difficulties because the school was in another tribal area and I could be disliked simply for my ethnicity. I hadn't given much thought to where I would actually live but my mother helped me.

She told me about a man called Musirimu who lived there. He was the son of my grandfather's cousin, whom I referred to as my second grandfather. My mother was confident that he would take me in and look after me though we could not be sure.

'So now all I need is money for the bus!' I said to my mother. I was referring to the trucks that were used to transport people over long distances on the dirt roads. This was a great adventure for me because up until then I had never ever seen a motor vehicle of any kind. It would take two days to walk to where we could catch *motogari*, the "bus", and I would need to get enough money to pay for this ride. Again I made bricks with my friend and this time we were able to sell them to local villagers. I still needed money for other things. Then I had another idea.

CHAPTER 9

My first glimpse of
the wider world

MY IDEA WAS TO WORK FOR A MAN WHO TRADED in sugar and soap and sometimes employed people to help with transportation of his goods from Lusenda, two or three days walk from where we lived. There were no roads or motor vehicles in our area and so people had to carry things in the old-fashioned way – tied on our backs or balanced on our heads. So I approached this trader, a man called Lawi to ask for work. At first he said I was too young and not strong enough to carry much but I insisted until he said yes.

The day came and I went with him and a group of other people, including my older brother Oreni. It is a journey I will never forget, not least for the spectacular scenery. Our area is at an altitude above 2000 metres and, after a long walk to the edge of the Mitumba Mountains, we had to make the long descent down to the shores of Lake Tanganyika. For the first part of the journey I was inspired by knowing that, from the top of Lusenda Mountain, a place called Kurimugono, I would see Lake Tanganyika. It was referred to in my language as '*Ikivu cya tanganika*' which translates literally as the sea of Tanganyika, which is not surprising considering that it is one of world's largest lakes.

I had never seen any stretch of water wider than a river and Lawi told us that the view was particularly spectacular first thing in the morning when it looks like "oily soup". He was referring to a particular effect caused by the sun shining at an angle through the air which is at a high temperature in that low area. This causes a mist that makes the gleaming lake seem to be boiling. I was not disappointed – it was a beautiful sight. The other reason I was excited about seeing this lake was the fact that it was the only place in the region where the fish sold in shops and markets come from. In my village we very rarely ate fish but we used to get small dried fish called *injanga* probably about once a year.

We "walked" – that is to say we went by our traditional fast walk/jog style of travel and for me, as the youngest member of the group with the shortest legs, it seemed cripplingly fast. As a business man, Lawi saw his time as precious and we had to complete the journey in two days in order not to miss the market. Lawi was very well known in the Minembwe area as one of the best fast walkers and my mother had discouraged me from going, saying she was very worried that I would not be able to cope. It was a business trip for Lawi so he would not have time to worry about me. Whenever I was desperate for a break or water, I kept remembering my mother's warning and felt under pressure to honour my promise to her. I knew that she wished I did not need to do this to earn school fees: I knew that she wished she could pay for me so I didn't have to suffer and that if it had been possible she would have done this walk for me.

We went through a large forest called Mukoko where the footpath was blocked by many trees and bamboos that had fallen in the heavy wind. We kept walking fast and jumping those obstacles. Next we crossed a large area of savannah, the noise of thundering waterfalls telling us we were getting closer and closer to the Mutambala River. Crossing that was very different to crossing the calm Minembwe River I was used to. The strong currents made it impossible to swim in and the "bridge" (the traditionally built swing bridge) had just been destroyed by the flood. We had two alternatives and both were risky: to walk over the thin, long, dry log that local Babembe villagers had put over it as a temporary measure, or to cross by wading and climbing onto branches of fallen trees lying in the river. With the first option, nobody knew how secure that narrow log was, whereas with the second option we could wade fairly confidently, climbing on to them in places, but would need to jump the last part where the branches did not meet the far bank. It was decided that this second option was the less risky for everyone but, as I was younger with shorter legs, I would have more of a problem than the others with that final jump. I made sure I did not go last so that, if I didn't make it, there would be someone at either side of the river to rescue me.

We had an overnight stop in the open air. Our guide, a man called Lumumba, woke us up before the intended time as none of us had a watch but we had already walked a certain distance before he realised that it was too early (probably about 3am). So we had to stop to sleep for a few more hours in the *agashigo* – open bush land. Between the discomfort and the excitement thinking of how beautiful the next day would be, I did not get much sleep.

As soon as daylight returned we continued at our gruelling pace. These few hours had been extremely difficult and my feet were hurting terribly. I held myself back from either crying or complaining as I knew I would only be told that I should not have decided to join the trip in the first place. On the positive side, I was desperately looking forward to seeing Lake Tanganyika.

Finally we arrived in Lusenda. My cousin Kayira, who worked at the store where Lawi picked up his sugar and boxes of soap, was furious to see me there and began to shout at Lawi for having taken me. I told Kayira to calm down, reminding him that the place we lived had no future other than looking after cattle and being regularly persecuted by government soldiers. I told him that if he had really cared so much about me he would have helped me to pay my school fees. I did not tell him, though, that I was planning to go to Uvira. As they continued to argue, I heard a strange noise, a noise I had never heard before. It was a car, the first I had ever seen. I ran after it as fast as I could to keep it in my sights for as long as possible. I was amazed by its speed and could not imagine that there was actually a human being controlling it. There was a white person in the car and this was only the third white person I had ever seen, the previous two being the Swedish missionaries, Adolf and Bertha. Adolf had driven over the dirt roads as far as Uvira to Bidegu which is where the road ended but he had walked to my village to preach. Bertha came later with our neighbour, a man called Joseph Mutambo, probably one of the three most educated men in the area. It was a three or four day walk from Uvira to our village.

In a hurry to complete his business, Lawi told us to get ready to leave in a few hours. He knew it was exciting for us to see this beautiful area so he told us it was our opportunity to go to the beach if we wanted. It was dangerous for us to go near the lake because Lusenda is a Babembe tribal area. Nevertheless, my brother Oreni and his three friends insisted that we should go to the beach so we went there. Seeing and touching the lake was an incredible experience for me. Lake Tanganyika being one of the largest and deepest lakes in the world, it was amazing to me – its huge size and blue water; I simply couldn't understand how that colour was possible. Looking at that vast expanse of water, we had no idea that it had an end somewhere and that there were people of other tribes who lived on the other side. Adolf the missionary had told us that his country was situated at the end of the world and beyond that was nothing but a stretch of endless water. Seeing this lake I found myself wondering if it could be something like this that he had been referring to. The waves were strong and we were amazed by their size and speed and the rhythmic order with which they struck the shore. At the same time as being fascinated by the beauty of the scene before me, I felt afraid as I listened to that rhythmic thud of waves on the shore, wondering what we would do if we were attacked by crocodiles.

My contemplations were short-lived, however, because within an hour we realised that we were surrounded by Babembe people. They shouted at us angrily that we were Rwandese, *Inyalwanda* meaning that we were foreigners and invaders. We could not really discuss anything with them because we did not speak their language and did not understand what they were saying. We were all terrified of what they could to us for being in their area. While we were surrounded, they kept speaking in Kibembe, though we tried to communicate in Swahili. We told them that if they would let us off this time we would never come back there again.

Then they called their friends to bring fishing nets and a canoe. They threw the net over us so we were tied together, pushed us into the canoe and said they would dump us in the lake to feed the crocodiles. My brother Oreni fought his best but his friends were terrified and did not help much. My brother managed to break through the fishing net but unfortunately the canoe was already in deep water. He couldn't jump in and leave us all behind and he couldn't fight them all off to rescue us. I had already seen many frightening situations involving violent attacks but this was somehow the most terrifying, perhaps because it was in a strange place, within the Babembe tribal area and on this huge stretch of water I had never seen before in my life. 'I don't want to die in that water!' I shouted. When they reached a deep place my brother Oreni told them if they wanted to fight they should not throw him in the water but face him on dry land. They ignored him and threw him over. He was a good swimmer so, though hampered by his clothes, still he managed to get to reach the shore. Then one of the older Babembe told them to stop. They paddled back to the beach and released us from the fishing net.

Feeling very shaken, we hurried back but we didn't tell either my cousin Kayira or Lawi what had happened to us. Lawi had prepared something to eat; it was a *giswaga*, a special food of the Babembe tribe which is made of cassava. It was good to taste something different and relax after our ordeal. We then started our journey. I was given ten kilogrammes of sugar to carry: I remember precisely how many kilograms it was because it was labelled "10 kilo". This was very heavy for me. Packaging for this weight of sugar was a thick khaki carton, well-sealed all around. It was decorated with beautiful designs and written on top in red and blue was "ONDES Kiliba" (Office Nationale de Sucrerie de Kiliba – the national office of the sugar industry of Kiliba). I carried it on my head in the traditional way of carrying or transporting heavy things. To protect and support our heads against the weight we use an *ingata* – a pad of banana leaves twisted into a coronet shape – on our heads. My brother Oreni had made two, one for him and the other one for me.

The first part of the journey was debilitatingly hot because of the low altitude. It took us the whole afternoon to reach Lusenda Mountain and I was exhausted by the time we got there. I had promised Lawi that I could do the job, so I remained silent and avoided complaining or asking for help. In my exhaustion, as we kept walking fast in the heat, the sweat from my head started to dissolve the sugar at the bottom of the package. The more the sweat seeped into the sugar, the faster a sweet stream poured over my cheeks towards my lips. It was delicious! I had tasted sugar once or twice before but I now I found myself with the opportunity of eating plenty. I put a finger through the damp part of the packaging so it was easy to reach the sugar but I had to be careful not to make it obvious so that Lawi would not find out.

After two days we arrived home but it took me many weeks to recover because my legs were swollen, the skin on my feet was chapped and cracked and I could not move my neck. It was particularly dispiriting as Lawi did not want to pay me. After a month I started begging him. At first he kept saying he would pay me 12000 francs, which is probably only about £2, but then he said he couldn't afford to pay me at all. My mother went and shouted angrily at him until he said he would pay the full amount if I accompanied him to Manunga market transporting other things for free. She did not agree to this and finally, after countless trips to his place, he paid the full amount. Unfortunately, by the time he had paid me my money, it had devalued. Still, it was better than nothing and I knew it would contribute towards my trip to Uvira.

My feelings towards Lawi were confused. On the one hand he had disappointed me by breaking the agreement; I had met my commitment to him but he failed to honour his commitment to me. This sort of dishonesty was one of the reasons that traders were perceived negatively in our culture but they were also mistrusted because of our traditional attitudes. Any activities that would affect moral standards were very much avoided. For example, we lived in an area very rich in minerals such as gold but we were strongly advised not to extract it as it would lead to love for money, greed and immorality. For these reasons, I was inclined to dislike Lawi and yet, on the other hand, I found myself admiring him for his courage in breaking the myths related to trading. He was a strong advocate for modernism and had an open minded view; he used to argue that it was possible to be involved in trading while maintaining traditional values. Politically, the whole village looked to him to know the news on political events and how they might affect our community. To a large extent we depended on him to know if we were likely to be attacked by government soldiers and so on. He was, therefore, a very significant person for us in terms of security as well as local development. In my view we needed people like Lawi to break the cycle of poverty in our area. Traditionally our wealth was about status, how many cattle we owned, rather than about material comfort and we needed to modernise. All of our people, whether wealthy in the traditional sense or not, lived with very little awareness of the world beyond us and, in my opinion, we needed to move with the times.

CHAPTER 10

The search for a new life in the city

OVER THE NEXT FEW YEARS I made several trips between my village and Uvira, each of them momentous and difficult, but none has stayed so clearly in my mind as the first one because it was such a new, exciting experience for me. With no roads or other form of transport in the immediate area, I had only ever travelled by foot but now I would for the first time travel by *motogari*, a public motor vehicle. The journey would begin by walking to the nearest road but then I would board this wonderful modern invention. It was sure to be a rather old Toyota Stout, continuously mended to the point that practically nothing inside the engine was what had originally been there; the braking system was likely to be a *frein à main* (hand brake), a stone that the boy chauffeur, the driver's assistant, kept at the ready to put behind a wheel when the vehicle stopped. Still, to me it represented my moving on to another world and I looked forward to my first ever trip down the winding, unsealed road through that beautiful precipitous landscape.

The first thing to do was to find people to travel with and I soon learned that there was a group of about seven who were planning to go to Bukavu, the main city in the Kivu region. Knowing that the road to Bukavu goes via Uvira, I went to speak to one of them, a young man called Jacques or Jake Muhindanyi. "Jake" is pronounced like the French "Jacques" so he was one of the lucky people whose Christian name had a rough African equivalent during the time Mobutu banned western-type names so he didn't need to change it unless he wrote it down. As the son of my grandfather's cousin, Muhindanyi Setefano, he was part of my extended family. He was very friendly and helpful, suggesting that I should find a suitcase and make sure I had spare clothes. I was worried that if I said I did not have a suitcase and spare clothes he might feel embarrassed to take me with him so, impulsive as usual, I immediately promised I would get these things, without any real thought of how we could afford them. My mother came to my rescue when she managed to find a relatively small old suitcase that belonged to my older brother Noah. There was very little to pack in it – just one pair of shorts, a shirt, a jacket and some beans for whichever family I would stay with but I was happy to look like the others, carrying real luggage.

It was good that my suitcase wasn't heavy anyway because we started the journey very early in the morning and walked for the whole day until we reached a Babembe village, Kilumbi, in the middle of a large forest. We had heard of it because it was known that it used to host Mulelist rebels. By the time we got there and settled down for a few hours' rest through the night, I had already started missing my mother. The leader of the group said that we must all wake up by 3am to continue the journey, which meant that we were going to leave before cockcrow – our usual way of knowing it was time to get up. We did not have any cocks to crow or any watches but we were confident that someone would wake the rest up at exactly the agreed time: we often rely on human wisdom to know the exact time we should wake up.

So at about 3am we started the journey through the dense forest of Kilumbi, which is part of the Mitumba chain of mountains, and I walked along half asleep. I was the youngest in the group but there was one girl not much older than me called Nyamajana. As we walked through the forest on a very narrow pathway, we had only one *ikimuri* (a traditional torch, a piece of burning wood) between us and that did not provide a lot of light. So our leader, Jacques, carried the "torch", shining it on the rough path ahead of us, and we all kept close to each other. It was very steep, muddy and in some places the footpath was right at the cliff edge. Underfoot the soil was muddy and slippery and, at one point, I slithered helplessly over the cliff edge. It was so muddy that I could not stop myself but just carried on down, terrified of what was going to happen to me. I shouted for help but they did not hear me.

Finally I reached the bottom where muddy debris had been washed down by rain and erosion. It was dark, full of termites and there I was, alone with my small suitcase. I was terrified, knowing this kind of place attracted all sorts of snakes, insects and other dangerous animals. I wondered when they would realise that I was not with them and worried whether or not they would be able to find me. At this point I started thinking that I should never have thought of going to this school so far away when all my friends had chosen an easier option. After all that hardship I had been through, could it happen that I would die here and no one would ever even find me? Without knowing how high the cliff edge was, I tried to climb up but just kept slipping back down. It started to get light but it was very cold. Finally, after what seemed like an age but was probably about half an hour, I heard the voice of Nyamajana shouting and echoing in this dense and humid forest. It is impossible to describe how relieved I felt as I shouted back. Jacques came to rescue me, making his way carefully through the dense, tangled undergrowth of the forest by the cliff edge and calling to me as he went to reassure me. When he had descended as low as he could, he then lay on his stomach so that he could reach a hand down to me and pulled me up. Jacques was very apologetic for what happened and reassured me that he would keep an eye on me from then onwards.

Eventually we reached a place called Nundu, the closest town from our village that was situated by one of the few roads in this area. The roads were not sealed but were simply dirt roads maintained from time to time by graders. People who need to go anywhere wait by the road until a *motogari*, generally an old Toyota pick-up truck, stops to pick them up. Being a driver was a job with relatively good status as it was about operating a motor vehicle – a very rare thing in our area. These vehicles are still a common form of transport and are often known by their model name: "Stout". Here we had to wait for the first vehicle that could take us the rest of the way. My excitement grew as we waited until finally a Stout arrived. We threw on our bags and suitcases and then climbed on ourselves. There were already plenty of sacks of fish and charcoal and, on top of them, many people. We were told to hold tightly onto anything we could reach and then the truck took off, crammed full of people and luggage, far beyond its legal capacity. It was not a comfortable ride over the dusty, bumpy bush road and we certainly did need to hold on tight to the sides to keep our balance. I felt a constant, painful dizziness as everything we passed seemed to be moving. Sometimes we were thrown against each other as the vehicle lurched and rocked and our nostrils were filled with dust. In some other places it had rained, making the road slippery. Through it all, the passengers kept up an endless concert of enthusiastic songs to encourage the driver with such words as '*kaza mwendo mungu iko pamoja nawe*', Swahili for 'carry on with the journey because God is with us'.

For a child on his first long journey by motor vehicle this experience was something I could never forget. Having travelled through the night, I lost track of time but approached my destination the next morning through spectacular scenery. Uvira is in a very beautiful valley bordered on its eastern side by Lake Tanganyika and by the mountains on the west. To the north-east is the Ruzizi River beyond which lies the north Kamanyola border with the republic of Rwanda along the delta of the Ruzizi River. Only one main road runs into town and people were dropped off in various places but I did not know where I should get off. I was not even sure that I had anywhere to stay but I knew there were a few people from my tribe living in Uvira at that time and the custom was that they would welcome other Banyamulenge people, especially those who were fleeing from hardship and hoping to create a better future for themselves. The distant relative my mother had told me about was called Musirimu and I intended to look for him.

I was wide-eyed and open-mouthed at my first views of "civilisation". My wonderment attracted quite a bit of smiling and teasing from the other people travelling with me and I did indeed feel lost when I was dropped off at in the city centre. Jacques said goodbye and then he and the others disappeared. I was completely overawed by my first experience of Uvira. It was a city indeed with roads, motor vehicles of all sorts, shops, a market and people milling around everywhere: it all seemed strange and nothing looked the same as where I came from. I felt shy and afraid amongst so many different people, few of whom looked much like the people I was used to because they were of other ethnicities. There were soldiers in uniform, beggars, children who seemed to be alone and neglected, children in blue and white school uniforms, people of all sorts being transported in dilapidated vehicles and others going about their work. I was intrigued by the handcarts being pushed by men stripped to the waist – presumably it was hot work in that climate – as they delivered crates of beer to the large stores. But for me the most impressive thing was the evidence of electric power: I could see the wires connected to poles and rooftops. I had of course heard of electricity at school, but its workings were a complete mystery to me, and the machines which it powered, were beyond my comprehension. I was really looking forward to seeing some of the things that operated by electric power – things I had only heard of, such as television. Another big difference to home was the temperature because we had left the mountains behind us and I was now in the heat of the lowlands by Lake Tanganyika.

Fortunately, Jacques had not really gone away. He had hidden and watched me to see if I could cope. He then took me to the house I was looking for and we were greeted by Musirimu's sister and one of his daughters. They both welcomed us and we sat under a mango tree for the whole late afternoon. There was a wonderful atmosphere as we relaxed together. It took me a while to realise that the beautifully cool air was because of the proximity of Lake Tanganyika – just a few metres from the house. Also, there was the constant, soothing rhythm of the waves. Musirimu himself was away in the Shaba region on business, supplying veterinary equipment including medication to a large government owned farm in the Shaba region. His wife had gone to church in Kimanga but came home later in the evening. I was nervously wondering if she would allow me to stay with them but I could not ask her straight away. It is not polite in our tradition for a newly arrived guest to talk of serious things like that before the evening meal. There were many people there, relaxed and chatting together in Swahili as it was a mixed group of different ethnicities.

As soon as I got up the next morning I told Mamma (a term of respect for older women) Musirimu that I had come to ask for somewhere to stay while I attended the school in town for which I had been accepted, Azahuri Institute. I explained that my decision to continue my education in Uvira was because conditions in my village were so difficult, particularly in regard to security and going to school. Unfortunately, she already had three other young people as well as her own children living in her house and she was clearly reluctant to take me too. The next day her husband returned home and he was also not keen to have me but, not knowing what else I could do, I just stayed on anyway.

CHAPTER 11

Starting Azahuri Institute

WHEN I WOKE UP THE NEXT DAY I was very anxious, wondering what would happen if they told me to leave. I was also worrying about whether the school would refuse me because I had been told that, as the school was predominantly of the Bafulero tribe, it was unlikely they would accept a child from my tribe. Remaining optimistic though, the next morning I just prepared myself to go to Azuhuri School, in Kasenga, for my first day. I knew the uniform was blue and white so I took out of my suitcase my only clothes other than the ones I was wearing – the clean blue shorts and white tee-shirt that I had saved for this big day. To get to the school I was guided by a boy from a neighbouring house, but he was so ashamed of me that he did not want it to appear as if we were walking together and sharing the same destination. He told me that we would use the "rail" route. This was the old and unused railway which had been abandoned since colonial times. It ran between the road and the lake, parallel to the road and was a route used by anyone avoiding the public or not wanting to be noticed.

I felt elated as I went on my way because, after all the problems I had faced, this would be the time when it began to feel worth it – I had finally reached a large city and a prestigious educational centre. Known as the *Complexe Scholaire Azahuri*, it was supported by the Pentecostal Church funded by Swedish missionaries. It was actually two schools side by side sharing some facilities such as the large playground and the compulsory church services every Saturday. One of the "twin" schools specialized in biochemistry, physics and maths while the other – the one I had chosen – specialised in agronomy (agriculture and veterinary science) and rural development. Even my father had to agree that being skilled in these areas would be useful to our people and I was excited to think I would have access to internationally recognised research centres and would one day be a well-qualified, educated person.

Arriving at the school, I was not disappointed. There were huge, modern buildings with hundreds of young people milling around, laughing and joking in Swahili, excited that a new academic year was about to start. My joy did not last long. I found and finally spoke to the headmaster, Nepa Kabayaho and my heart sank as he told me, 'Yes, you have been allocated a place here but I cannot give you a place because we are full.'

As politely as I could, I argued with Nepa that I had a right to study at his school because it was the regional schools authority that had allocated me a place there. He then started looking at me and laughingly asking if I were Rwandese though, as an educated man, he would know perfectly well that my group of Tutsi people, the Banyamulenge, were citizens of Zaire. 'No I am Congolese' I replied.

'You look like a foreigner and you'll have to pay a foreigner's fees! How dare you assume that you would be given a place at this school? *Munyarwwanda* (you Rwandan), this is not a school for people like you!'

My heart sank. I had never been to Rwanda or any other foreign country and, at that time, I didn't fully understand the racial divides in my country – that my ancestors had originated from the area now known as Rwanda but had been forced to more or less settle in the Kivu area. I sensed immediately, though, that his comments were prompted by racial prejudice. It was clear from my physical appearance that I did not belong to a tribal group of that area and I spoke a different first language. Having grown up through troubled times, I was accustomed to racist comments from other tribal groups but I thought here, in an educational setting, I would be free of such things, especially from the teachers themselves. Perhaps I had even hoped I would be welcomed as the first person from my tribe to reach that school and that I would not be judged as "primitive" despite my background and obvious lack of sophistication. I was not sure if he was simply being unpleasant or if he found it unbelievable that I had travelled so far to study at his school. It was a bitter disappointment to me to find that a headmaster – an important, educated man – could judge me in this way. Unfortunately I had also made a serious error with the uniform: at senior secondary school level they expected every student to wear blue trousers – not shorts like I was wearing – and a white shirt. The headmaster then sent me away but said he would consider my case.

It was an anxious time for me as I waited. Many of the other students were looking at me and laughing, insulting me by shouting 'RRR', an acronym standing for *Rendez-vous de rendre les Rwandais au Rwanda*, a French expression suggesting Rwandans should return to Rwanda. It was certainly becoming hard to take: my first day at school and no-one would accept me.

I returned home and informed Musirimu about the outcome of the day, which was difficult because as I spoke to him I didn't even know whether I had a place to stay. Musirimu just ignored the issue of where I would be staying and started getting involved in the business of my enrolment. He was upset about Nepa's response but he did not seem as surprised as I had expected so I quickly gathered he was used to the facing discrimination. He had warned me that I would be the first child from my ethnic group to study at that school and he was curious to know whether I would be considered. He then wrote a letter for me to take to another school headmaster, who was influential because of his involvement in the management of the Pentecostal church that controlled the school Nepa headed. When I gave the letter to this headmaster, he smiled and asked me to go with him to Nepa's office. I waited outside while they had a long talk together and then, about an hour later, Nepa called me into his office. I was trembling and impatient to hear what he would say. Despite his racist comments, he seemed to be a very capable person who took his job seriously. His decision was that he would allow me to join the school provisionally. If a child from one of the local tribes requested the place, my place would be withdrawn. Also, before I could start I must have the correct uniform.

Well of course that was something of a relief but I now had to resolve two difficult questions: where would I live if the family was not able to look after me and how could I find new clothes? I had just sufficient money to pay the school fees so how could I buy a uniform? I decided to prioritise issues: obviously I couldn't even try to start school without the uniform so I would start by getting that.

I went back home using the railway route, full of joy but at the same time nervous, thinking of my two problems. I had lunch together with Musirimu's children, which seemed strange to me as I was used to eating very early in morning and then not again until the evening. After lunch I went to Mulongwe market with Musirimu's daughter who helped me to choose some clothes. I bought blue jeans, my first ever long trousers, and a white shirt.

Back with Musirimu's family, I just kept quiet, not asking if I could stay or not. I knew that in our tradition, they couldn't really throw me out but at the same time I was concerned that there might come a point where they would ask me politely to leave. I knew that, though they might be annoyed at having me with them, they would probably just accept it. I did not have a choice anyway as I could not go back by myself and it would be a long process to arrange to return home. Besides, I knew that Musirimu was indebted to my father for various things and our families had strong links. I also knew that he might change his mind if I did well at school because I overheard him saying that he didn't mind children staying at his place if they were hard working and could pass their exams.

So I decided to work hard, be helpful and well-behaved and impress him in the examinations that would take place after my first three months. These first three months would be a sort of probation period for me. Meanwhile I was also very worried because I had used my school fees to pay for my uniform and did not know how I could pay for my schooling. I started praying whenever I was alone in the house and could see that everyone else was outside and couldn't hear me. Though I had written a letter to my father, I had not told him about my problems because I didn't want to worry my family; so I was completely surprised when, a few weeks later, a man from my clan came to find me with money from my father. What a wonderful surprise! Although he was becoming more supportive in his attitude, this was one of the very rare times he actually intervened financially.

Ahead of me were other challenges. I soon found out the enormous problems I would face just getting to school every day. I had to walk about 7km each way and people who saw me, recognising me as a Tutsi, would throw stones at me. So, for a whole year I avoided using the main road; I kept using the old, disused railway track where there were fewer people and so fewer stones. At school the other students insulted me and kept spitting at me, constantly asking me in a mocking way where I came from. And all the time my biggest worry was not what they were doing to me but whether the headmaster would withdraw my place if he found a local child. Most of the teachers were quite abusive too, calling me names such as *ngombe* meaning cow (a reference to our herding tradition) or *Museveni*, the name of the president of Uganda who was perceived as Tutsi or Rwandese by many Congolese.

There was one exception: a very clever maths and physics teacher called El Kika. He had been in the area where I come from and so was not prejudiced against my people though even he jokingly referred to me as Rwandese. I knew he didn't really mean it and I enjoyed his lessons feeling that at least there was one teacher I could trust not to mark me down in the results. I was soon supported also by another Banyamulenge in the school, a boy called Mutebutsi Kayaya. It was a relief to have someone to share the burden of bullying and insults. He was very articulate as well as strongly built and had become used to defending himself against attacks from Babembe young people in his previous school, so he was less afraid than I was and encouraged me to be strong at all times. He was protective of me and would step in whenever I came under attack. We spent as much time as possible together for mutual support.

Of course I was bitterly unhappy and homesick but my unhappiness made me all the more determined to succeed. I persevered and passed the exams. Musirimu was impressed; he had expected them to find a way to fail the first Tutsi to access that school. I explained to him that I had worked extra hard to make sure I passed well because if I had been borderline they would probably have failed me. He agreed that I could stay at his place that year though his wife was still dubious about how the family would cope with being responsible for accommodating and feeding so many other people.

Towards the end of my first year, I started suffering repeated attacks of malaria. I had it eight times in twelve months and it made me feel physically weak. However, finding out at the end of the year that I had passed the annual exams made me extremely happy. I had not received great marks but this was still a great achievement considering what I had been through – illness, open discrimination from the teachers, lack of money, feeling homesick and so on. I went home during the long vacation and, as usual, I had to join my father to search good pastures for our cattle. I avoided telling him everything about my first year in Uvira but he realised I had overcome a lot of problems and came to trust me: he realised that I was determined enough to succeed and things were not as hopeless as he had thought.

After the long vacation I returned to Uvira to start my second year there. This time I was more prepared: I knew how people from my ethnic group lived in fear every day. I was still only about fourteen years old and had never lived in a place free of ethnic tensions so, although I recognized the dangers, I came to accept this way of life as normal.

CHAPTER 12

Malaria and worse

WHEN I FIRST LEFT THE HIGH PLATEAU of Minembwe, I hadn't appreciated how much healthier it was to live there than in places at lower altitude. One of my strongest early impressions of Uvira was the frequency of funeral processions there. My walk to school from Musirimu's place took me fairly close to the principal cemetery of the city and almost every day I would see a crowd of people taking someone to be interred. The worst of all was when I could see that it was a child or baby who had died, which was very often. Though it was an everyday occurrence, passers-by were always extremely respectful of the procession, stopping all they were doing to stand in silence to show respect for the corpse. When the mourners had passed, singing as they went '*wende pamoja na Yesu safari ni ndefu na njia ni ndefu wende kwa bwana*' ('safe journey with Jesus! The way will be long but you are going to be with Jesus') people would ask one another, 'Do you know which family it is who has lost a child?' Invariably, there would be someone who knew the family and who could say what the cause was. It was always malaria.

There are preventative treatments for malaria but, because people can't afford them, malaria is widespread in this tropical region and most people suffer from it at least once a year. Children are victims more often than adults because older people are more likely to have resistance, having survived it earlier. The disease is more prevalent in the rainy season, especially December, when there are more mosquitoes to spread it. The symptoms are the same for everyone except that they vary in severity and some people have more resistance than others. I had never suffered from it in the lovely climate of my home and so it hit me hard now; usually I had it about three times a year. The worst attack I ever had was at the end of the first term of my second year. It was December, coming up to Christmas and I was preparing for end of term examinations. Towards midday I started to shiver and feel extremely cold, even though the temperature was as hot as usual. I asked permission to leave the class so I could lie down in the sunshine for a while but the warmth of the sun didn't help me and my shivering worsened. I decided I would have to go home and asked a school friend to bring me my books. I had no money for transport so was forced to walk the long distance as usual but by the time I reached the bridge over the river Mulongwe, my condition had deteriorated. Now I was in the hot phase with fever, headache and vomiting. I moved a little away from the busy road to lie down under a palm oil tree; this was in a place that is normally very pleasant but I was oblivious to it, completely unaware of the traffic, the people or the river. I was dehydrated with no strength to do anything and was lost for a few hours. There were no emergency services and I had no money to pay for transport to hospital. People passed me by because it was fairly normal to see a sick person vomiting at the side of the road.

Towards the end of the afternoon, I was woken by the noise of children playing nearby, and began to wonder what I could do. The city is a lively place at this time of day with noises from all directions as people go about their busy lives along this main road: students going home from various different schools, old cars, men pushing hand carts, people returning from working in their fields, women on their way to fetch water, with large pots balanced on their heads. Feeling isolated and worried that other pupils from my school might see me in this vulnerable state, I covered my face with my white shirt. Soon I fell into another phase: my temperature felt normal but I was covered with sweat. When I tried to get up to carry on, I realised that I would not be able to make it all the way home, about eight kilometres. I had to find somewhere closer to stay. I thought of someone who lived nearby, a man I knew of through my friend, Akim. Called Shekwa, he was a good friend to many Banyamulenge families though he was a Mufulero (singular of Bafulero) himself. He was a good Christian and belonged to the Pentecostal church on that side of town. Telling myself that I did not want to die without anyone knowing, I gently began to move, vomiting as I did so, though there was nothing left in my stomach other than saliva.

When I reached Shekwa's place, I found him sitting under the tree outside, mending shoes. He was not a wealthy man but struggled to support his family as a cobbler. Though he looked a little forbidding with his white hair and eyebrows and red eyes, his warm smile told me he was kindly. To reassure me, he spoke in Kinyamulenge, '*ese kusa nuhaye utinya*' ('You look as if you are afraid of me') adding '*ndakangana sindyana*' which means, 'I look scary but I can't hurt anyone!' At first I wondered why he didn't ask me how I was feeling because it was clear that I was in a bad way. Then I realised that this older man had the same sort of wisdom I would expect of my father: he could see I was ill and knew immediately that it was malaria but, not being able to do anything about it, couldn't see any point in asking me.

He told me he hadn't got any medicine but gave me water and let me rest there. I told him that I lived with Musirimu and it was obvious he knew him. Then he offered me the only advice he knew: '*nitakwicya urakira*' (if it doesn't kill you, it will go). It was at this point that I began to be delirious and in my nightmares I thought again of those early impressions of Uvira when I had been so shocked by the funeral processions. The song they sang as they accompanied the bodies rang in my ears, 'Safe journey with Jesus!' I wasn't worrying about dying but I could not stop thinking of my mother and wondering if I would ever see her again. Did she know how I was suffering?

As night started to fall, Shekwa told me I could stay with him if I wanted. I decided to force myself to go home because I knew the family there would be worrying and we had no way of communicating with them. So he would not try to stop me leaving, I tried not to show that kind old man how bad I actually was. He said a prayer for me and told me to be careful. I took to the road again but was forced to stop for a rest after about half a kilometre; then I continued until I was about half way between Musirimu's place and Shekwa's place. Here I passed out and slept for a few minutes under an acacia tree. When I regained consciousness, I couldn't move at first but just lay there listening to the noises around me. Men, women and children passed by speaking several different languages, some calling to their friends while others sang as they went; it was relaxing just to lie there listening. Finally, at about nine o'clock, I managed to find enough strength to get up gently and struggle on home.

By the time I arrived, Mamma Musirimu was really worried because what was usually a one-hour journey had taken me at least four hours and she had been unable to get news of me. She immediately gave me chloroquine tablets and I felt very relieved to have medication at last. Unfortunately I had an allergic reaction which meant that, on top of all the other symptoms I was suffering, I now had constant itching and couldn't stop scratching. As a result, I didn't sleep for several days. Then I was given quinine, which made me dizzy. With no money available, there was no other possible treatment and I was extremely grateful to Mamma Musirimu for giving me her medication and doing everything she could to help me.

After a whole week of staying at home in agony, I summoned up enough energy to get out of bed and Mamma Musirimu suggested I should go to see a nurse called Bose, another man from Bafulero tribe who was a good friend to Banyamulenge. She knew he would let me have treatment on credit. Having done a test, he confirmed that it was a severe form of malaria but he had nothing other than quinine he could prescribe.

I had a further week of illness, still unable to go to school. By this time I was getting worried that it might be cerebral malaria because it was affecting my sleep and I had hallucinations and terrible nightmares. Images from the day would float before me but then they distorted into hideous, terrifying figures. I saw buildings toppling down onto people, cars piling up on top of each other, men who changed into animals, lorries that changed into motorbikes and people transformed into leopards and snakes. It was sheer chaos and it exhausted me because I felt myself involved in it all, straining my mind trying to create a formula to reduce that chaos.

After this close encounter with malaria, I no longer felt afraid of the disease that killed so many children, but another terror began. During that same academic year, security problems grew worse in Uvira. I had to do all I could to try not to be noticed by the secret service agents, hiding myself from them as much as possible. The reason for the worsening of the situation was because of social and political developments at that time. There were many Rwandan refugees living in Uvira, people who had fled the 1959 revolution there (*see timeline*) and these were, of course, Tutsis. Now there was an underground movement to recruit young men, children of these original refugees, to train them to fight for the liberation of Rwanda and the right for exiles to return. This was the beginning of an armed insurgency against the Hutu regime in Rwanda, an insurgency that eventually led to the 1994 genocide. The majority of the population of Uvira were Bafulero, Bavira and Bebembe, all of whom had sympathy with the Rwandan Hutu regime. Because of this increased tension, Tutsi men, whether Congolese or Rwandans, were often arrested, beaten and tortured. There were frequent curfews and, as usual when there was any problem, there were plenty of opportunities for throwing stones at Tutsis. In addition, there was a great deal of looting because soldiers hadn't been paid for months and so resorted to this method to pay themselves. Tutsi people are quite easily distinguished from other tribes by their physical appearance and so all were vulnerable: ordinary people who had never been involved in violence or illegal acts of any kind began to live in real fear. What had previously been just mistrust and dislike from people of other ethnic backgrounds had now grown into a hatred that was frightening in its intensity.

On my way to school I continued to use the railway route, hiding as much as possible. I could not avoid walking through the Uvira "parking" (a large open area) – so, when there was known to be violence there I would miss school. Although at school I enjoyed Mutebutsi Kayaya's support, we often used to walk to school separately so that we didn't get so noticed in public. Some political situations in this troubled land had repercussions for everyone in the school and there were frequent closures but this particularly situation was, of course, something that affected just the Tutsis so it was always difficult to tell the headmaster or teacher that my absence was due to insecurity reasons. I was afraid that he would not be sympathetic because he had not wanted me in the school in the first place and might grasp any excuse to be rid of me. So I would usually say that I had not been well or something had happened in the family where I lived.

One day after school, I was sitting under the mango tree outside our house revising for my exams. No-one else was home except for a boy of about my age (one of Musirimu's relatives who went to another school in Uvira) who was sitting with me. Suddenly we became aware of a group of youths, only half dressed and giving the appearance of being high on drugs, circling the house. They made it clear that it was me in particular that they wanted so my companion managed to run away. They shouted abusively, accusing me of having destroyed a car tyre pump, and told me I would have to go to the *Mbwa mabe* (bad dog pit). Even though I knew I had done nothing, I wondered what Mbwa mabe was, but assumed it was some sort prison and was terrified of being sent to it. Of course I was completely innocent of the "crime" they accused me of. Not only had I never even seen a car tyre pump but I wouldn't have had the slightest idea what to do with one. I had arrived in the city relatively recently and I hadn't mixed socially with people beyond the family where I was staying. I had been completely preoccupied with those things that were of vital importance to me – my education and so on – and there was no way I could have been part of a gang that had committed an act of vandalism.

What I didn't realise was that this was simply a gang of young hooligans, made up of local ethnic groups and always looking for any excuse to attack young people of my ethnic group. They had metal objects with them to use as weapons and they sang songs of violence, saying they would eat me without bothering to cook me first. They didn't mean this literally of course but were simply threatening to hurt or even kill me. I shut myself in the house with all the doors and windows locked. I felt real despair and deep in my heart began to ask myself if there could ever be a place where I might find peace. They threw stones at the doors and windows and onto the roof. They yelled that they wanted to destroy the house and burn me in it. I was terrified and trembling with fear. I had no idea what to do. There were no telephones in Uvira at that time so I had no way of communicating with the outside world to ask for help so my only hope was that boy could find someone. There was a gendarmerie (police force) but the only way to ask for help in times of danger was to report an incident and whether or not they did anything about it would depend on the bribe offered and the ethnicity of the person in danger.

After a few hours, they still hadn't managed to break in and were becoming tired of throwing stones. Suddenly I heard the voice of a woman who was a friend of Musirimu's family; she suggested ironically that they could throw stones at her if they really wanted to hurt someone that evening. Then they left. When everyone else came home I was still shaken but they didn't even seem surprised at what had happened. It was quite normal apparently! They were able to tell me what *Mbwa mabe* meant: it is an expression in the Lingala language meaning literally "wicked dog". It refers both to a degrading and cruel place and to the prisoners themselves, suggesting that it was a place where prisoners should be treated as if they were dogs living on any scraps or rubbish available.

FROM THIS TIME I LEARNT TO LIVE IN FEAR of this threat but nothing could have prepared me for what I experienced there when my fears became reality. On the way home from school one day I was confronted by men who worked as secret agents in an organisation known as CADER. They started physically and verbally attacking me. I was still only a boy of about fifteen years old and I felt small and insignificant as they pushed me along against the wall. The cell they finally pushed me into was about four metres by four metres square with a barrel in the middle to serve as a toilet. There was no light at all. The only light prisoners received was when the guard wanted to speak to someone at interrogation time; then he would open a small hole in the middle of the door and briefly a little light would enter, enabling us to see each other. Ten of us were in there and it was the height of the dry season so the temperature reached 32 degrees Celsius in the day. The smell was hideous and the only food was when the guards allowed relatives or friends to bring something to eat.

When I was thrown into that dark hole, the other prisoners yelled at me, '*Tupatiye cigareti, leta tumbaku weye petit*', meaning 'Kid! Give us cigarettes, bring us tobacco!' On seeing me arrive, the only time they had enough light to actually see me, they exclaimed '*Nimunyarwanda, ni mutusi, c'est un Rwandai, un Tutsi!*' ('Look! he is indeed Rwandese, he is Tutsi!') Fortunately for me there was another young man of my ethnicity, Ngoga, and he had already been accepted by the others. He persuaded them not to beat me. He had not seen me but he recognised my voice and soon became my friend, telling me how he too had been arrested. We squatted beside each other in the darkness and exchanged our stories of how and why we had been arrested. Like the other prisoners, we sat close to the wall, as far away as we could from the stinking barrel, but we were the only Tutsi. The others had been arrested for various reasons, like petty theft or being drunk, and they were frighteningly tough to a boy like me. Some of them were part of a local gang group called Kadafi; they used to sell petrol in cans as there was no petrol station around, but they also dealt in drugs. This lucrative trade gave them power because they became wealthy enough to bribe the local gendarmes (police) and they became almost untouchable. This time, apparently, their luck and influence had run out because they were in this terrible place with the rest of us.

Every morning we had to leave the cell, walking on our knees, to be interrogated by the guards. This was time that I would notice my cellmates' faces. They were tough, hard-looking men but I could see fear in their eyes. As I scrambled along on my knees, my stomach felt as if it was in a knot of fear and then blinding light hit my eyes and made them stream with tears after so many hours in darkness. 'Leo utakula mavi', the guards shouted, meaning, 'Today you will eat shit!' I begged them not to make me do this, saying that I was not hungry and would prefer any other torture. They said it was up to them whether or not I ate and whether I ate this or that. One morning, they left me on my knees and kept hitting other people for hours. Beating was called tasse de thé or chai (cup of tea) because this is what every prisoner received in the morning as breakfast. They used a plastic cord of rounded shape called kiboko or cordlette, an instrument specially designed to give long lasting pain on a naked body.

The family I lived with were not informed of my arrest: they only found out that I was in prison when a young man called Eva spotted me being interrogated the morning after the day of my arrest. They were not very surprised because they knew there was no need for me to have committed a crime: the crime could be invented after the arrest. Besides, being a Tutsi automatically meant being guilty before a crime was established. The guards told me they had arrested me for two reasons: firstly, that I was "Rwandese" because I was born Tutsi, secondly that there was a fight at a Tutsi church when an old man called Sebu was seriously injured. The fight had indeed happened because of a church and charity leadership conflict but I had nothing to do with what had happened and I was too young to be involved in this matter. Although a third "crime" was not mentioned, they continued to interrogate me, asking whether I supported the Rwandese Tutsi movement that had started in Uganda. As my answer was no they kept beating me with the kiboko to make me change my story. On my second day in prison, while I was being interrogated, I saw my best friend, Busoka, being chased away by the guards as he had brought me some food. Seeing him made me cry for the very first time since my arrest but it was not because he was unable to give me the food and water: I knew I could not eat in that prison cell with its stinking communal toilet no matter how desperately thirsty and hungry I felt. I had had nothing and the oppressive heat had made me feel as if I could die of thirst but still I could not have swallowed anything in there.

I did not reflect a great deal about what was going on because I accepted it as an ordinary situation that could happen to any Tutsi. However, this was perhaps the beginning of my political awareness and my later strong feelings about injustice. President Mobutu had created a political system that did not encourage belief in a better future. He used to say 'Avant moi c'etait le deluge et après moi c'est le deluge,' that before him it was chaos and after him it would be chaos. After three days and nights I was released and charged with 'causing insecurity to the general public,' I was told I must report to the Court two days later. Musirimu took on the responsibility of following this up. 'How on earth can authorities act like fools?' he said angrily. 'How could they do this to an innocent child and what is the judge going to ask him when the cases are fabricated?' The charges were dropped after several trips to the court by Musirimu because he knew so many important people. A day later, I learned that my friend Ngoga had also been released and charged with similar 'crimes'; we met, talked about our experiences and discussed how fearful we were of going to school. Luckily for Ngoga, he only had to walk one kilometre to his school, whereas for me the journey was ten times longer and the route required passing by the Mbwa mabe prison.

I was traumatised by this terrible thing that had happened to me and lived in fear of what might happen to me next. Also, after this experience of prison I developed an eating disorder and found it difficult to eat. Before long I had malaria and, being thin and weakened, I seemed to have little strength to overcome it. There was one positive outcome of the prison incident however: it made me mentally and emotionally stronger and I felt that I had become a man. I began to see my victimisation as an initiation into my community's struggle. I knew that it could have been any Banyamulenge who had been treated in this way. If it hadn't been me it would have been someone else from my community. Because of this collective aspect to my experience, I gained respect and a great deal of support from the Banyamulenge community in Uvira including, of course, Musirimu's family.

Returning to school, I never mentioned where I had been on the days I was absent as I knew most people there would be more inclined to believe I had done something to deserve what had happened than to feel sorry for me. When I was arrested I was with a school friend called Mwenyemali and I was worried that he could have informed the school office or other students about my arrest. I had a hope he might not have done, especially as he was a quiet person, proud and focused and not one to indulge in idle gossip. Indeed he had not spoken about it and I asked him not to. 'Don't tell anyone! It's none of anybody's business. In fact many would wish that I had died in prison or that I was forcibly sent to Rwanda, a country that nobody in my family has ever lived in!' I told him and he respected my wishes. School rules about being absent were more strictly applied for an absence of more than three days but I managed to get a medical certificate from a local nurse even though I had not been to a hospital clinic.

Things were never quite the same for me after that. I experienced several events that brought me or my friends close to further encounters with Mbwa mabe. I found myself constantly on the look-out for those non-uniformed secret agents called CADER or others who might be working for the security services.

CHAPTER 13

Tension rises

UVIRA IS SITUATED JUST OVER 18 MILES south of the Kamanyola border with the Republic of Rwanda along the delta of the Ruzizi River. The city itself is narrow, huddling between the great lake and the Mitumba chain of mountains. It is home to more than two hundred thousand people from various tribal groups speaking several different tribal languages with Swahili and French as the official languages of communication. With its many shantytowns, the result of urban drift, there was always a high level of petty crime as well as hundreds of people seeking work. Added to these problems was a severe economic crisis linked to the political problems and lack of security. Overall, it was not a happy place to live despite its beautiful surroundings, particularly for those of us of the "wrong" ethnicity. For us, life consisted of trying to survive each hour and each day as it came. For me personally, this lack of security and the violence we endured was compounded by the problems I faced as an adolescent so far from my family. Not only was I too far away from them to have their support and comfort but I had to bear alone all the difficulties of raising my school fees and finding money to pay for medicine for the malaria that plagued me. With all of these problems I felt so oppressed that it was as if I were stifled, as if this hot place so far from the cool hills of home was pressing down on me and suffocating the life out of me. There seemed to be no hope for a better future but, though I often despaired and thought I couldn't cope, I did cope because I had to, there was no alternative: I knew that security at home in the village had worsened and I also did not want to return there as a failure. I made up my mind to hold out to the end at all costs like a man.

The persecution and exclusion of Tutsi was becoming more official. Two years before, in 1987, all Tutsi had been excluded from voting on the grounds that they were "not nationals" or even that they were "invaders" (*see timeline*). Certain Banyumalenge contested this manifestly unfair legislation and became so angry that their actions escalated into the destruction of urns at polling stations. This protest was seen by the government as a criminal act of violence against the State itself and security was tightened against Banyamulenge everywhere, not least against our community in Uvira. It became increasingly common to be humiliated and attacked in the streets and adults were frequently arrested and tortured. The simple fact of being a Tutsi born on Congolese soil was enough to rouse this hatred – we were seen as foreigners, intruders. There was a great deal of political unrest in general but, whatever the original reason for the unrest, any political demonstration or military show of force was accompanied by stone throwing at the Tutsi. We were the scapegoats for any problem.

The majority of Banyumalenge still lived the traditional village life so, in an urban setting, we were quite noticeable for our less sophisticated ways, such as the clothes we wore. Besides, amongst local tribes it's usually easy to recognise a Tutsi – often tall and slim with narrower faces than the other tribes. Though I wasn't particularly close to the stereotype, it was pretty obvious that I belonged to that hated tribe. So I went to school trying to hide my face, though this rarely helped, to avoid the insults that were screamed at me, names that were meant to hurt and dehumanise us like *serpent, chien* (dog), *criminal, microbe, vache* (cow), *parasite* and *cancrelat* (cockroach). Some, like *squelette* (skeleton) and giraffe were mocking our racial features while others, like RRR (*Rendezvous pour rendre les Rwandais au Rwanda*), *sale etranger* (dirty foreigner) and *sans domicile* (homeless) distinguished us as outsiders rather than true Congolese. When trying to hide myself didn't help, all I could do was to tell myself that, as long as I managed to avoid physical attacks, I could put up with the verbal abuse. What I heard mostly from the crowds that insulted me was *munywarwanda UYOO* meaning that I was a Rwandan who should be attacked, an unwanted person. To be called Rwandan was more than simply to be noticed as a foreigner: it had also accumulated strong negative connotations. The children in the crowds would shout '*funga kinwa Zair iendelee*', Swahili meaning that people who walk with their mouths open (a racial insult referring to our different facial features) were holding back progress in Zaire (Congo). As a man, I can now recognise this as extreme xenophobia but, as a teenager, I was bewildered and suffered the pain of insult unable to defend myself in any way. During times of political disturbance, abuse went beyond just the verbal and Banyumalenge, whether adults or children, could not leave their homes without the fear of being recognised as Tutsi and attacked by stone-throwers. At such times they had to rely on friendly non-Banyamulenge neighbours to supply them with food and any other shopping needs. Sometimes these nice neighbours would find themselves in serious trouble for having helped us: their houses would come under attack from people throwing stones and rotten eggs at the windows.

There were plenty of times when I couldn't go to school and what made this worse for me was that I could not justify my absence afterwards because it was something that affected only me – the rest of my classmates being of accepted ethnic backgrounds – and security problems were simply not recognised as a reason for absence. I was obliged to keep quiet about what was happening and keep my anxieties bottled up within myself, hidden from my schoolmates and teachers. This was a heavy burden to bear and every night as I tried to sleep I would be worrying about what awaited me the next day when I took that long route to school from Mulongwe to Kasanga. To keep my spirits up, I would think of the story from my childhood of the little lamb who survived so many dangers. I could all but hear my step grandmother's voice as she spoke for the crocodile, snake and other fearsome animals to tell the lamb, 'Go – today is not your worst day!' Then I could tell myself tomorrow would not be my worst day either and plan my route to avoid the worst places, either going by little-used paths or slipping in with groups of other pupils on their way to school.

Though I was much more secure amongst these groups of other schoolboys who were not so xenophobic, I felt an outsider amongst them for other reasons. I could hear their conversations and it was as if they belonged to a different world. They chatted about not just their homework and examinations but their families and friends, sport, popular music, fashionable dress, the girls they fancied and so on –

all the normal interests of teenage boys that I had no time for. None of this applied to me because I was completely preoccupied with simply surviving from day to day and all my hopes centred on a time when I could live in peace – sweet peace with no fear and insecurity. I could not join in their conversations because we seemed to have nothing in common. Having no spare money to help me dress as they did or to join clubs and take part in other leisure activities, I felt like an outsider with no friends. I couldn't even go to the beach on beautiful Lake Tanganyika for fear of attacks by extremists. So I had no outlets beyond school and simply spent the rest of my time at "home". Musirimu was a kind man who treated me as his son but he could not be a substitute for my real family and friends. So I was very unhappy and my social life was practically non-existent.

Fortunately I knew people who inspired me and encouraged me, giving me the will to live. These were others who had shared my experience of exclusion and persecution and they understood my vulnerability because they were older and had more experience of it. Firstly there was Jacques who had been a support to me ever since I first arrived in the city when he helped me to find my host family. I smile when I think of some of the things he had to teach me in those early days. For example, it was Jacques who first introduced me to the idea of underwear, telling me that other pupils at school would laugh when they noticed I had none and that there would be no way I could swim in the lake without. Taking his advice and the money he gave me, I decided to buy some. First I tried at the pharmacy but quickly ran out again when the shop assistants laughed, too embarrassed to ask them what was funny. Next I managed to find a shop that genuinely did sell underwear but I mistakenly chose women's. The shop assistant asked me if I was sure and, when I said I was, she no doubt assumed I was buying the panties for someone else. When Jacques saw them he was astounded and laughed uncontrollably but I would not return them to the shop. As long as the item covered my nakedness, I could not see that the details mattered. He then took over and bought me some for me himself. The whole incident was a nightmare for me at the time and it was the first of many times when Jacques helped.

There was also his sister's brother-in-law, Gerevazi. The two shared a strong friendship that went beyond family relationship and together they took an interest in me. Neither was gifted academically or well-educated so they could not help me with school work but they were socially talented and had practical skills. Their experience and maturity put them in a position to help me a lot and this they did right from my early days in Uvira in a non-obtrusive way, trying not to seem over-protective of me. They introduced me to certain survival techniques they had found necessary to overcome poverty and persecution. 'We know you can pass your exams,' said Gerevazi, 'but that won't help you much when it comes to surviving daily life here.' At the time I didn't really understand what he meant but I found out later.

One day they invited me to meet them on the beach for a swim, assuring me that all would be fine and if anything happened we would just have to defend ourselves. When we met, they explained to me in detail the problems we Banyamulenge faced in the city and how I should face up to them. 'You're not going to carry on being the meek little lamb, the naive little boy from the bush. That would just attract more attention and wouldn't help you at all to make the sort of contacts you need to help you in school!' This way they inspired me to harden my attitudes so I could confront situations that, like other members of my community, I was sure to encounter. We met regularly to discuss survival strategies and, even as we did so, the social and political situation was becoming even trickier.

During my second year in Uvira, we learnt from the radio that war had broken out in Rwanda and a rebel movement called the Rwanda Patriotic Front (RPF) had been formed to defend the rights of Rwandan refugees who had been exiled from their country for thirty years. Because in the beginning the majority of the rebels were Tutsi, this rebellion was bound to have a massive impact on our lives. The general Congolese population and the government authorities did not distinguish between Congolese and Rwandan Tutsis so they immediately began to accuse the Banyumalenge community of being part of the RPF. Rumours were rife that every individual in our community conspired in smuggling arms to the rebels. Furthermore the government reacted immediately to the developments by sending in Congolese troops to help the Rwandan government. Effectively this was supporting the Hutu government of Rwanda to fight Tutsi rebels so that meant that Tutsi became the enemy of the state. Adults were often stopped and interrogated and young people were assumed to be RPF sympathisers. Even at school verbal attacks became vicious.

Fortunately for me by this time there were more Banyamulenge boys in my school though, of course, they were in other classes. There was Damacene, my very close friend Kayaya, Byicaza and Gapinja and my cousin Ndoli. In my culture a cousin is such close family that he is practically a brother and this was especially so with Ndoli, the youngest son of my father's older brother. As mentioned earlier, he was my *abonse rimwe*, and we were like twins.

With this cousin-brother as well as my friends, I felt much less isolated at school. During breaks, when the others were playing or going for food, we four would get together and share advice on how to survive our difficulties. We would share what we knew about what was happening in town – which parts we should avoid and so on. Above all, we let each other know which pupils in school were the most aggressive so we could avoid them. Ironically, though our meeting like this was a result of our trying simply to live a peaceful life, it led the other pupils to accuse us of plotting a rebellion against the state. It was amazing to me how the Banyumalenge could be so unwanted and vulnerable and yet still be seen as dangerous. It seemed absurd that an isolated young person with no money could be accused of arms traffic or a planned military action against the state. None of us had experience of life beyond our little village and this oppressive life we struggled hopelessly to survive in Uvira.

A few weeks after this escalation of difficulties, Ndoli, Damacene and I started to question the way we were constantly under accusation and began secretly exchanging news about what was happening in Rwanda. As our fears and insecurity grew, we began to wonder if the RPF might one day liberate us from the oppression we suffered. We did not involve Kayaya as we were not sure whether he would support our views. Kayaya was a very intelligent and opinionated young person but also had some scepticism about the new ideas. All of us, though, were losing our childhood innocence and trying to take a more adult approach, thinking of our future. Ndoli told me he had been given a prophesy by a Christian spiritualist that one day he would be a senior commanding officer in the army. I told him that was a utopian dream. It seemed impossible that we could ever escape the extreme exclusion we suffered to the extent that we could not only integrate into the army but take a commanding role in it. A few days later, Ndoli and I met up with his closest friend, Gakunzi, who was at another school called Mwanga. He was Banyamulenge like us but, unlike us, his family also lived in Uvira; his father had a steady job and no financial difficulties. Though he was only the same age as we were, Gakunzi was much bigger and stronger physically, so we were interested to know if he received the same kind of treatment as we did after the recent events in Rwanda. He was angry about how we were being treated and told us there must be an escape route for us.

We continued to meet secretly and discuss what we could do to help ourselves and also how the rebellion in Rwanda was progressing. We received this news from the secret radio station, Muhabura, set up by the RPF. We knew listening to the radio would mean real trouble if we were ever caught by the authorities but that didn't stop us. Ndoli, Gakunzi and I would hide behind houses near the bush at five every morning to listen to the forbidden radio station. One of the popular songs that were played regularly on it had an incredible impact on many Rwandans and Congolese Tutsi who were persecuted. It has remained in my mind ever since those times spent secretly listening to Muhabura radio. Sung by Cecile Kayirebwa, a Rwandan refugee woman in Belgium, it says:

'Turaje Ibihumbi n'ibihumbii
Turaje ibihumbi by'abasoree
Turaje ababyeyi babyiruye, bamwe bananiwe
Turaje abakobga b'abaga, n'abana b'ibisage
Turaje impinja n'incyuke
Turaje nimuze tuje iwacyu, amahanga tuyimuke
Turaje n'imusase bugari igihe kirageze
Turaje gushira hamwe twese
Turaje nimuturebe mutumenye turi bene mugabo umwe

Ntarwango k'umutima ntanzinka nkizashize
Turaje tubafitiye amakuru, y'majambere n'ukuri, umurava n'ubufura,
  turakumbuye cyane.'

It was a message from the thousands of exiled Rwandans scattered all over the world for the previous 35 years to the Rwandans who were still in Rwanda under the extremist Hutu government. The words mean:

'We are coming in our thousands,
We are coming with many young people:
Mothers, women who are pregnant, heroic girls,
Children with beautiful hair, babies and toddlers.
Come! Let's all go back home and leave exile forever!
Countrymen still in Rwanda, please prepare for our coming
Because now is the time to reunite.
We are one people and we are coming!
Recognise us as brothers and sisters of one family!
We have no hatred and are not planning revenge as happened before.
We are coming with good news for the whole nation,
News of building our country together!
We are very determined and sincere with these promises.
We miss you so much!'

As we listened to this song every day, we dreamt of freedom and togetherness. It gave us encouragement and hope that one day the injustice we suffered would be over and that we would not all be exterminated. Other songs that kept up our spirits were from the South African musician Lucky Dube, especially the song called "Different colours, one people". It was an inspiring song about how people of different backgrounds could work together to build their country, promoting cohesion and harmony between white and blacks in South Africa during the harsh apartheid regime.

Just before the end of the first school term in 1989, the Congolese troops that had fought against the RPF rebels in Rwanda abandoned their positions there and returned to the Congo. They were spread over an area that included Bukavu and Uvira and were mobile, having broken into showrooms to help themselves to Kawasaki motor bikes. Feeling humiliated and angry at their retreat, they roared around the country keen to avenge themselves on any Tutsi civilians. As usual during times of extreme insecurity, the Banyamulenge communicated secretly to warn others of danger. The soldiers were terrifying, their faces set in an expression that suggested they were drugged. They were accustomed to killing and had pillaged the town, seriously beating and injuring anyone who looked Tutsi. So we hid in our homes and I couldn't reach school but Gazunki, Ndoli and I continued to meet and encourage each other that one day there would be justice. My friends began to drink a lot while they listened to Lucky Dube and the other music that inspired us. Music and drinking became a way of coping with anxiety and putting up with our problems. We lost ourselves in the exciting rhythms and released a lot of nervous energy as we threw ourselves around.

One evening about a week after the retreat from Rwanda the three of us went for an evening of music and dance in a bar at Nganda du Grand Lac, about five kilometres away. This bar was called Grand Lac (Great Lake) and was owned by a Tutsi called Asieri. As we left afterwards, we learnt that the RPF were recruiting young men for their armed struggle and my two friends told me that, if asked, they would accept and join the struggle so that they could one day return and liberate their families. Within two days, Gakunzi had disappeared without saying anything to us. He had been secretly recruited! We knew that, though it was easy to get recruited, it wasn't at all easy to actually join the RPF rebellion. It involved getting secretly through Burundi where there were people gathering recruits to send north to cross the border from Burundi into Tanzania. This meant walking through forests and bush avoiding the official Tanzanian security forces.

Gakunzi's mother was distraught. She sent for us to see if we could tell her what had happened and cried inconsolably, 'My son, my son, you are very young! My God why that?' not knowing if she would ever see him again. Her tears flowed and nothing could comfort the pain in her heart. Watching her, I felt her pain keenly but could think of nothing to say that would make her feel better. I knew how much she was attached to Gakunzi and had always wished my mother had been as demonstrative as she was. She would cherish him and touch his face, something I personally had never before seen a mother do to an older child. Seeing her sorrow, I felt confused. Although I admired Gakunzi for having taken such a bold decision, for his mother's sake I regretted his disappearance and it was painful to think that this meant he might not come back.

Ndoli and I continued to meet without our friend Gakunzi. About a week after he had left, there was a social gathering of Banyamulenge at the Hotel de la Victoire. This was a very unusual event for us – the first real social gathering we had tried to hold since the insecurity had been so bad. It was organised by ISOKO (a name referring to people of common heritage) which was a group initiated by a few Banyamulenge university students in Lubumbashi; here in Uvira it was being set up by Gakunzi's brother and two other young men. The event went on throughout the night and the songs that were played were very moving: songs about freedom by musicians such as Yvonne Chaka Chaka and Lucky Dube. At about 5am I found Ndoli in tears, weeping for our lack of human rights and liberty.

When I looked for him again at six o'clock he was nowhere to be seen and I could only assume that he had gone home though this would have been odd because it had been agreed that we would all walk together in case we were attacked. The next time I went to school there was no trace of Damascene either. They had both disappeared. I was in a dilemma and didn't know what to do. I was afraid to go around alone, feeling as I did that I was unwanted in a society that had no sympathy at all for me. By that evening I had learnt that both my friends had been recruited and were on their way to join the RPF with the idea that they could contribute to the liberation of their families from the oppression and violence they suffered.

Now I was not only lonely but also really afraid to go to school because other pupils would see the defection of my Tutsi friends as simple proof of what they had been accusing us of – that we supported the rebellion in Rwanda. When I finally found the courage to go to school, I was attacked verbally in the strongest manner yet. Luckily for me, there were still three other Banyamulenge in the school, my friends Byicaza, Gapinja – and Kayaya, who was strong in my defence.

CHAPTER 14

Jimmy is born

SOME DAYS LATER when the town was relatively calm, a friend called Bukuru Ndakanirwa invited me to go with him to Nganda du Grand Lac and there I got to know a young Banyamulenge called Isaac Rumenge. He was tall and strongly built, very calm and with a discreet, proud manner. I saw in him a protective figure. That same evening two men, Bosco and Gaston, came to talk to me, Bukuru and Isaac. Bukuru knew them personally already; I knew of them as both were Tutsi from North Kivu but living in Uvira, and were quite visible in the town. They explained to us that the war in Rwanda was about liberating the Rwandans from dictatorship and allowing refugees to return to their homeland. The refugees were, of course, principally Tutsi and were scattered throughout the world but particularly in our region of eastern Congo. Then we were introduced to another man, a man we had never seen before and whose name we were not given. This man began to explain to us that whatever happens in one African country impacts on another. The war in Uganda, he told us, had started in Tanzania with some links to the revolutionary war in Mozambique and the ANC in South Africa, and we should therefore not think that a war just over the border in Rwanda could leave us unscathed. Whether we acted or not, it would have an impact on the lives of the whole Rwandaphone community and we really had no choice but to become involved – our fate was either to be willing to risk our lives or to continue to just survive a wretched life of fear and persecution.

He kept explaining that it was not just a war to liberate Rwandans but also a liberation movement for others under similar oppression in Africa. He was eloquent and knew how to persuade idealistic young men; it was no longer difficult for me to imagine how Gakunzi and Ndoli had agreed to be recruited. We young men were, he said, the future generation on whom our tribe depended. It was our duty to understand our present danger and to take into account ways of escaping it. His strength of conviction reminded me of how Gerevazi and Jacques had inspired me but, whereas their advice was simply to help me as an individual survive, this man seemed to have a far broader agenda, one that I couldn't, at that age, fully understand. I did not need to understand it in depth: it was enough for me to feel that I was doing something to avoid the prospect of my people living with persecution for generations to come.

Within a few days he had persuaded Isaac and me to join a clandestine movement whose task it was to fund the RPF, negotiate routes and encourage recruitment. From now on, he told us, we would need to operate under false names and communicate in code so that no outsider could access our information or know who was involved. We would have to take great care about to whom we spoke and what we said. Gradually I was coming to realise why Ndoli and Gakunzi had simply disappeared without telling anyone. In addition to his powers of persuasion, the man had a pistol and I was genuinely afraid that if we didn't take part in his meetings he would pursue us.

Then a week later I found that my friend, Bukuru was also playing an active role in the group. They told me they were absolutely convinced of the necessity to prepare for the worst and to support the RPF. In my naivety and innocence I did not need a great expert to convince me but was easily won over by the enthusiasm of my friend. Bukuru impressed me because he was very dynamic and worked night and day in very risky situations. I had known him a long time and trusted him implicitly. So, though there were people I hardly knew, like Isaac, between the rhetoric of the nameless man and the enthusiasm of Bukuru I was won over: I felt myself ready to do anything, almost as if we were a group willing to get ourselves killed for the good of our community.

A week after this dramatic conversion, my best friend from the village, Tokos, arrived in Uvira. He was as likeable as ever – always positive and optimistic as well as highly entertaining. Being about four years older than me, he had always been the leader when we were together and now that I was away from home and a bit older, one of his first questions was, 'Do you ever drink alcohol?' I replied that I hadn't any money for beer and, luckily for me, I hadn't enjoyed it at all when I was given the opportunity to taste it. Still, he said he would like to chat 'over a beer' so we went to a bar called Oasis where four other young men were waiting, one of them a young man called Sunzu that I knew well.

As we drank, Tokos proceeded to update us on what was going on in politics and assured us that extermination awaited the Banyamulenge. Our only hope was to join the RPF and then come back to save our relatives. As he spoke I felt as if my head was in a vice and life was weighing down on me, forcing me to respond to what he said. But I was too young to be able to give an opinion on such a weighty issue. I certainly couldn't contradict him because he was clearly correct in saying that there was no visible path towards peace for our people. I will never forget sitting there in the bar feeling the effects of alcohol for my first time ever while these life-changing decisions were being made. I felt light headed and excited, aware that I was now a man amongst men, men willing to give their lives for the benefit of our people. I met Tokos again the following day and again we spoke for a long time over a beer. He warned me to be vigilant and told me he had confidence that we would meet again one day. When he said goodbye, he told me that would be our last meeting for a long time. He and all the others I had met previously in the Oasis bar went to join the RPF rebellion, as did many other young Banyamulenge.

Meanwhile Isaac and I were becoming involved in another aspect of the war. We knew many of our friends had gone to fight over the border but the nameless man told us our work was even more crucial than theirs. Working with various groups in differing locations, we were to maintain the security of the secret routes over the border and the flow of funds. We were trained in such skills as coding and other aspects of espionage. I no longer felt helpless and suppressed as I took on my new role. As well as the constant fear I was accustomed to living with, there was now the excitement of feeling useful, of feeling that at last I was fighting back and standing up for myself. Our secret meetings were from late in the evening until the early hours of the morning and we were told to carry a Bible so we could claim to be going to a prayer meeting if we were stopped by security agents. As well as the training we received there, we were inspired by the songs we sang and the RPF ideology that the nameless man taught us. Amongst this clandestine group, I became "Jimmy" – a shadowy figure no-one beyond our group knew and I found myself happier as this person than I had been for many months before. By day I seemed to be very much more alive than when I was the oppressed schoolboy. As the verbal abuse hit me, I had the satisfaction of knowing that there was now some truth in it – I truly was helping the Rwandophone cause. I had skills none of my accusers knew about and so, within myself, I felt a quiet confidence. I kept my cover as the quiet, studious schoolboy but that gave me the opportunity to be useful to Gaston, Bosco, the nameless man and, above all, our great cause. It gave me fulfilment socially too because I shared a common goal with other young people who were involved in this political military movement.

Later, when I was more experienced, I was given a specific secret service group, concerned with political mobilisation and spying, to lead. As well as the regular, clandestine political and military meetings, my work involved organising and facilitating the movement of recruits, helping them to cross over the border into Burundi. Making informal links, I obtained identity cards and documents so they could travel. We made contact also with the people in Burundi who were to receive them, sending coded letters that said, 'Here is your luggage and money. I am sorry for the delay and next time I will make sure that you are reimbursed as promised'. The recruits were instructed never to travel as a pair so that anyone caught could speak only for himself. To ensure their safe arrival, we needed to use unofficial and dangerous channels, communicating secretly with relevant people. Informal or illegal channels were used, hiding from the Congolese and Burundian officials by crossing the dangerous terrain of stagnant, muddy water that borders Lake Tanganyika. In the Tanzanian area there was difficulty in crossing the Akagera River and National Park with dangerous wild animals. As well as the physical danger of the journey itself, there was the constant threat of being arrested. We worried constantly about what happened to the young men we sent across the border in this way and we were always eager to hear news of them and all that was happening on the front line. Our leaders didn't tell us much about any losses though – they told us only about the positive news.

A few weeks after I had committed myself to the movement, I came home from school one day to find a great surprise awaiting me – my cousin Kayira had arrived out of the blue having travelled the long distance from Minembwe just to see me. He was a very strong friend of my family, who helped us in all sorts of ways. He often supplied my father with veterinary products and he would also help me with school fees when I was desperate. At other times, like this, he acted as our messenger. He had come to tell me that he knew about Ndoli leaving and he was worried that I would follow him. There was great anxiety in the village he told me. It was not just that everyone was anxious for the young men who had gone off to join the RPF but also they feared for their relatives and friends who were certain to be questioned by the authorities; this meant of course that they and other members of the community were in an even more dangerous position than usual. Because I was bound to respect him as an older person, I could not refuse Kayira when he asked me to go back to the village with him to see the situation at first hand. In our tradition a strong word from an older person is equal to physical force in ordering someone to do something; so when he said 'I want you to get ready and follow me', I simply went. He paid the transport costs for both of us.

After so many months of longing to see my mother, meeting her was not the happy reunion I had always dreamt of. Her face was drawn and soaked with tears as she hugged me and told me, sobbing, that Oreni had gone to join the RPF. I could hardly prevent myself from crying too. Oreni! I had so looked forward to being with my closest brother again and telling him of my experiences. There was so much I wanted to tell him, so many thoughts and feelings to share with him. I knew we would think alike on many matters and he was, of all the people I knew, the one who could best relate to the way I felt. Others close to me also had left: Ndabananiye, my second cousin, the son of my cousin Kenasi and my cousin, Petero nicknamed Anti-Choc, who had become an adopted brother following the death of his parents, and my cousin Gitingi.

I spent a week in the village. Though in many ways it was wonderful to be with my people again, it was also difficult because there was so much bottled up inside of me that I could tell no-one. My mother was worried already about Oreni and the others so it was absolutely imperative that I should let her think that I at least was reasonably safe. Also, had anyone in the village known what I was involved in, they would be considered guilty too if the authorities found out. As it was, they could claim with complete innocence that I was just a schoolboy. So, here in my beloved home, I felt a bit like an outsider and it was with a heavy heart that I returned to Uvira after a week. My secret work, to which I was committed three times a week, was waiting for me. I was sad that some of my plan had changed: when I had become involved in the RPF movement, my assumption was that if anything happened to me, Oreni would be there for my mother.

Then I had another terrible shock when I heard that my cousin Kayira had died suddenly. He had become unexpectedly very ill and, as we did not have access to hospitals or medical facilities, there was no way of saving his life. A group of men had carried him to the nearest hospital in Nundu, then to Uvira and then on to Bujumbura in Burundi but it was too late. Afterwards we learned from an American doctor that the illness had been a straightforward problem with the urinary system.

From now on my life would be very different. I had become more isolated because I had lost so many people dear to me – Ndoli, my brother Oreni, my best friend Tokos and my cousin Kayira.

CHAPTER 15

Tutsi "crimes"

IT HAD BEEN A LONG DAY AND I WAS HAPPY to be on my way home, though I was wishing I didn't still have that long journey to do from Kasenga to Zone where my host family had moved to. I had grown used to the walk of 14 kilometers return journey a day but now this was even further. I was also wishing I didn't still have so much homework, in particular that tricky essay where I needed to get my head around hundreds of scientific names to explain the origins of various plants. Still, this first part of the walk was refreshing and I had a classmate with me, a boy from the Bafulero tribe who seemed quite friendly. The river Mulongwe was browner because of recent floods but it glowed in the late afternoon sun and the air was becoming cooler after the long, stifling day. I always loved crossing the bridge of the Mulongwe River and feeling the breeze on my face after a day at school. As well as the spectacular view of Lake Tanganyika, there was also a glimpse of the city of Bujumbura, the capital of Burundi, in the distance. The whole scene always looked beautiful and peaceful in the late afternoon as the temperature cooled and the sun got lower in the sky.

But today there was a difference. There were many more than usual of the mobile police around the main street of Mulongwe, Uvira's city centre. It was normal to see some in their usual green and red uniforms and carrying arms because they made money by creating minor "crimes" and then accepting bribes; but today there were noticeably more of them. Also they were more heavily armed, as if they were ready for action. I felt a bit apprehensive as I saw them but not really afraid because I knew there was often a disproportionate response to minor incidents and I knew that I had done nothing wrong. 'Someone is unlucky today!' I commented to my companion.

To my great surprise, as we continued to walk in the direction of the Mulongwe "parking" area, I was shouted at by a person who was obviously of my ethnicity, 'Be careful as you could find yourself part of this!' He obviously did not want to be specific and he seemed to be hiding his face as he walked quickly away from the crowds. We carried on anyway and, when we got as far as the house of someone I knew of, Musafiri Mushambaro, who lived in the city centre near the "parking", he was standing outside. He explained what was happening. He told me that it was something that could affect our whole community. I felt myself start to tremble as I remembered what had happened to me previously: I was terrified of being beaten again or thrown into prison. I was hungry and tired and just wanted to go home.

The issue was that two young Banyamulenge had been arrested on suspicion of poisoning or bewitching the river Mulongwe. Belief in witchcraft was strong, the tribe most strongly associated with it being the Barega. It was reported quite regularly that a member of the Barega had been caught flying over the lake or the city to send down magic power. When the only television antenna in the town had broken down, rumour had it that Barega had been seen installing sorcery into it because it interfered with their magic power in the area. This time, however, it was Banyamulenge who were accused. Apparently these two young men had been on their way from their home village of Kundondo to Uvira, a two day walk, but had stopped to rest by the river. They were carrying a large packet of butter, a luxury gift for their relatives. In no time at all, someone had interpreted their rest by the river with a large packet as an act of sabotage by witchcraft. This allegation against the two suspects quickly became a general conspiracy theory. Rumours circulated that the intention was to bewitch the main reservoir as well as the river, so producing poisoned water that was intended to destroy all ethnic groups within the city that were not Banyamulenge. It was claimed that this mysterious poisoned water would affect only non-Tutsi people living in the city. I was completely astonished at this bizarre accusation and said so to my companion. 'How ridiculous this is! Even if it were true, which it cannot possibly be, does it require a police force to be involved?' I said.

Considering he was a well-educated boy only two years away from his final secondary school certificate equivalent to baccalaureate, his answer was shocking: 'I heard something like this was happening.

There were stories going around this morning about your people starting a new strategy to kill us,' he said.

Astonished, I asked him 'Can you honestly believe that, despite the fact that Banyamulenge are excluded from any modern facilities and higher education, they could still have the sophisticated power to develop materials that would poison a river?' I also reminded him that the reservoir was built by French engineers with no Banyamulenge involved. 'And anyway, even those French engineers couldn't build a pump that sends clean water to my people and poisoned water to yours!' I laughed as I spoke. The idea that a tribe who had been excluded from all public sector employment could have had any way of sabotaging a state enterprise seemed to me completely ludicrous, even if some scientist somewhere had found a way to separate poisoned and non-poisoned water on an industrial scale.

But there was not so much as a hint of a smile in his ice-cold reply: 'The truth comes from the fire for you people! When it comes to evil forces, Tutsi are snakes and capable of anything, including magic!' He was referring to a common African belief that lies can be destroyed by heat but truth cannot. Among many tribes there is a traditional way of detecting lies by using boiling water. If two people have a dispute they would be asked to put their hands in boiling water; the one who withdrew his or her hands first would be considered guilty. (It may have worked by reminding the guilty person that the consequence of dishonesty is traditionally extremely dangerous, much more than just burning hands; no doubt this could cause confession before the test is completed.)

I terminated our conversation and our budding friendship by saying, 'It is amazing that God acts in many ways when it comes to protecting oppressed people. It is amazing how you extremists and xenophobes make us out to be bigger and more powerful than we are.'

Although I had been made aware of what was going on, I didn't realise just how serious it was, how high the authority behind it went. In fact the line of command went right up to the *Commisaire de Zone* who had issued an order that any Banyamulenge acting suspiciously should be arrested. Had I known that, perhaps I wouldn't have started to argue with my companion. As it was, he walked off and left me when a group of soldiers approached me for questioning. I was a Tutsi with no "truth from the fire" but the fire was on its way to me. Simply because of my ethnicity I was arrested by security agents and beaten. I was not released until a day later after a claimed scientific analysis of the chemical composition of the butter. It was, of course, found to be butter though I have my doubts that it was ever really analysed.

This wasn't an isolated incident: petty acts of violence became a way of life that I was starting to accept as normal. A few months after that, there was another incident I will always remember and it happened just when I was starting to feel happier and used to living in Zone with my host family. One thing that made my life much happier there was that we had been joined by a relative and good friend from our village, Busoka. We often went for walks together; we liked to chat without the adults sometimes so we could feel our opinions were our own and not just theirs. Also, we had other things to talk about, like our exams or the books we had read. Sometimes we talked about our good friend Tokos and his theories. Like Tokos, Busoka always had plenty of jokes to cheer me up and help me to think positively; it took away my worries about lack of money and the things I felt I needed to buy. Busoka also had a high regard for my academic work and thought we could help each other in many ways; he often started discussions leading to school work for this reason.

On this particular evening we were chatting as usual when suddenly we saw a crowd running towards us. We stopped to ask what was wrong but we had no chance to find out: it all happened so quickly and we were completely unprepared for it. They began by knocking us around the head and pushing us aggressively towards a large, impressive yellow house – obviously the home of someone influential. There, everyone in the household, the mother and father as well as numerous young people and the security guard, surrounded us. They called to other people from the neighbourhood and we became the centre of attention for a large crowd, all keen to humiliate us in every conceivable way. They ripped off our clothes, threw us to the ground and began trampling and spitting on us. We shouted for help but had no idea what else we could do. We were in a private house and the owner seemed to be a wealthy person of high status so it was unlikely anyone would intervene on our behalf. We knew that he could do what he wanted with us if he had a significant social or administrative position, such as with the police or the judiciary, including having us killed.

He spoke in Lingala, '*Lelo bokokufa*', meaning 'Today you'll die!' I saw Busoka's eyes: they were red and he was breathing painfully as he said to me, 'What have we done to deserve this?' We asked the man who had threatened to kill us, 'What have we done?' and were told we had committed two crimes. Firstly we were Tutsi and secondly we had broken his precious windows. It made me think of the old French proverb, *En voulant tuer un chien on l'accuse de la rage* ('If you want to kill a dog you accuse it of having rabies'). He then produced a pile of broken glass and threw it on the ground in front of him. We pleaded with him, 'We are certainly Tutsi by birth – we had no choice in that – but we had nothing to do with breaking your windows!'

He then decided to take us to the Mbwa mabe, a decision that made me tremble as the memories of the last time there were still vivid in my mind. He also said he would torture us in electric chairs. There was nothing more we could say but, to our great surprise, he then decided to call the neighbourhood chief. Neighbourhood chiefs are a part of the local tradition: they have no official power in the modern state but still wield considerable influence amongst their own people. Because the man who had accused us was obviously influential in the modern state, we didn't really expect any help from this chief. Fortunately however and much to our surprise, the chief said, 'Do you really believe they did that? What proof have you?' and went on to say that we ("your prisoners" as he referred to us) should be allowed to have a mediator to speak on our behalf. He suggested a mediator from our own tribe and said he himself would be the second neutral mediator. We nominated a man called Senda and someone was sent to tell him.

As soon as he came, the mediation began. We were still being spat on by the rich man and, as we had no money to offer bribes, we feared the worst. We remained tied up though the hearings took several hours. Finally the chief gave his judgement: 'These young people are the innocent victims of aggression and injustice. You could kill them if you wish because it is within your power but in my opinion you should let them go because they are innocent.'

'Even if they are foreign invaders?' replied the rich man. He then continued kicking us in the face.

'You have children yourself,' I pleaded with him. 'Would you allow them to be beaten up because of their ethnicity?'

Finally, late that night, we were released. We were traumatised and wracked with questions about why we should suffer such injustice and if it could go on like this always. Mostly we just wished we had been born with another identity completely so we need never be noticed as different. But, at the same time, we knew we had been lucky and it was as if by a miracle that we had been saved. We were indeed very lucky that day because, as I found out later, that rich man was the president of the national transport society and also had considerable influence in the secret police.

A year after the incident I saw that rich man again, completely by chance, as I walked through Uvira past the commercial bank opposite the secret police offices. At this particular time Uvira was close to a state of emergency because of regional political instabilities. The secret police were insisting there was a lot of arms trafficking; in reality, by convincing the public at large that a huge security threat existed they created for themselves an opportunity to extort higher bribes from innocent people. I was walking quickly, not only to avoid him and because I was aware of the security dangers but to avoid being splashed by mud as it had recently rained and I was wearing my one and only presentable shirt.

Suddenly I was approached by a very tough-looking man who ordered me to stop immediately and said he was going to examine what I was carrying in my plastic bag. In it he found two chargers for mobile phones that I was taking to Asieri, the owner of the Grand Lacs bar, for one of his friends, Kayitare. At that time I was very naïve about such things because there were no landline phones in Uvira and Kayitare was one of the very few people who owned a satellite mobile phone. I didn't really understand what the chargers were and, though I knew my friend would not give me something that might put me in danger, I began to fear that they might make a good excuse to arrest me – that it might be claimed they were something used to make bombs. In any case, it was usual to be arrested for no reason other than being Tutsi so I was not really surprised when he gripped my wrist and announced, 'You are under arrest! Don't move!'

He hustled me over the road to the secret police offices where his colleagues joined him. All of them were very large, their large bellies being a sign of affluence, the badge of the rich who could afford to eat a lot. They all yelled at me together, interrogating me as if I were a terrorist. They filled out official documentation for my arrest and forced me to sign it, which I did not want to do as it was a legally binding document that stated that the 'forces of order' had arrested a 'Rwandan Tutsi adolescent carrying grenades and other explosive materials.'

I was then thrown into a small cell where I was alone while they continued to threaten me for the whole day with their guns and bayonets. Inside myself I was terrified but I tried not to show weakness and continued to assert my innocence. They wanted to know about the traffic of arms in Uvira, saying it threatened the security of the town, but I continued to say I knew nothing at all. As I was involved in the RPF movement under my secret identity as Jimmy, I was inwardly terrified, thinking that an informant may have given them information about my involvement in the movement and about its operation in Uvira. By this time I had become heavily involved in fund-raising. For example, I helped organise events that, to seem innocent, linked in with other local celebrations such as Independence Day, Christmas day and New Year's Day, or any other significant occasions. The wealthiest and most influential people in the town were invited and we arranged for them to be welcomed and served drinks by beautiful girls who encouraged them to spend their money. However, at these events, we organisers would pretend to be guests like anyone else so it was unlikely that I had aroused suspicion by these activities. What was really worrying me was that I had mentioned the name of the owner of these telephone chargers, Kayitare Anselme. He was a Rwandan Tutsi who fled Rwanda in 1959 following the Hutu revolution there when so many were forced to leave. Kayitare was relatively rich and had a role in sponsoring the RPF movement. We had become friendly through our work together and because his wife was a Congolese Tutsi from North Kivu. It would be terrible if I unwittingly implicated him in terrorism offences. I knew I was in deep trouble because arms trafficking was considered equal to murder.

Luckily for me though, Musirimu had been notified and had spoken to influential lawyers. As a result, I was given a letter to take to court and released fourteen hours later. When I told Musirimu about the letter he laughed and told me not to bother reporting to the court; he commented, 'They are stupid to arrest a young person like you on those grounds but be careful too with what you get involved in'.

I knew from this comment that he had become aware of my involvement in the RPF movement. It was impossible to keep it from someone I lived with because he knew about my early morning training. Three days a week I had to be up at five in the morning for a 10km run along the shores of Lake Tanganyika towards the border with Burundi. To avoid suspicion from the local people, this had been organised as just a social activity but Musirimu had obviously guessed that it was preparation for possible military activity. He knew that otherwise I would not have taken on such a tough keep-fit regime when I had to be at school by eight o'clock like the other pupils. Also, it was noticeable that I was sometimes late home from school, a result of meetings after school where I was involved in discussions about frontline development and new ideas for fundraising.

His comment and the whole incident reminded me of the danger I was in but, at the same time, strengthened my resolve to continue with my secret work.

CHAPTER 16

Ambush

THOUGH I WAS INVOLVED IN MY CLANDESTINE WORK and living in constant danger of arrest, school life had to continue to be as "normal" as possible. During our secret training, it was impressed upon us that we should be hard-working and live up to our ideals of equality, integrity, dignity and respect for others. We were told to avoid bitter feelings of revenge and to "turn the other cheek" by never trying to hit back or hurt those who hated us. At school I continued to work hard and tried to get on with everyone but I felt under constant strain. By the time my second year drew to an end in July 1991, I was dreaming of returning to my village from where I could go off and herd cattle for a while with my father, just as in the happier days of my childhood.

Realistically I knew this would not be easy because the political unrest and violence was not confined to Uvira. In rural areas, not least in Banyumalenge territory, tension had been growing, particularly amongst young people, ever since the destruction of the urns that had followed the exclusion of the Banyamulenge from voting. Banyamulenge youths resented the way their community was discriminated against and became increasingly less willing to simply accept the authority of their parents and the scorn of other tribal groups. They saw themselves as members of a developing country and wanted their fair share of it. For that reason, they began a movement called Celaza. The name originated as *Communautes des Eglises Libres du Zaire* (Community of the Free Churches) but did not really have that meaning – it just had a certain ring to it and gave an impression of liberty. When this movement began, I was far away in Uvira and took an interest in it only when its actions became especially interesting: often they were minor and laughable but sometimes they were violent and more disturbing. In June 1991, a Banyamulenge man was killed by Babembe in Mibunda, in the west of Minembwe (*see timeline*). In revenge, a member of Celaza killed an important Babembe man. His name was Ndulwe and he had been a highly respected elder and church leader so his assassination caused tensions throughout the whole region; attacks against the Banyamulenge multiplied until it seemed that no opportunity to attack our community was ever missed.

Apart from the difficulty with security, there was another problem to overcome before I could go home: I had no money for the fare. There was no chance of paid work in Uvira but I decided I absolutely must earn some money. Musirimu made his living in the cattle industry: he sold veterinary medicine to the big cattle industries both within the Congo and in other countries. He was paid partly in cattle that he sold to the abattoirs in Burundi and he often needed people to drive the animals there, something I was well trained for from my childhood. So it was agreed I could do some work for him taking the cattle to Burundi. This sort of work was done by night, not only to make the long walk less exhausting for the animals but also to avoid motor traffic on the main road where the journey began. The return trip was forty kilometers and much of it was dangerous – through marshy savannah with threats of snakes and crocodiles – but I was not afraid because I knew the routes well from journeys I made as Jimmy, escorting recruits who were going to join the FPR. Also I was not alone because Jacques agreed to come with me and being with him made it something of an exciting adventure as we herded about one hundred and fifty cows through the darkness to Burundi. Being paid afterwards was even more exciting. We were paid a sum equivalent to $20; I had never had so much money of my own and I asked Musirimu to look after it for me until my journey home was organized.

Of course, working like this in the night did nothing to help my studies at school in the day so I failed some of my exams in June and had to stay for resits in July. It was tedious and annoying that I couldn't get straight away in June but I was buoyed up by the thought that I would soon be with my family at home or out herding cattle with my father. That July was warmer and less rainy than usual but, generally, it seemed quiet and mundane as it had been the year before. That had been my first July in Uvira, at the end of my first year at the senior secondary school when I was so homesick but had no money to pay for a trip back to the village.

Now I was excited, knowing that this year I could go back; I was impatient to get away but had to wait for the results of my resits. I was worried with a lot of questions on my mind. Not wanting to make the journey alone, particularly as I knew there were security problems, I agreed a date with some other Banyamulenge who were going back to various villages in my area. One of them was Matani, a cousin of my sister-in-law. He was a couple of years older than me and had always treated me like a younger brother. We planned to take a *motogari* (passenger vehicle) along Lake Tanganyika and then walk up the mountains to our villages. 'We'll go as far as Nundu before climbing into the mountains,' Matani said, 'because the Babembe of Nundu are not so dangerous as the Babembe of Lusenda and Baraka.' As well as being very sensible and an experienced traveller, he was one of the biggest and strongest in our group so we all accepted his decisions and treated him as our leader.

We met on the agreed day, early in the morning by the statue of President Mobutu, between Mulongwe and Kimanga, a place where vehicles stopped to pick up would-be travellers. I was the youngest in the group of about fifteen, all male, mostly Banyamulenge returning to their villages after studying in the city.

The next motogari was as usual a Toyota Stout. It already had a cargo and some other passengers going to various places along the route; we were told to make ourselves as comfortable as we could on top of the sacks of charcoal and bags of fish. We hung on, tumbling on top of each other as the heavy truck struggled slowly along the narrow, unsurfaced road riddled with ridges and potholes. It took us more than half a day to travel our first thirty kilometers because we had a breakdown at a place called Swima and it took hours for the driver and two *convoyeurs* to get it going again. (the *convoyeurs* were the driver's right-hand men. They organised the loading of the trucks and, even more importantly, they leaped down as soon as the vehicle stopped to put stones behind the wheels to supplement often faulty brakes). The Banyamulenge passengers all hid behind the vehicle while the repairs were going on because we had heard the Babemba of Swima were very keen to avenge the death of Ndulwe, which had happened just a few weeks before. It was a relief when the vehicle finally started and we were able to continue to Nundu, a small town set in a hollow between the Lake and the mountains.

It was late afternoon when we arrived there and, jumping down from that uncomfortable truck, we felt as if a nightmare had just ended. With satisfaction and relief we watched the Stout disappear into the distance with its remaining passengers, little realising that a greater nightmare was ahead. Despite being tired, we were cheerful as we collected all our belongings together and started to walk into the town. We were hungry and needed to get something to eat there before starting the arduous two-day walk up the mountain to our villages. Matani told us to walk quickly to the little market next to the hospital but to keep a low profile, walking in pairs with gaps between so that we didn't look like a group. He went in front to lead the way, occasionally looking back to see if we were following. At the market we quickly bought some food – bananas, cooked cassava and so on – and then continued our quick but careful walk.

What none of us knew was that news had already been passed on about us and a group of Babembe was waiting for us. Soon, though, we began to notice that people we passed were looking at us in an unusual way: we didn't realise it at the time but they were assessing our condition to tell those waiting in ambush what to expect. Matani began to get anxious about losing some of us and told us all to hurry. Just before reaching the bend in the road before the bridge, what seemed like hundreds of adults and youths suddenly appeared out of the bush and surrounded us. It was the first day of the long holidays for the regular secondary schools so the mob was enlarged by many youths who might otherwise have been in their classes. Nearby was a brick oven, which they broke open so that they could hurl the hot bricks at us. Suddenly it was if the sky were raining bricks

We had no idea what we could do to defend ourselves and Matani, still acting as our leader shouted, '*Mwirwane ho, mutabazwe namaguru yanyu, aha na h'Imana gusa*', meaning 'Every man for himself! Run if you can! Only the grace of God can save us now!' Though our aggressors could see that we were seriously hurt, they showed no sign of wanting to stop and began attacking us by punching, head-butting or wielding anything they could lay their hands on. Some of the men in our group were so hurt that they could do nothing to defend themselves as they lay helpless on the ground. Everyone had serious wounds and blood all over their clothes. We wanted to get to the bridge but, at the same time, we were afraid that if we reached there the crowd might throw us in the river and let us drown. Suddenly I was dragged off into the bush by three men. I was yelling that it wasn't me or anyone else in our group who had killed Ndulwe. I was convinced they were going to kill me but in fact they saved me to some extent because they only stole my suitcase and then left me alone.

When I became aware that I was no longer with the other Banyamulenge, I began, for the first time, to cry. I wondered where Matani was. I was sure he was still alive and couldn't believe such a kind, trustworthy friend could let me die alone. I headed in the direction of the bridge again and then could see that the fighting was still going on. I could even make out one or two people from our group trying to save themselves from being thrown into the river.

Suddenly, above all the noise and confusion, a deep, booming, commanding voice began to speak. It was one of the Babembe elders shouting in the Kibembe language, telling his younger clansmen to stop what they were doing. There was an eerie calm, a deathly silence, as if loud cacophonous music had suddenly stopped. Then the chief's voice resounded, 'Do not sully the streets of our city with innocent blood! Do not kill children here before our eyes! That would be a curse against us, the Babembe!'

While the weapons (sharp sticks, stones and bricks) were laid down, we glanced around, noticing that some of our group had disappeared while others were badly wounded. Seeing Matani, I ran to him and embraced him as if he were my father. He was obviously happy and relieved to see me, the youngest of the group he was trying to lead, and he then shouted out to anyone who could hear him, '*Niba araho mwihishe ntimurebe inyuma duhurire kumusozi umwanya hacyiye agahengwe!*' which means, 'If you managed to hide somewhere, now is your time to make your getaway. Don't look behind, just look after yourself and we'll regroup on the mountain.'

We all left as quickly as we could without a backward glance. Some of us could hardly walk but staggered along, almost crawling on all fours. Of course we had all lost our luggage and food but that didn't seem to matter when we had been so close to death – we could think only of survival. When we had gone a short way up the hill and finally felt safe enough to look behind us, we could see that the crowd had disappeared and the brick oven was completely destroyed; broken bricks were all over the road. As we waited apprehensively, afraid that those who were not with us were dead, we saw a figure emerge from the bush to the left and then another from the right. Gradually, one by one, every member of our group appeared. All were limping, all bleeding but all alive! It had been, as Matani had told us, a case of each person looking after himself and then regrouping. Those of us less severely hurt tried to look after the others but no-one had any medical training and we had, of course, no first aid kit either. We used shirts to bandage wounds to try to stop the bleeding. It seemed like a miracle that we were all still alive and, before we moved off, we said a sincere prayer, 'Thank you, God, that we have been spared!'

Because I had missed several minutes of the violence when those three men took me aside, I was one of the least severely hurt. Unfortunately, being so young and quite slightly built, I was not strong enough to carry any of those grown men on my back. I was able, though, to offer support to someone who could only limp. We were a pathetic group as we tried to climb into the colder mountains in so much pain. We knew that it was getting colder as night fell and, also, that resting would only make our painful bodies stiffen more. 'Wounds are less painful when they are fresh,' we told ourselves, drawing on traditional wisdom. We knew that the first village, Kabemgbwe, was a long way away but we pushed on through the night, though there was one man in so much pain that he couldn't help crying out at times in agony. At around midnight we saw the village in the distance and began calling out in our own language, knowing that fellow Banyamulange would not hesitate to help us.

The villagers woke up and looked after us, warming water to bathe our wounds, the only medical treatment available as there was no clinic in the area. They gave us food and a place to sleep, as is customary in our tradition of *Gufunguza*, welcoming visitors and offering them milk and something to eat. In the traditional way we were shared amongst the houses; because we were all young men, we went mainly to the little houses for unmarried men.

Though it was a relief to lie down and rest amongst friendly people, it was not easy to sleep with so many things racing through my mind. I was in pain and was worried that I might have some kind of internal haemorrhage. I longed to see my mother to tell her what I had been through that day. I turned over in my mind what had happened: I could see the crowd, wild and violent, and then that old wise man with his words of wisdom that had quietened the mob. I pictured the crowd evaporating at his simple but profound words. Then I saw again the hectic escape into the bush, not knowing if any of us were dead. Finally I turned over and over in my mind how this violence had arisen. Why had the Banyamulenge youths killed a respectable Babembe man and how could vengeance for acts like this ever stop? Why would politicians encourage this hatred and violence? Couldn't they see the bad feeling that was being created unnecessarily? I was young and idealistic and didn't want to lose my faith in human nature. I had grown up fearing this tribe because when I misbehaved or cried my mother sometimes threatened, 'I'll call a Babembe to you!' My family, though, had a close friend from the Babembe community called Asula Senge and he had changed my views because I knew he was a good man who wanted peace with other tribes and friendship with my family. I had started to believe that other tribes are people like us who strive to live in peace too. So, as I lay trying to sleep, I thought of the wise old man who had dispersed the mob and of Asule Senge. I wanted to keep my faith in human nature and renew my hope for the future. Then I said my prayers of thanks and finally slept for a few hours. Most of us continued on our journey the next day but one had to stay longer to recover from their wounds.

CHAPTER 17

Another perilous journey

WE HAD A GOOD HOLIDAY IN THE VILLAGE with our relatives and friends and I spent three peaceful weeks herding with my father. The return trip to Uvira was relatively uneventful and I soon settled into my life in Uvira again. This time I knew exactly what to expect so it was not too hard for me to accept and I resolved to work really hard at school in the hope that one day I would be able to rise above all my problems. My dream was that the war in Rwanda would end and a more just society could be built throughout our trouble-torn area of central Africa. I tried to keep positive by remembering the good people I knew from other tribes like Asula Senge and the chief who had saved us at Nundu as well as plenty of boys and teachers I knew at school. Many were very supportive. There was a clever and influential Mufulero boy called Fikirini Ramadhani who would challenge others when they teased or bullied me and who often walked part of the way home with me. There was also a Mubembe boy, Mutama Aoci, who was very helpful in so many ways. He avoided talking about politics and would simply go quiet when the subject of excluding or exterminating the Banyamulenge arose. His father had paid for him to have extra classes and he found a way of inviting me to join him there without embarrassing me. This was extremely useful, particularly when I had missed important lessons because of being ill or not being able to pay my fees.

On the whole, I was becoming more confident in school. This was largely because I did not feel so much of an outsider as I had at first. I now understood that there were many different social and tribal groups, some more influential than others. Divisions were not just along tribal lines but also based on socio-economic and geographic regions. For example, there was a contrast between urban and rural and between the deprived areas of town and the more comfortable areas. Another category was *Batoka mbali*, meaning those who came from far away because, the Congo being so huge that another region can seem like a world away. Moving a far distance sometimes brought with it a positive social status because those who had travelled to the area were often highly educated intellectuals whose skills were sought-after. More often, though, it was a disadvantage to be an "outsider" from far away. In my class, there was one boy who fell into that category and he became a close friend, probably because we united in the face of so much social exclusion. Between us, we developed a form of self-defence that showed itself in jokes that humiliated our attackers.

No longer allowing myself to be bullied, I even went as far as attacking a teacher in this way. Though the majority of the Bafulero teachers were nice, this one was an extremist who had been abusing me about my ethnicity for some time. I stood in front of the whole class and reduced them all to laughing and screaming by saying, 'It stinks in here! I think the teacher has just farted!' With the lesson completely disrupted, I was sent to the headmaster. Even there I held my own: 'Yes, I did say that,' I agreed, 'but he really did fart and it was so loud and smelly that we simply couldn't handle it!' Though he was angry, I could see that he had difficulty keeping a straight face and I suggested he should call for witnesses. These witnesses backed me up but I still had to take my punishment and be beaten. Later, a nice teacher had a word with me, warning me that Tutsi were a tiny minority in the school and I should be careful what I said. 'This is their school and they can do what they want,' he reminded me. Still, I felt empowered by my new strategy of fighting back and accepted my punishment with pride.

The next step for me was to get good grades in my final examination and I tried to concentrate on that. It was not easy though. I still had a 14 kilometres walk every day and had great difficulties raising the money for my fees and other things I needed for my studies. As there were no jobs, I relied on friendly people to give me some or sometimes I earned money by taking Musirimu's cattle to Burundi. I was still working, without pay of course, clandestinely in the night. This was important to me because it made me feel that I was doing my bit already towards a better future. This combination of worry and work was not good for my health: it seemed to make me less resistant to malaria and I suffered from it at regular intervals, as people do when they have it in their system. Overall it was not easy to stay positive when I felt surrounded by problems, problems which categorised into two main groups: the collective socio-political difficulties faced by all my community and difficulties of finance and personal relationships that affected me as an individual.

I had now spent three years in the city with all its insecurities but I was at least used to living with Musirimu's family and felt secure once I was home from school. There was some kind of mutual arrangement between him and my father based on various reciprocal favours; but the main reason he let me stay so long was because of our traditional attitudes towards helping other members of our tribe, especially as we were from the same clan and our families were very close. So I became virtually a member of the family with somewhere to sleep and a bed, a bed that was shared with visitors or other boys looked after by Musirimu's family.

The Musirimus' help couldn't go much beyond this though because they had seven children of their own and were not well off, even though Musirimu had a good job. He was a wise, thoughtful, patient and intelligent man but he also drank quite a lot. He always said this was a good way of making contacts with important people and people from other communities who had the potential to be his enemies. He was a very likeable man who did a great deal to help other people, especially those trying to improve themselves through education, and Busoka and I were not the only additions to his family.

Having spent more than three years with them, I felt like part of the family and we had shared some dramatic moments that seemed to bind us together. For example, one night the river Kalyamabenge flooded and the roof of the house was ripped off by wind. Neither Musirimu nor his eldest son were present at the time and I was the strongest male there to help his wife and children. Without a roof above us and with the water rising and no emergency services or other authorities that could help, it was quite a dramatic time. I ran off to town to find friends who could help and then returned to help the others move to a temporary home with friends.

There were other frightening moments we shared too, mostly connected with the intermittent political violence that could erupt at any time. On one occasion when Musirimu was a long way away in Shaba on business, I and two of the children fell seriously ill with malaria. Having no money to buy medicine or pay for a doctor, Mamma Musirimu resorted to using out of date compresses, all that she could find in the local pharmacy. The result was a sort of paralysis where we had stiff necks, could not walk easily and had problems with our jaws and mouths. Because of financial hardship, we would only seek medical intervention in desperate circumstances, because it meant getting into debt. Finally a Ugandan doctor visited us with an arrangement to pay him later when we had money. We recovered shortly after his visit. This incident is typical of the dangers of out of date medication sold in many part of Africa to desperate people.

Life went on, swinging from one crisis to another, and I continued to dream of that peaceful life herding cattle with my father. I generally couldn't afford to travel home for the holidays but instead used to stay in the city to make contacts that might help me raise my school fees. After taking my third year exams, however, I was determined to go home. Musirimu was away on business and I had no way of earning any money for the fare but I had a friend from my village, Sabune, who was nearly as poor as I was and equally keen to go home so we planned to go the whole way on foot – a trek that would take four days. We were less than eighteen years old, fit and impulsive and determined to see our families. We knew our host families in Uvira would forbid us if they knew what we had planned so it was a well-kept secret that we intended to walk that violence-torn area south along the great lake to Nundu. Political and security problems had continued to escalate and it would have been fairly risky even for a group travelling together by motor vehicle so to attempt to walk it was something the adults simply would have forbidden us to do. To avoid causing concern, Sabune told his uncle and I told Mamma Musirimu that we were travelling by motogari but we actually set off on foot early one Sunday morning. We were very apprehensive about the first part of the journey because we knew that a few kilometres along the road to Bubembe there was a military position that we would need to pass at the port of Kalundu. We comforted ourselves with the thought that it was Sunday and so there would be fewer people. 'The soldiers won't bother us – they'll have other things on their minds,' said Sabune but really he was trembling and more afraid than I was. My work with Umuryango, the secret movement, and my times in the jungle with my father had made me more used to dangerous journeys.

Lorry loads of fish suddenly appeared as they left the port with their cargo of dried fish. We dodged out of their way but at the same time used them to hide from the soldiers. We had hoped to hide ourselves behind *bomora* (handcarts of fish) but, because it was Sunday, there weren't many. 'Even fish vendors have a break on Sunday!' I remarked wryly. The soldiers noticed us and looked at us intently. I kept my head high and told my friend that it was important to look innocent and give no impression of fear – we must act like men. Sabune had a little money, just enough to buy us food on the journey and to offer a bribe if we were in danger.

We were discussing the possibility of bribery when we found ourselves surrounded by three older soldiers in camouflage uniforms. 'Only buses and cars come this way – go round!' they ordered in threatening voices. I tried to ignore them and carry on because I was fed up with the excuses soldiers came up with to victimise innocent people; I would have preferred them just to carry out their injustices without inventing some pretext of legality. '*Yoo tokoboma ayoo*', 'You are going to get yourself killed!' one of them snarled at me. Sabune gave me a look that meant we shouldn't argue and then gave them some of his money. They looked in a dissatisfied way at what he had given them and said they were not in the business of negotiating and we had better give them more before we were attacked and locked up in prison. We knew that this was no idle threat and could actually happen within minutes. Sabune gave them more money until we had hardly anything left for ourselves. They then took it upon themselves to frisk us and, of course, found the rest of the money in Sabune's pocket. They searched our bags also and took all our clothes and spare shoes before telling us to disappear as quickly as we could because they didn't want to see any more of us.

Despite having no money left for food and no idea where we could sleep, we continued on our way along Lake Tanganyika, a route that took us through spectacular scenery between the huge expanse of the lake and the towering mountains on the other side. So beautiful and yet so dangerous! We knew that we could be attacked at any of the villages along the way and we also knew that, generally speaking, it was the young men who were violent and we could relax more with the adults and old people.

Between ten and twenty kilometres from Kalundu lay the villages of Kabimba and Kigongo where the majority of the people are Bafulero or Bavira. A group of youths were sitting under a mango tree playing mancala, the board game common in Africa. They gave us a curious look but they were intent on their game and said nothing. I noticed that Sabune smiled with relief but ahead of us lay the more dangerous villages of the Babembe and settlements of Hutu refugees from Burundi. We passed Makobola and Swima, both Babembe places, and started to wonder if we should spend the night there as it was starting to get dark – the time of day when soldiers patrol the roads and bush. Some had seen us already but they hadn't noticed we were Tutsi because the light was fading and we hid our faces.

The problem with finding somewhere to rest was that the villages were dangerous too but I had one hope: I knew that somewhere in these villages there lived a man from my clan and sub clan called Mukiza who, though he was connected with the army, was Banyamulenge like us. Sabune was incredulous, not believing anyone of our ethnicity could survive life in this area, but it seemed to be our only option to try to find him. Avoiding young men, we approached various old men to ask if they knew a man called Mukiza; to our great relief, we finally found someone who knew him and led us to his home, a small hut house in very mediocre situation.

Mukiza seemed hungry, which was not surprising because soldiers received very little pay and sometimes went unpaid for many months or years. He had joined the army so that he could help Tutsi people in situations of injustice, but this meant he had to endure extreme discrimination himself. 'How is it possible for you to be here?' he exclaimed in surprise when he saw us. He didn't know us but he could immediately see that we were two young Tutsi so he welcomed us in and gave us food. We spent the rest of the evening talking and exchanging news and then we slept deeply, relieved that we had found somewhere to stay. Worried about what might happen to us, he tried to prevent us from leaving the next day but we insisted, knowing that he had barely enough food for himself, and set off early. We each had some money he had given us so that we could buy fruit or something on the way. As we left, he said, "*n'Imana yonyine ibahurutsa*', an expression my people use when there is danger beyond the control of people; it means 'Only God can protect you!'

The next place we were heading for was Nundu, the same place where I had been ambushed two years previously. There was no avoiding it because we had to go through the town to reach the road to the mountains. When we reached it at around 9 am, we kept to the main road and passed through the same local market to buy fruit. Fearing what could happen this time, I told Sabune we'd have to buy some bananas very quickly and not stop in the town. I was no longer naïve but watchful and looking at every movement of people around us; I kept warning Sabune not to bargain or waste any time there. One good thing about the Babembe people is that, generally, they are known as not likely to base an attack on a previous one: once their 'revenge' is done, that's it. So my hope was that, since the time they had attacked us previously, they had finished their attacks on Banyamulenge. Sabune agreed and added that we should try to hide our faces. So we quickly bought the fruit and then ran on. When we reached the place where our group had been attacked the last time, I remembered what Matani had said to me and the others and repeated it to Sabune, '*Nturebe inyuma cyangwa kuruhande*', which means 'Don't look behind or to the sides!'

Thirty minutes later we were in the mountains. We were exhausted and covered in sweat but not yet out of danger. We pushed on but Sabune fell ill after a few hours and so we were obliged to stop and rest. He slept for a few hours during the afternoon but we absolutely had to carry on. He was too heavy for me to carry so he put an arm around my shoulder and we limped along like that. It took us about ten hours, from early in the morning until the evening, to reach the first Banyamulenge village, Kabembwe.

As we staggered into the village, we were greeted by a crowd of friendly people who asked us where the adults were. They couldn't believe we had made the trip alone. They treated us as if we were their own sons and Sabune soon felt better with their care. We slept well that night and then spent a complete day there to recover before carrying on to Minembwe. Our families were, of course, overjoyed to see us but shocked that we had undertaken such a dangerous journey alone. They made us promise to go back by a safer route and raised the fare for our transport.

CHAPTER 18

Homeless

DURING MY FIFTH YEAR of upper secondary school in 1993, I went on a class trip to the *Institute Nationale de Recherche Agricole* (INERA – the National Agricultural Research centre), a residential college for agricultural studies. Like the rest of my classmates, who were boys from various tribal backgrounds, I was excited about this trip to Mulungu, 250 kilometres away and all funded as part of our course. It actually turned out to be quite nerve-wracking because there were four Burundian pupils in my class – three Hutu and one Tutsi, Ntakandi – so the shadow of the tension in Burundi followed us there. A Hutu president had just been elected (*see timeline*) after years of Tutsi dominance and his followers were jubilant.

After a few days at INERA, the organiser spoke confidentially to Ntakandi and me to warn us of danger from our Burundian Hutu classmates because they had threatened to kill us. So Ntakandi and I stuck together and agreed never to both sleep at the same time. Also we agreed not to eat the prepared food when it was the turn of the Hutu boys to help in the kitchen because we were genuinely afraid that we might be poisoned. Because most of our class were not involved in the Burundian problem but had more knowledge of what was happening in Rwanda, the Hutu boys told our classmates that we listened to the banned radio channel, RPF. My reply was that in the Congo there was not a conflict between Tutsi and other tribes – we were all one nation; they should keep their political problems in their own country, whether Burundi or Rwanda, and try to live in peace. By saying this I managed to get support from the majority (largely Bafulero) boys because they could see the justice of recognizing regional differences rather than ethnic conflict. In fact most of my classmates supported me warmly. Still, with all this tension, the school trip I had so looked forward turned out to be a very long month indeed and I was quite relieved to get back to the relative safety of Uvira.

When I arrived back, though, another bitter disappointment was waiting for me: it was not going to be possible for me to live at Musirimu's place any longer. Mamma Musirimu was a resourceful person who coped well with her large family but having so many additional people to feed was a problem for her. Her husband was frequently away on business (as he was at that time) and, having no income of her own, she had to rely on him sending her enough money in time for all the household needs as well as the rent; it wasn't easy. I had tried to pull my weight and had always helped with household tasks such as fetching and carrying shopping and firewood, but there were others to help now also.

Before asking us to leave, Mamma Musirimu had negotiated other accommodation for Busoka with Musirimu's business partner in Uvira and she assumed that my brother Noah would manage to sort out something for me. When he lived in the village he had always helped me with school fees by selling cattle and now he had a job as a teacher in a village in Burundi so it was assumed that he would be in an even better position to support me financially. Unfortunately this was not the case, though I was not sure at the time why. When two other "guests" arrived for a potentially long stay, Mamma Musirimu decided that it was time for me and Busoka to leave. With Musirimu away on business and unlikely to be back for another six months, we simply agreed without dispute that we would leave within a few days.

I had always deliberately tried to keep in touch with various people who might be able to help me when I experienced particular difficulties and I now wrote to one of them, a man called Jules from the south-west of Congo who worked for a non-government agency. In my letter I said that I was looking for somewhere to live and would be able to pay the rent towards the end of the year. I didn't want to give the impression of being desperate, even though I was, and didn't say that I would soon be homeless.

When the day came for us to leave, Busoka went to his new home and I left giving the impression that I had somewhere to go too. I was too proud to admit I hadn't. 'Ntawakwimena inda' says the old Banyamulenge proverb – 'Don't reveal the insides of your stomach to everyone!' My good friend Tokos had updated this saying to 'Never tell people your problems because 70% of them won't want to help you, 20% will laugh, and 10% are worse off than you anyway!' In an unequal society such as the Congo, it often seems better to hide problems than to talk about them and the Banyamalenge were always keen to maintain their personal dignity and integrity. So it was that I packed up my things and left my family and home of five years with no idea of where I was going, letting everyone apart from Busoka believe that I knew where I was going.

The day I left I hadn't the heart to go to school but instead spent the day trying to organise something for myself. I took all my belongings in two bags and left them in a kiosk in Kimanga Street. Kiosks are part of the way of life in Uvira – small lock up shops that sell a variety of things and the owners were usually friendly. 'Could I leave my things with you for a few hours?' I had asked and I wasn't refused. I then went to see Jules in person as I hadn't had a reply to my letter. He immediately agreed to accept me into his own home but, not wishing to seem like someone with absolutely nothing and in a desperate hurry, I said I would be along the next day. Meanwhile, I had to survive the rest of that day.

By the time evening came I was hungry. Busoka had given me a little money and it was just enough to buy me a meal in the slum area in a restaurant called Tundisa, which in translation means "it doesn't matter what you eat if it fills you up". I ate quickly and left because I was afraid to be in that neighbourhood after dark. It wasn't just the possibility of being attacked by violent men that frightened me: being alone at night brought back to me all the stories of witchcraft. In every corner of the town there were witchdoctors, the only source of hope for sick people who believed in these methods and who couldn't afford modern medicine. I knew that the powers they were reputed to have were not always benign. In particular, I became very aware of the dogs – their barking in the distance or their shadowy forms moving along. Dogs wandering in the night are often assumed to be sorcerers – humans transformed into animal form to commit evil acts. I was also terrified of *kanyonya* ("bloodsuckers" in Swahili). These are mythical beings looking for blood or human organs, and those dark streets, whether the backstreets that never had lighting or the main roads during one of the many power cuts, seemed to me the ideal habitat for them.

For a few hours I wandered around in this state of fear and then, overcome with worries and tiredness, sat under a mango tree. I tried to sleep but couldn't because I was too afraid. Then I remembered a very nice man I knew who might help me. I decided to go to him and say there were a lot of visitors at Musirimu's place that evening and would it be all right if I slept there. I was afraid the lie would be found out the next day but decided to try anyway. When I went to his house and knocked, I was told they had no spare bed and, putting on a casual air as if I didn't really mind, I didn't let them know how much I was in need but just smiled and walked off. In a way I was relieved because I was worried about telling such an untruth when it might be found out. I then tried something else. I walked a few kilometres towards the city centre to the home of a man called Ziriguru whose daughters and wife were very friendly towards me. I knew his house had an annex for visitors and I would ask whoever was in the annex if I could stay there. So I knocked on the annex and when someone I didn't know opened the door, I acted as if I were an expected friend of the family. I slept there on a pretext, not wanting anyone to know the situation I was in and feel sorry for me.

I left early the next morning before anyone could find out about my problem. After recovering my bag from the friendly man in the kiosk, I headed for Jules' place, full of hope. What Jules hadn't explained to me was that he had two wives and they didn't get on with each other. The first one was indignant at my suggestion that I would be staying in her house. She was a strong woman with a lot of influence over her husband. 'He made no mention of any such thing to me!' she told me in a way that meant I'd have to find somewhere else. The other wife was gentler towards me and wanted me to stay at Jules' place but the first wife insisted I should leave; as a compromise she suggested that she could introduce me to a nurse called Henri who worked in the Catholic dispensary in the heart of the Parokia Parish. However, this introduction would be several days later and, in the meantime, I had nothing – no idea whatsoever of where I could sleep or eat.

My new strategy became to spend as long as possible in bars, particularly Nganda du Grand Lac because it did not have anti-Tutsi elements. It was owned by Asieri, a Congolese Tutsi from North Kivu and would be full of people who had a moderate attitude towards Tutsi people. Of course that couldn't stop me being anxious about spending the night with a crowd of strangers getting drunk, especially as I was aware that I was supposed to buy drinks but had no money. Still, I managed to distract the security guard to get in and then just tried to be inconspicuous as I listened to music. Sometimes I even managed to snatch a little sleep on chairs or benches. In the daytime I just wandered the streets, ashamed to speak about my situation to anyone I knew or go to school as a homeless, unwanted vagrant. By the third day I was getting very hungry. Luckily there was plenty of water in town and I knew that I could survive with just water as I had done before. Then, by sheer good luck, I bumped into a man from my direct clan. Though he would not have realised that I was no longer living with Musurimu, I think he could see that I hadn't eaten for a while because he gave me some money. I thanked God and felt a huge problem had been resolved because the money would be sufficient to eat in the Tundisa for a few days, which meant I could last until Jules' wife took me to seen Henri.

Meanwhile, I lived as a boy of the streets, sleeping in bars, until the time came to meet Henri. He readily agreed to take me if I agreed to pay him a sum of money the equivalent of a head of cattle in value, though he knew that would not be immediate. I had written to my father to let him know he would have to sell one so that I could pay this man, but I was not sure whether my father had received the letter or how soon he could send the money. I had not told him I was homeless so he might not realise how urgent it was.

At this stage I didn't know why my brother Noah hadn't managed to find a way to send me some money so I felt hurt, angry and desperate to find out why. I made up my mind to go and visit him in Burundi before moving in with Henri. Noah was the eldest of my brothers and he had experienced a lot of the same kind of difficulties I had in becoming educated. It was a great achievement for him when he completed his teacher training but he then found his ethnicity barred him from teaching in the Congo. He didn't give up though: instead he found a post in Burundi in a remote rural area; not being Burundian, he had been unable to find anything in the towns so accepted this job in a village called Gishubi in the northern province of Gitega. As there were extremely few Tutsi in that area, it was not considered safe enough for him to take his wife and four children with him so he had gone alone. For the Banyumalenge, women being left in the village while their men go off to work is a normal situation. As well as security considerations they knew also that going to a totally different region without our cattle-based lifestyle would pose dietary problems for a family who depended on milk.

I longed to see my brother again, not only for obvious brotherly feelings but because I was so perplexed at the way he seemed to have abandoned me by stopping the financial support and leaving me in my homeless predicament. At the same time I knew he had problems of his own and there could be good reasons for why he had forgotten me, but I needed to find out what had happened. My friend, Budagu, helped me with some Burundian currency and I planned my journey to go via Bujumbura, the capital city of Burundi, stopping afterwards at Gitega where I knew of someone who would put me up overnight. This was a brother of Musirimu, Elias Ntuyahaga. It took a day by bus to reach Gitega where I was warmly welcomed by Elias's wife, Mamma Kamaliza.

She was shocked to see me: I had lost so much weight and did not look healthy. I could not explain to her how I had been homeless because that might have caused trouble in her family as Musirimu didn't know what I had been through. I was extremely hungry because I had no money to buy food when the bus stopped at roadside markets, so it was wonderful to share a good meal with that friendly family and I slept well afterwards, happy and relaxed to be with Banyamulenge people again. Very early in the morning, Mamma Kamaliza came with me to get the bus. She warned me that I would still have a very long walk from the "bus station" in Gishubi to the very remote village where Noah was. She was right. After a very dusty few hours travelling on dirt roads, I still had a six hour walk. Of course I had to ask the way as I walked through the villages and I received surprised looks from the people who were not used to seeing a Tutsi walking alone through their territory.

When I finally made it to Noah's village in the evening, I was dusty, tired and hungry but I forgot all of that when I saw my brother again. There had been no way of letting him know I was coming so he was taken by surprise and overjoyed to see me though, like Mamma Kamariza, he was shocked to see me so thin. Any misgivings or anger I had towards him disappeared immediately and we were soon laughing and exchanging stories. Though there were so few Tutsis there, he had some friends amongst the other teachers and his life was reasonably comfortable. He had employed someone to clean and to cook for him on the wood burner; this felt like a luxury in a place that had no electricity or other amenities. One day he took me to visit the rabbit farm that had been set up to improve nutrition in the area (though, of course, it did not help Banyamulenge like Noah since we are almost vegetarian). On the whole, though, his life was hardly any more comfortable than it would have been back in Minembwe, especially since his pay cheques were so irregular and he hadn't received any for a year. Our family thought of him as successful and relatively rich but I could see him now as cut off from the rest of us and not very well off financially either. He still relied to a large extent on money he earned by selling cattle back home. Despite this financial hardship, he gave me enough money for my fees and some extra to help me get back.

After I had spent a few days there, we were listening to Burundi radio when there was a terribly shocking announcement: there had been a coup and the newly elected Hutu president, Melchior Ndadaye, had been arrested by Tutsi members of the Burundian army (*see timeline*). This was terrifying for us because Hutus form 85% of the Burundian population and we knew they would react violently. We remained glued to the radio and within hours there was an announcement from the Prime Minister, Sylivie Kinigi. He said that everyone should stay in their home and no-one should move from one area to another.

Early next day the news got even worse: another announcement came to confirm that President Ndadaye had been assassinated!

Ndadaye had been a hero for Burundian Hutu so their anger was extreme. Killing of Tutsis had started everywhere in the country just after he was arrested and now it could only get worse. In Gishubi, the atmosphere was extremely tense because it was the birth place of a very influential Hutu politician, Sylvestre Ntibantunganya. Villages were surrounded by militia groups hunting Tutsi in the area. We joined some Burundian Tutsis, staying in one room together, while all around us there was noise and confusion. Around the village, people were shouting, banging drums and blowing whistles to alert people to start the "work", by which they meant killing Tutsi.

'You must go,' Noah said to me. He then went to see his neighbour, a Hutu man who owned a motorbike, and gave him money to take me to the nearest military barracks. As people had been forbidden to move around and many roads were blocked, this would not be easy but the man agreed to try.

We set off at about 4am while it was still dark and took unofficial paths. In the distance we could hear shouting and screaming as people were attacked. Then, after about an hour of travelling, as if we hadn't got enough problems already, we had an accident. Both of us were quite badly hurt and the motorbike was out of action. Suddenly, despite the historic and horrific moment that the country was going through, I found myself distracted entirely by my own personal problems. I was bleeding quite heavily but I made an effort to stay calm and thought, as usual when I had problems, of that old story of the little lamb. Yet again I said to myself, 'This is not my worst day!' Our clothes covered with blood, we walked to the nearest village and, luckily for me, the first house we arrived at was home to a very friendly, welcoming Tutsi woman. She washed our wounds with warm water as there was nothing more she could do. By this time my worry was not the injuries, but the killings that were taking place around the country. I could tell that the woman was very afraid too. When she had done all she could for us she went out and stopped a car and asked the driver whether he could take me to a place called Matana. She assured the driver that I was not Burundian and said I was not Tutsi either. So I was given a lift and pretended that I did not speak Kirundi.

About 30 minutes later we were stopped by a gang of killers. 'This is it!' I thought to myself. It was a terrifying moment. They looked in through the car windows, saw me and ordered me to get out. This could have been disastrous because, though my face does not look like a stereotypical Tutsi, I am tall and slim. Thinking the same thing, the driver told them, 'This is a Congolese boy' but they spoke to me again, repeating that I should get out. Still pretending I didn't speak that language, I tried to look as if I didn't understand but I was afraid my facial expression would betray me. I tried hard to stay calm and look as if I didn't know what was going on. As luck would have it, a few cows appeared. The men were distracted by this and ran after them to kill them for meat, leaving us at the road block. 'Let's go!' I yelled. The driver started the car and we made our escape.

As relief spread over me, I thought again of the story of the little lamb and said to myself, 'No, this is not your worst day!' Arriving in Matana military camp, I found thousands of other students had also gone there for protection. From there I was able to travel in a military vehicle to Bujumbura but I could not continue because the border with Congo was closed so there was no legal way of getting back. I stayed in Bujumbura until I found someone to help me to cross into the Congo. Once I managed to get back into my own country I started to be aware of the pain caused by my injuries in the accident. Worse than that was the anxiety about what might happen to Noah.

CHAPTER 19

Hardship

THE UPHEAVALS IN BURUNDI HAD, of course, a significant impact on life in Uvira with its large number of Hutu and Hutu sympathisers, making life for any Tutsi people even more precarious. There was a great deal of stone-throwing and even some Banyamulenge deaths. Extremist gangs proliferated in this climate, making certain areas of town extremely dangerous, including the "parking" that I had to cross on my way to school if I didn't take the longer route by the old railway track. This area was notorious for drug-tracking, sales of smuggled gold and ivory. Nevertheless I looked forward to getting back to a relatively normal life living in a house and going to school.

Collecting my bag from the kiosk I was hopeful my accommodation problems were over but I was soon disappointed. From my very first days there, life at Henri's place was extremely difficult. He left the house early every day and left no food for me. I had somewhere to sleep but nothing to eat. I was starting to feel ill with malnourishment and had become very thin. Busoka visited me and helped by bringing food but I didn't tell him just how unpleasant my life was there, or how Henri would insult me and repeat over and over that he was convinced I would never pay him. At one time when he knew that I had not eaten for a few days, he left money all over the house to test whether I would steal some to buy food; he repeatedly used this method to test my integrity and honesty which I felt was an insult both to my traditional values and my Christian upbringing. What he did not know is that it was embedded in my family values that I would never beg, otherwise I would not be at his place in the first place: I was there on the understanding that my father would fund me by selling a valuable animal. He didn't seem to understand that we Banyamulenge might suffer but would always be prepared to "die like a man"; in other words, we must keep our dignity and values whatever trials we endure.

Now I was settled into a house and had money for my fees, I felt able to return to school without being worried that people might find out I was an unwanted, homeless person. As a proud Munyumalenge, I couldn't face being seen as weak and vulnerable and wanted to be able to hold my head high amongst my classmates and those around me. I was doing quite well at school and particularly enjoyed science and social science subjects. My best results were in biochemistry, economy, *zootecnia* (animal husbandry), topography, biology, urban and rural development, history and geography. Generally, I was passionate about all my studies and committed to learning. I saw education as a way forward for my country, a way out of the violence, misery and hatred. Many of the things my friend Tokos had told me years before continued to inspire me, especially stories about a country called Japan. This country, he had told me, had risen to be one of the world's leading economies by fighting poverty through developing education, knowledge and skills. I was desperate to learn, not only for my own future but for the good of others and the country.

The boys at school were from varying backgrounds and tribal groups but one or two were strikingly different. One of these was Magumu. We were all rather in awe of him because he was significantly older than the rest of us and clearly belonged to one of the tough gangs in town; this was apparent by his red eyes – a sure sign of drug-taking – and some of the things he said that surprised and shocked us. He was trying to get away from the gang culture to turn his life around. Seeming "different", he didn't mix much and was seen as a rather eccentric character but one we were rather afraid of. We kept a wary distance, sensing he was dangerous. Life must have been tough for him, living a double life and trying to keep up with students who had taken a more conventional path towards being educated.

One thing I really liked about him was his complete lack of social snobbery. For example, although Bafulero were the dominant tribal group in Uvira, their language for some reason had very low status and both students and teachers would avoid using it. Not Magumu though. When he came to school still a bit high on drugs, he would speak to the teachers in their own dialect and, when they pretended not to understand, would mock them, saying, 'Are you denying who you are? Are you not so and so from the tribe of such and such? You were born rural and are the first of your clan to make it this far!' This was huge mockery to direct at a teacher but he was unafraid. On one occasion, I went back with him to his place. It was a barren, stony place where his mother laboured on the infertile land to raise a few crops. Both parents seemed hungry and very poor but Magumu showed them enormous respect. Even in school he constantly praised his mother. No doubt he had resorted to trafficking and drug abuse in anger at his own "failure" but now he was determined to make a future for himself and his family.

One day on my way home to Henri's place, I felt so tired after the first few kilometres that I decided not to take the longer but safer route on the old railway track but to cross the "parking" – that wide stretch of open land that could sometimes be dangerous. I hadn't eaten for a long time and was very tired so the temptation to go by the shortest route was just too strong, even though I knew it was an area famous for the Khadafi gang. This gang, drug-users notorious for selling petrol illegally, had become practically untouchable to the authorities because they had the means to bribe themselves out of difficult situations; their acts of violence passed generally without comment. All sorts of illegal activities went on in this area: theft, drug trafficking, gold and ivory smuggling, currency exchange, selling petrol and anything that made money.

Within seconds of my decision to take the shorter route, I was noticed and yelled at with '*Munyarwanda, munyarwanda*,' a term meaning that I was Rwandan but in the worst possible sense, referring to that ethnicity as a filthy, unwanted Tutsi tribe. At this time when people were seeking revenge for the assassination of the president of Burundi, it was even more dangerous than ever: Tutsi were seen as legitimate targets for justifiable revenge. They leaped on me immediately, spitting at me and using all sorts of insults, asking me for the president's body. I replied that I wasn't Burundian though it was a useless defence as they knew that well enough. My being Tutsi was sufficient for their anger and I could see by their wild, red eyes that they were not in a mood to be reasonable and accept any explanations I might give. Again I felt the strong injustice of being condemned simply for my ethnicity. Only a few weeks before I had needed to convince the military in Burundi that I wasn't Burundian myself but now things were even worse: my nationality made no difference at all and only my ethnicity counted.

'This is your last day!' they jeered at me and I believed them as I looked around and saw other Banyamulenge they had taken hostage. Their leader, a youth called Cesar who was well known in the town, gave an order to bring petrol and when I felt some being poured onto my head, I was convinced that my "worst day" had indeed arrived. My chest felt as if it could burst with the pounding of my heart and I was dizzy with confusion and despair.

Suddenly, an authoritative voice rang out: 'Don't hurt him! Don't do him any harm! If you want to kill him you will have to kill me first. Look how many you are, all trying to kill such a slip of a youngster! And all because he's not your favourite race!' It was my schoolmate Magumu who was an influential member of this gang, one who was respected because he was strong, dangerous and shared their lifestyle. He pulled me roughly away, telling me to disappear as quickly as I could because Cesar was a fierce extremist and had meant what he said. I got away and so did the other hostages in the confusion that followed Magumu's intervention.

After this incident I felt dull, tired of everything. I seemed to see the world from a distance as a small and petty place. I turned over and over within myself how, like others of my ethnicity, I was virtually a hostage imprisoned in a place from which there was no way out. It was only by a miracle that I had escaped that gang. They were ruthless and had a strong group consciousness and a determination to act together to cause violent harm. Characteristically, that violence was not to be directed against other vicious gangs but against those people they judged to be "unwanted", namely those they labelled as strangers and invaders: the Tutsi. To support themselves they were involved in all sorts of criminal activities; the fact that such gangs could exist and remain untroubled by the forces of law and order reflected a breakdown in society that I found totally depressing. Furthermore, it seemed to me that, in Uvira, people were accustomed to following the majority without real thought and, as a result, they could so easily become xenophobic. There was little in-depth questioning of what was going on in society or what individuals could and should do to change things. The only way a gang could be made to act in a particular way was through offering money.

A few months later I was taken hostage by a youth called Vicky, the leader of a gang based in Kimanga, a poor area in the south of the city. Because I had no money to pay for my release, I was beaten up relentlessly and finally left on the ground with the threat, 'Don't think you are free! We'll get you another time because you haven't paid yet!' I was only one of many young Banyamulenge whom Vicky threatened with death if a bribe wasn't paid, though many were released even without the bribe. This constant danger in the streets of the city meant that we were restricted in our movements if we wanted to be safe; so not only were we outcasts from society but we were limited also in how often we could meet up with other young Tutsi. I didn't venture out much in the evenings.

Even greater than my worries for my own security were my worries about Noah because I had no way of finding out how things were going for him. The killings in Burundi went on for a month and, in total, about 300,000 people were killed there during that time, including twenty seven Banyamulenge working as teachers. Among these twenty seven, there was Busoka's brother Benayi, who had been my teacher at primary school, an incredibly good man who was a great support not only to Busoka but to many other young people. It wasn't until a few months later that I learnt Noah survived: he had managed to escape to Bujumbura but he was deeply affected by all that had happened. His Burundian Tutsi colleagues that I had met when I visited were not so lucky and had been killed. Again I found myself with conflicting feelings: on the one hand I was happy to learn about Noah's survival but at the same time I was very sad for Benayi and all other teachers that I had met in Gishubi. They had all been such nice people and truly dedicated to their work.

I continued to worry also about my friends who had joined the rebel movement and I didn't see the others often; Busoka attended another school and Kayaya had gone to another region. Luckily though, a year or so before I had met another boy from my tribe, Budagu. He was not in my school but he attended its "twin", the science/maths specialist arm of the Azuhuri complex. The two schools shared a common playground and compulsory Saturday school services and this is how I had managed to meet him. Being a shy kind of a person, my new friend appreciated some of the "streetwise" advice I was able to give him. For my part it was good to have someone to confide in and I found it difficult not to tell him everything though I kept some things from him. My work for the RPF had to remain secret. Although Budagu and I had different problems, we had many things in common and our friendship became really strong, He inspired me in many ways and became my mentor and counsellor.

At one point, Budagu and I made an arrangement to put some money together in Burundian currency as we were aware that, due to inflation, Congolese currency would lose its value. Starting with some of Budagu's Burundi francs, we bought a few T-shirts wholesale and then sold them on to friends. Unfortunately, our business idea did not really work because I simply could not keep up with the increasing capital so we shared our profits and gave up. What I earned helped me enormously as I could buy food and a few things I needed for school.

Through Budagu and Busoka, one man came to hear of me and how I was suffering from malnutrition. Having met me he invited me to move in with his friend. It was wonderful to leave Henri, especially as the situation had become even worse with him; I paid him the agreed cost even though I hadn't spent the full year with him and it gave me great satisfaction to say goodbye to him this way. Living with these two friendly men I felt a lot better as I began to eat properly and sleep well. Some nights, of course, I didn't sleep so well: those were the times I was secretly going to meetings as Jimmy. My new hosts were furious when they found out that I had been over the border into Burundi and said I was obviously not the serious student they had taken me for. So after several happy weeks when I had started to feel settled, I was told I must go. Their reaction surprised me because they were well-educated Banyamulenge themselves so I had assumed they would be sympathetic to the cause. Also, they must surely have realised that if I was not a serious student I would not have continued to live through so many problems in Uvira and still pass my exams. As it was, they ignored all this and threw me out knowing that I had nowhere to go. As well as being upset, I felt angry at their lack of sympathy which was not at all in accordance with our tribal traditions where we always help one another. Feeling unable to face them to tell them how disappointed I was, I wrote them an angry letter, saying they had not fulfilled their promises and they should have left me at Henri's.

So once again I took my bag to the kiosk and became a street boy. It did not seem such a frightening thing to do this time because I had become hardened to life on the streets and had various survival strategies. I knew how to sleep in bars and I found other places too, such as a large cement store where the guard allowed me to sleep sometimes. Occasionally I used my earlier trick to stay the night in Ziruguru's annex.

A bigger problem was finding food but I got around that too. The first evening I paid a friendly visit to Bidurwa and chatted in a friendly way with his children until it was time to eat; of course, I was given a meal too. The next two nights I used the same technique with another lady I knew, Nanna. Then, after a week or so, I started to visit Kayitare, the man whose phone chargers I had been delivering when I was arrested. Being a businessman from Rwanda, he was much better off than most people but he was modest and friendly. His wife was also Tutsi but from North Kivu and the whole family was extremely pleasant. I went to their place every morning. Being a mother and used to young boys, Mamma Kayitare immediately sensed that I was hungry but also knew that I would be uncomfortable if she asked me about it. Instead, she would bring food to her children and their cousins who lived at their place so that I could share with them. Sometimes her older son would be surprised to find himself being fed again and would tell her that they were not hungry. 'Just eat out of politeness!' she would smile. But none of my friends, not even this kindly woman, suspected that I had nowhere to sleep. I continued to spend the night in bars, the cement store or Ziruguru's annex.

CHAPTER 20

Things get better

A FEW WEEKS LATER, I learned that the Kayitare family was moving to Burundi or even possibly Rwanda as the war was thought to be finishing. So I went to see them, timing my visit to coincide with their evening meal hoping I would be invited to join them. Of course I was invited to share the food but my visit had even more good luck: he asked me if, with some help from a friend called Butoto, the twin brother of Bukuru, I could look after his house for him when he moved. He needed someone to stay in it and check out possible tenants to rent it in his absence, showing them round when they visited. When he asked me, he had no idea that he was talking to a homeless person desperate for somewhere to live and I didn't want to tell him how perfectly his suggestion suited me. Instead I let him believe that I was doing him a favour by accepting. It seemed as if my life had taken a turn for the better and I was overjoyed.

I moved in soon afterwards and was transformed from a down-and-out living on the streets to someone living comfortably in a house that had been valued at about half a million dollars! I felt like a king. Not only had I suddenly found a beautiful place to live but it was full of modern devices that I had never experienced before. I had it all to myself though Butoto came to see me sometimes so that we could both try to find a tenant for Kayitare's house. Food was still a problem because, thinking I would be going regularly to Musirimu's family, no-one had bothered leaving any for me though they had left some money in Burundian francs as well as rice and dog food for the dogs that lived outside in a small house. On my first night in that house, I lay in my comfortable bed so excited and happy that I could hardly sleep. What a coincidence that this marvellous opportunity had come my way! Also, I turned over in my mind how strange it was that rich people's dogs live a thousand times better than poor people do. Kayitare's dogs had their own home and were fed regularly by someone who cared for them. They even had pocket money! Well, over the next few weeks and months I found myself sharing their money and their food. Dogs have low status in African eyes so I found it degrading to be doing this but I realised that I should just be grateful that I had enough food to live on and I was eating it in this superb modern house with all its luxury items. Yes, I was eating dog food but I was eating it in style, from a nice plate at a large table listening to music on a stereo system!

The house was a long way from my school, almost as far as Musirimu's place. I had another great stroke of luck, though, by meeting someone who was able to give me a lift most days. One very hot morning, I was walking along as usual by the main and only road into town when a Samurai car with tinted windows pulled up beside me. As the electric window wound down, I saw a friendly face offering me a lift. It was a Rwandan I had met a year before when I was taking part with the rest of my class in the INERA project in the Bukavu area and he was on business there. He had been surprised and impressed to find a fellow Tutsi studying at a relatively high level of education and, being an older person, had done his best to encourage me. As Kinyarwanda and Kinyamalenge are mutually intelligible, we were able to chat in our first language, which made us feel close too. His name was Ndamage Mutwa and he was the manager of an Asian company called Kotecha at offices about a kilometre before my school. He had experienced difficulties in Uvira with his ethnicity but, being a successful businessman and naturally friendly person, had always been able to make friends or bribe his way out of tricky corners. The tinted windows of his car were to avoid recognition as an "outsider" and he would know that I had the same problems trying to hide my Tutsi appearance. As we got to know each other better, he became a sort of father figure to me and he came to respect me for my experiences as a "town boy" who could survive on the streets. Once he gave me the job of distributing his company diaries and then he gave me some extra ones free to do whatever I wanted with. I gave them to influential people, like shopkeepers and customs officers, so that I could secure some relationships that might be useful to me in the future. My friends at school noticed the change in me and I felt I was more respected – I was even called "Kotecha" by some. Ndamage also encouraged me by taking an interest in my schoolwork but he was always discreet, never letting it be seen publicly how close we were.

I spent a lot of time studying and catching up with school work that I had neglected when I was facing more severe problems. Living in comfort made it easier for me to prepare for the *Examen d'Etat*, the Baccalaureate final examination at the end of secondary school, which would, I hoped, open the possibility of a good career one day. It was when I filled out the forms for this exam that I changed my name to Alexis Ntung; the name I was given at birth was clearly Banyamulenge and I didn't want the examiners to discriminate against me because of it. As I had no official birth certificate, nothing else was required of me to become this person. "Ntung" looked rather like a shortened version of my original name and I had been known in school as Alex since 1990, when president Mobutu had allowed us to take western names again. Of course, to my family and friends from my home, I remained (and still remain) Mvuka.

I wasn't in a hurry to find a tenant for the house and, when people came to look at it, I set the rent high hoping they could not afford it. My work as "Jimmy" had given me the confidence to negotiate in this way because I had met several high-ranking RPF officers through it. The difference was, of course, that with these visitors from the frontline, everything had to be secret. Their presence in the town was highly confidential. Along with my team, I had to ensure that we were aware of likely security issues and identify homes where the meetings could be held. Each host family and everyone involved in the meeting were identified only through coded messages; special guests would have to be verbally registered by a secret name with nothing written down. Guests were impressive people, often carrying a pistol, and they would give presentations about various aspects of the RPF movement, their number one priority being to stress its core ideology which was the philosophy of unity. These meetings had given me self-confidence but, at the same time, they were stressful because of the dangers involved. In contrast, meeting rich and important people interested in renting Kayitare's house was relaxing and pleasant. Acting as a businessman in this way, I found people's attitude towards me change. Rich people invited me out for a drink so we could negotiate the price and I thoroughly enjoyed this new life where I could feel influential and important.

Finally Butoto told me that a very rich man had made an offer that we simply couldn't turn down. He had no idea that I would be literally on the streets as soon as we found a tenant and, even if he had known, he couldn't have done anything to help me because he lived with Catholic priests. So the prospective tenant came and paid six month's rent at $600 a month – an enormous sum. I was terrified of handling so much and asked him to pay it into Kayitare's account. We arranged for him to move in after one week and he gave me $25 for having organised the contract. This was the largest sum of money I had ever owned. The new tenant wanted to buy the dogs also but by this time I had grown very fond of them; it even felt to me that they were fellow Banyamulenge and I was reluctant to leave them, especially to someone from another tribe. So I worried not only about what I would do myself but what I would do about the dogs, knowing that Kayitare was unable to take them.

Then, just one day before this new tenant was due to move in, the bell rang. When I opened it I was surprised to see Ndamage. It turned out that he was interested in renting the house on behalf of his boss, Mr Kotecha, and I was very sorry to have to tell him that it had already been promised to someone else. He was disappointed to have missed it and then, to my astonishment, he invited me to move in with him when the new tenant took that house, even though I had never told him that I couldn't return to Musirimu. It was perfect timing for me when I was dreading being on the streets again so close to the final examinations at school. He even agreed to let me keep the dogs, Milu and Leopard.

Some days later, I went with the dogs to the lovely big house that Ndamage had just had built by Lake Tanganyika. It was in an area known to consist largely of houses built by people who had become rich by shady means, illegally or through corruption of one sort or another, but, in Ndamage's case, the money was his legally. He was a well-educated, intelligent man in a highly-paid job. Amongst my people divorce is practically unheard of but Ndamage was more "modern" and was separated from his wife; sadly, he had lost touch with his children because he didn't know where she had taken them. He missed them greatly and was lonely and so I suppose our friendship meant a lot to him and we became very close.

By this time I was over eighteen years old and had learnt many harsh lessons from all that had happened to me. In our society, status is earned both by passing certain stages in life and by age: younger people respect their elders and older people look after the young. So between Ndamage and me there was a relationship of mutual respect while, at the same time, he was practically a father figure to me. He had three people working for him: a Tutsi cook (it had to be a Tutsi for security reasons) and two others to act as guards and do the general work of the compound. They all treated me with the respect due to a member of the family or honoured guest. I had my own room and all my washing and cooking was done for me. As I was tall and slim like Ndamage, he gave me some of his clothes and he also gave me some pocket money.

I had never lived so comfortably and, though I realised that my life could change at any time, it gave me the confidence and relaxation I needed to face those final examinations. Because my schoolmates knew that I lived in this prestigious neighbourhood and saw the sophisticated way I now dressed, they treated me with a new respect. Girls started to notice me too and I was amused one day when some rather pretty school friends approached me to ask where I had bought my volleyball cap; it was the latest and most fashionable one at that time. From then on I called it "my magic cap" but I did not let myself get carried away by the girls' flattery. Between us I sensed a big barrier, a barrier that had been created by all that had happened to me before and by my secret knowledge that I had two identities. I made some effort to become more like other boys by joining a basketball team in the neighbourhood where I lived but I lacked the confidence to play well and still felt like an outsider. Really I became rather introspective and thoughtful for one so young: I was constantly thinking about the injustices of society, particularly the exclusion of the Tutsi, and dreamt of creating a fairer world. I even rehearsed in my mind a speech I would make when I became the secretary general of the United Nations!

I was determined to succeed in my education and now, with such a comfortable home and a father figure to encourage me, my studies went well. I approached my final exams with a lot of confidence, optimistic for my personal future if not for the political future of my country. I wanted to become an engineer and also a politician, in which role I hoped to improve the lives of my people.

CHAPTER 21

Catastrophe

RACIAL TENSION WAS AT BREAKING POINT. Myths about the origins of "Bantu" (not really a distinguishable ethnic group) and Tutsi grew even stronger. Some claimed that "Bantu", distinguishable by their different physical features such as flatter noses, were "autochthons", beings who were a natural part of the environment because they had sprung out of the land and were its original inhabitants. Tutsi by contrast were said to be Nilotic invaders from the North. Conspiracy theories grew and there were even rumours that a regional Tutsi empire was about to emerge. The Congolese authorities and leadership did not refute these ideas but actually encouraged them, failing to accept the diversity of Congolese people, many of whom have cross-borders identities.

Everything came to a head on April 6th 1994, a date that I can never forget because it irrevocably changed my life and the lives of countless other people. On that day a plane carrying very important people was shot down. The people killed on it were all Hutu: the Burundian President, Cyprien Ntaryamira, the Rwandan president, Juvenal Habyarimana and other government officials. They were returning from Tanzania after peace negotiations with the RPF (Tutsi) movement so it was ironic as well as tragic that what had started as a bid for peace should end this way. Although it was not definitely known who shot down the plane, the immediate general assumption was that it was the RPF. Later there were speculations that it could be the Presidential guards and Hutu extremists who did not support the peace talks and possible return of Tutsi refugees; it was even suggested that the French troops in control of the airport were responsible. This debate was to continue for many years and is still not resolved, but, back in 1994, most people believed without question that the RPF were to blame. We knew immediately that an event of this political significance would have tragic consequences not only for those individuals immediately involved but for the whole of the Great Lakes region. Reprisals were sure to take place not only in Rwanda and Burundi but also in Eastern Congo because all Tutsi would fall under suspicion, not only the RPF.

When the news first broke we avoided leaving the house, staying indoors glued to the radio for further news of what was happening in Rwanda. Ndamage had television too but it gave news only through a French channel that we did not trust to give impartial news, France being implicated in the fighting. Sometimes we used a Dutch Swahili station and other times the BBC World Service. Whichever we used, we had to be careful to do it late in the evening and on low volume so as not to come under suspicion. Some of the stations we picked up were of extremist Hutus who were encouraging their fellow tribesmen to kill Tutsis and we knew any such actions would not stop at the border. While feeling afraid for ourselves, we were even more afraid for the Tutsi of Rwanda. In my case, I was particularly worried about my cousin Samson, who was so admired in my village as the first of our clan to go to university and leave the area. For Ndamage the anxiety was much worse as his whole family lived in Rwanda. He pinned his hopes for their safety on intervention by United Nations troops, hoping they would intervene if massacres began. This is why he listened so intently to overseas news as well as more local reports.

Very early in the morning of the day after the incident with the plane, we learnt that the killing had begun. We had expected trouble but the sheer scale of what happened was beyond anything we had imagined. The television showed things we could hardly believe: corpses littered around in hundreds or floating down rivers like useless and unwanted logs. These human beings had not been killed for any other reason than that they were Tutsi, the same ethnicity as us; the revulsion we felt is impossible to describe but it was like being physically ill and we couldn't eat for days. We felt a mixture of horror, extreme grief, despair and also anger that nothing had been done to stop the massacres. The United Nations troops, under orders to be "peace-keepers" rather than intervene, had been helpless bystanders letting it all happen. We will never be able to understand this lack of help from the outside world.

I stayed home out of trouble's way that day and for some days after, supposedly studying for my final exams though it was impossible to concentrate on my work. Ndamage stayed at home for the first day too because he could not let his grief show in front of the people who worked for him. As manager of the largest corporate company in Uvira, he was expected to maintain his dignity. A long absence would be noticed though so he soon returned to his daily routine; at least work might take his mind off the horrors and he felt secure driving with those dark windows.

When he returned late in the afternoon one day, I noticed something unusual: he wasn't wearing his glasses. As he got out of the car, he avoided looking at me and I could see that he was crying – something men of my tribe would never do unless under extreme circumstances. Without going into any details, he simply told me that many of his family in Rwanda had been killed. I didn't know what to say and found it difficult to imagine what he was thinking. It would have been disrespectful for a younger person to ask questions so I remained silent. There was an unspoken understanding between us that these were our people who had been killed and we ourselves could be next in the firing line. I cannot describe the despair I felt at the injustice of it all or my frustration with the United Nations. My previous high hopes of one day working for them had transformed into bitterness and anger and there was an empty ache inside where once my idealism had been. Sometimes it seemed that all I had left to sustain me was my Christian faith and I continued to pray fervently.

Within days, the impact of the massacres reached Uvira when a large number of Hutu refugees reached the town, trying to escape the danger in Rwanda. We knew that among them could be extremists who would take revenge on any Tutsi they met. The RPF was fighting for Kigali and trying to find protection for Tutsi and moderate Hutu. The danger these moderate Hutu faced was graphically illustrated by the murder of the Rwandan Prime Minister, Madame Agathe Uwiringiyimana, and other political leaders who had tried to defend Tutsi. As well as receiving civilian refugees, Uvira became a sanctuary to Hutu soldiers who arrived in armoured vehicles with their weapons in retreat from the front. There were also some

French military personnel from what was known as the Turquoise operation, a security measure undertaken mainly to protect French economic interests in the area and the lives of French people and other expatriates.

The city rapidly became a zone of military action. In response, the Congolese government sent the presidential guard to make it secure. However, as soon as these "security forces" arrived, they began to pillage from the Rwandan Hutu refugees and hunt down any Tutsi. Life became even more dangerous and Ndamage occasionally would say something like, 'These people might kill us one day!' referring not only to the military men but to the Hutu extremists among the refugees. At the same time, he remained a basically friendly and trusting man who tried to get on with people of various tribal backgrounds. One day, he came across a Hutu refugee from his own home area in Rwanda where he himself hadn't been for years. The two men were instant friends, being from the same area, exchanging stories and building up trust to the point that Ndamage bought the car the man was selling. Shortly after, this Hutu man returned to Rwanda to collect some belongings he had left there but was immediately arrested and accused of having slaughtered a whole village, men, women and children. This incident unnerved us both. We simply could not tell which Hutus were innocent victims of the war and which were perpetrators of the genocide; with so many people having been slaughtered, it was evident that there were literally hundreds of murderers and it was impossible to tell who they were. We became suspicious of everyone who wasn't Tutsi.

Through all of this we were trying to get on with our normal lives. Going to work in his dark-windowed car gave Ndamage an outlet to offset the anxiety about his family. Because he did not know where his ex-wife had gone with the children, he still did not know if they were safe though he knew his parents and many other relatives were dead. To some extent, he relied on my street knowledge to decide what the security situation was like. He rarely met ordinary people himself because he just drove to work and then back to the compound at the end of the day. Sometimes he might have gone elsewhere or was late back but, out of respect, I could not ask where he went. I occasionally saw him on the balcony of a hotel by the lake and guessed then that he was avoiding security problems on that particular day. I was very worried about him because he was not a robust man physically and now had so much heartbreak to cope with. He did not talk about his problems with me but we could sense between us mutual concern, like a family bond. He knew my best hope for the future was in getting a good education so he encouraged me to persevere and take my final exams in June. I was supposed to go to school for group studies but sometimes the security situation made it impossible for me. Then I would study somewhere in or near the compound. Ever since I was a small boy in the village I had enjoyed learning outside – in the bush somewhere or in a tree with the soothing call of birds in the background.

One day I saw Ndamage's car enter the compound as if he were coming home from work. However, the dark windows were down and I immediately noticed that it was not my friend driving. As I approached to see what was happening, I found there were eight soldiers in camouflage uniform packed into this five-seater estate car with no sign of Ndamage. From the car they shouted out in Lingala that they were from the Departement de la Garde Presidentielle (DSP). This was the first time I had ever seen anyone from this organisation but I had heard it was a sort of secret service conducting complicated operations and secret assassinations. They were popularly known as "les escadrons de la mort" (death squads). I noticed that their uniform was much smarter than that of ordinary soldiers and they looked very well fed and equipped. Their eyes had a glazed and wild look that suggested they could be drugged and not likely to be very reasonable. I stood there alone, the houseboys having leaped over the compound wall to escape, with only Milu and Leopard, the dogs. These were barking furiously and one of the soldiers wanted to shoot them but another told him there would be no point. As the soldiers got out of the car I was shocked to notice blood on their hands but, before I had chance to consider what I should do or even how I felt, one of the soldiers thrust an old German bayonet at me; it went diagonally across my chest but I was extremely lucky – it only tore my jacket and shirt before falling on the ground. At that point, feeling in a state of shock, I became aware of Ndamage's voice shouting from the car. I had had no idea at all that he was in it because he had been forced down onto the floor between the back seats and the boot, his hands handcuffed behind him and several large army boots holding down his head and body. These soldiers had forced their way into his office, taken all the money they could find and beaten him up. The beating had continued right through his perilous journey home.

He shouted to me in Kinyarwanda, telling me to give them everything they asked for. I wasn't in a position to give them anything though because six of them began to ransack the house of their own accord while the two others thrust my head against a cement block wall. They asked me if I was the one who had shot down the presidential plane and told me that this night would be the last for all Tutsi. I had an idea to save myself and told them I had something for them. When they let go of me, I went and found some bottles of whisky. By this time, Ndamage had staggered out of the car and he told me to find his jacket so we could bribe them with cash. He also begged them to let me find his wedding ring dropped in the car; they just shouted he should care more about his life than a wedding ring. Despite the $600 I found in his jacket and the whisky, they would not let him go but drove off with him in the same way as they had arrived. I was left behind, very shaken but relieved to be alive.

I spent a restless night, terrified they might return and extremely worried about Ndamage who was by now a fragile person in no condition to withstand this kind of treatment. I was not alone because the houseboys returned as soon as the DSP car left. As soon as it was light I got up and went to tell a Tutsi woman called Perse who was married to someone in the president's family. I asked her to help me find out where Ndamage might be. In those days there were no phones so we drove around in her car, which was recognisable as belonging to someone important, to approach various military officials. When she got out to speak to them she told me to wait in the car. After a few stops she came back looking pleased because she was finally able to tell me which prison Ndamage was in. I was really relieved and asked her to take me back home to get some food and drink. As soon as I arrived home I asked the cook to prepare some food and water for Ndamage and then I walked the four miles or so to the prison to see what I could do to help my friend. When I arrived I was not allowed to see him but instead was interrogated myself, accused of not having stood still when they were raising the flag and singing the national anthem early that morning. I was not even there at that time! However, they let me go a few hours later and I tried all I could think of to get freedom for my friend. Firstly I asked Perse what we should do and then I reported to the Kotecha authorities that Ndamage was under arbitrary arrest. Hours later, they lobbied on his behalf and he was eventually released – shaken and looking ill but generally unharmed – after two days. He was not given his car back though – that was confiscated.

When he came home, Ndamage decided that the Congo had become so dangerous for Tutsi that we should plan to leave soon before things got even worse. In Rwanda the situation was extreme with massacres continuing but the RPF seemed to be winning so there was at least hope for us there. He told me that, despite what was going on, I should sit my exams. 'One day there may be peace and, you never know, you might still be alive!' he said.

Another person who encouraged me to carry on with my studies was Daudi, also much known as Papa Mister, one of my extended family who had recently appeared in the Uvira region. Because he didn't look Banyamulenge, he was one of a very small number of Banyamulenge who had succeeded in joining the army and, as a soldier, he moved around quite a lot; his wife and children were based in Fizi mostly. By now he was middle aged and had lived through a great deal of trouble, which had begun for him when his father was killed by Mulelist rebels (*see timeline*) in 1966. His life had been hard so he spoke to me in a tough way, telling me I should stop complaining and get on with my education. Everything could change once I was educated, he insisted. 'Young ones like you are our future,' he said. 'Your survival is not just for yourself but for all of us because, when you have achieved a place in society, you can help us.' With this sort of encouragement, I did manage to rise above all the intimidation and anxiety and go to school to take my final exams

173

in June. I was fairly confident I had passed them all, though it had been difficult for me to study with so much on my mind.

Once I had completed my exams, aware that my family would be worrying about me, Ndamage gave me money to cover the cost of a trip home. I arranged to travel with a relative, Naum and we got a lift with a man called Muller who was driving that way and agreed to take us too if we contributed something towards the petrol. He was an NGO worker and, because he was someone who did useful and welcome work across various different communities, he was well respected and unlikely to be stopped or attacked in any way as he passed through the various villages. As a result, this was the most comfortable journey I had ever had to the village. For once I travelled in an uncrowded vehicle that did not smell of oil, a modern four-by-four Pajero. Muller took us by an old, unmaintained colonial road that was often impassable but was relatively easy to drive that day because it was dry. He drove us right into the mountains to a place we called Zero before continuing his journey to Mumibunda. The ground being so dry, we made good time as we walked the rest of the way, Naum to his village and I to mine.

Of course it was wonderful to see my family and friends again but my time with them cannot really be described as happy with so many terrible things happening. Also, I knew I could not stay for long because I sensed that the presence of someone like me, a young man who could have had contact with the RPF, made village people even more vulnerable; with this in mind I had already arranged to leave after only two days. In some ways, the village seemed much as it had always been because the villagers were doing their best to act as if nothing particularly unusual had happened and they were going about their normal business. Some things were noticeable though. For one thing there were more children around because Government funding for the schools had stopped two years previously and the school was not fully staffed. Parents who could afford it paid fees to fund a teacher but school attendance had become patchy, according to who could pay and how often. It grieved me to see bright children unable to get an education, especially as it included my little sister, Benite. She had been excelling at school, which was considered unusual for a girl in those days, and I had always encouraged her by writing her letters. Another noticeable difference was that there had been a religious revival and an increase in prayer as people turned to their faith in God for help. I was very moved when I heard a woman praying out loud. 'Dear God', she pleaded, 'why are we seen as strangers in our own land? Thou knowest the truth, that this is our homeland. Thou knowest that we have nothing and that people like us are being slaughtered in Rwanda. Dear God, help us, I pray!'

Everyone knew what grave danger the Banyamulenge were in. 'Ntabgoko buberaho gushira' my father told me. This is an optimistic expression that my people use at times of great danger and it means that no one group of people is destined to be completely exterminated. He told me that we should scatter, all going to different places, so that at least some of us would survive to carry on our family and tribal line. This policy would not include him and my mother, of course, because they were bound by *itongo*, the concept that an old person must stay in the place that he had made his own, where he had lived his life, raised his children and so on. The young respect the old and the old themselves take great pride in their long lives and will not run off and leave what is theirs; to do so would be considered *guphira mugahinga*, which means dying deserted and unwanted in a place that is not their own. But for children there is a different proverb: 'The bird that will not fly does not find the best fruit,' they say. My parents wanted as many of their children as possible to move away to find a better life and increase the chances of some of us surviving; there was no question at all of them challenging my decision to go to Rwanda with Ndamage. My brother Samuel had recently married and wanted to move somewhere else though he did not know quite how he could. All my other older siblings were already in different places. My two older sisters had married men from other Banyamulenge villages as is our custom. My oldest brother, Noah, was still in Burundi and we had no news of him since he had escaped the massacre in 1993.

Oreni, my closest brother and my closest friend, had gone to join the RPF as soon as recruitment first started. This was a source of great anxiety for us because there had been rumours that he had been killed in battle. Though he did not say it, I sensed that my father blamed himself that Oreni had run off in this reckless way; I think he felt that my strong-headed but very gifted brother might have made different decisions if his family had encouraged him more at school because Noah and I had used education to get away. Recently however, we were given hope because the friend who had been with him when he originally joined the rebels had succeeded against all the odds in running away from the RPF and was now safely back in the village. Oreni, he said, had been in another battalion but he thought my brother was still alive. Our relief in hearing this was tempered by the stories he told of the harsh regime the RPF practised. He said that discipline was so strict that it was not uncommon for them to execute members of their own fighting groups, either by starvation or by a hammer blow to the head. Such stories not only made us worry for Oreni but shocked us too because we couldn't understand how our fellow Tutsi could treat their own people in this way. In my case, I suffered nagging doubts deep within myself about the support I was giving to the RPF. Stories of how fighters behaved were terrifying for my parents who were worried that my younger brother, Jean Claude, might be forcibly conscripted by one side or the other in these extreme times. My other younger brother, Bonfils, was away looking after the cattle and they hoped that this would keep him out of such danger.

After two days in the village it was time for me to leave. Really, according to custom, I should have gone to visit my sister Angeline because she had just lost her son. He had been a fine, healthy boy but had died suddenly of some unknown disease because there was no clinic or hospital for her to take him to; his death had shocked us all. I didn't go to visit her though because the only way to get to her would have been by walking. Previously, the lovely Minembwe landscape was somewhere I loved to roam but now I knew that danger lurked everywhere and I simply couldn't risk going to see her; though I knew it disappointed my mother, I said nothing and just prepared to leave.

All of my close family who were home at the time walked with me as far as the Minembwe river, not wanting to leave me. Here we said goodbye as we had done so many times before but this time was different. We avoided looking into each other's eyes and there was a strong sense that none of us wanted this goodbye. Parting at the river made the occasion even more moving because in our tradition it symbolises a very definite separation. To some extent, I was able to hide my tears as I bent to take off my shoes and roll up my trousers. Then I waded through the metres of marshy ground to the *ikiraro* (string bridge made of bush materials) and walked over "our" river for what I thought would probably be the last time ever. When I reached the other side, I turned and we waved again. They stood and watched me until I was out of sight and to this day I can still picture them there, my little sister Benite, adored as the baby of the family, drying her tears on my mother's wrap. I kept turning round to look at them until they were hidden by the hill. Then I climbed the Lundu hill, right next to the village where I was born. From there I said goodbye to this beautiful region with its gentle hills, convinced in my aching heart that I would never see it again, and set off towards Zero, no longer trying to fight back my tears.

CHAPTER 22

Escaping from Uvira

UNFORTUNATELY FOR NAUM AND ME, Muller was a rather westernised man who had even travelled to Europe several times. This meant that, when he reached Zero before us, he felt he had deadlines to meet and was not willing to wait. Worse still, he didn't know any of the traditional ways of leaving a message, like putting a stone on top of a long leaf or leaving marks in the earth. He didn't even think of shouting over those vast valleys, in the way of village people, so that anyone within hearing distance might be able to pass on a message to us. We had no way of knowing he had gone, and spent the rest of the day searching for him. We walked in the direction where we thought he should be coming from and eventually came to a hamlet of two huts where we learnt that a car had gone past that morning at around *gukama inka* (calf feeding time, morning) which meant, frustratingly, that we must have missed him by only minutes. No other vehicles would be travelling that route so we had no choice but to walk back to Zero and from there take the long way through the forests and down the mountain to Nundu from where we could get a truck to Uvira. It would be the usual two day journey.

Back in Uvira, security was worse than ever and there seemed to be constant bad news. One particularly strong blow for our community was when we heard that Daudi (Papa Mister), my soldier relative, had been killed in Burundi. The community had not yet fully recovered from the shock of hearing about all the Banyamulenge teachers slaughtered there in the 1993 massacres. Daudi had only gone to Burundi to get medical treatment. He had been walking in a predominantly Tutsi area called Ngagara when he was stopped by the *Sans Echecs* (meaning Stop at Nothing) – a militia group formed by young Tutsis in response to the massacres of 1993. He didn't have an obviously Tutsi appearance and, when he spoke, they took his Kinyamalenge language to be a spy's attempt to speak Kirundi. They stabbed him through the heart. When the Burundian police found the body, they realised from his ID and other papers that he was from the Congo and was in the country for medical treatment. His body was then taken to the Congolese Embassy where it was kept until some of our young men went to bring it back; I waited on the Congolese side of the border to see if I could help.

Nowhere was safe. We were wary of the thousands of Hutu refugees from Rwanda scattered around the city and especially around schools because we didn't know if any of them would be hostile towards us. Arbitrary arrests and violence were common also, as officials were still trying to crack down on support for the RPF. Now the RPF had won Kigali and taken control of Rwanda, the feeling that Tutsi had no place in the Congo became more widespread. Local military groups threatened violence and said Banyamulenge should leave the country but, at the same time, there was no official order to leave and no legal way of going. Leaving the country was not easy because the three frontier crossings we would normally use were all heavily guarded at that time both by the regular military and by the presidential guard. Nevertheless, it was generally accepted that it would be better to go of our own free will than to risk our lives by waiting till we were forcibly removed. With all the confusion and fear, many Banyamulenge instinctively kept close to their own people to feel safe, arranging to meet secretly to discuss the issues and how they should act. Others, knowing it could be dangerous to be seen in groups, kept themselves to themselves and slipped out of the country quietly and alone. If someone hadn't been seen for a couple of days, it was understood that he had left.

Obviously, it was easier for single men than for families to slip out in this way and Ndamage told me I should go as soon as possible. He gave me $80 for transport through Burundi to Rwanda where I should look for his one surviving sister in the south. He would join me later. Being in charge of a large corporate company, it would have been irresponsible of him simply to disappear. He must have felt extremely insecure and isolated at this time though. His only contact with his Asian employer 150 kilometres away was by radio and he had no close friends at work because he had to maintain a managerial distance. Besides, the other workers were all from local tribes and already perceived him as a "foreigner"; he had to make sure that none of them knew that he was planning to escape. All these problems were on top of having lost most of his family in the genocide and still not knowing what had happened to his wife and children. Still he maintained his dignity though he was drinking quite a lot by now. I was worried about him but had to hope and trust that he would be able to use some of his many influential connections when the time was right for him to leave.

After making a few arrangements, I was ready to go. On the morning of my departure I disguised myself as best I could. My face is not particularly Tutsi in appearance and I tried to pad out my slim body by wearing a lot of clothes. At least this saved me from needing to pack much into my bag! After saying goodbye to Ndamage, I took a motogari and headed towards Kanvinvira where I crossed the border into Burundi. I knew the tactics to use: bending my knees so as not to look tall, I mixed into the crowds with goods to sell and passed some money to a friendly guard who gave me something to carry to a guard on the other side. Once I was over the border, I paused for a while to look back and collect my thoughts. I told myself that I should try to remember that view, perhaps my last, of the beautiful chain of mountains that I was so used to climbing to reach the high plateaus my people call home. I had left Minembwe, my village; to find a better life elsewhere in terms of safety and access to education and now I was forced to leave my country to find that safety! I felt tears in my eyes and uttered a little prayer: 'God, why have you abandoned us?'

As well as feeling sad and isolated from my friends and family, I was perplexed: I had never been to Rwanda and my connection to Rwandan Tutsi was only as a result of victimisation. Myths had grown around people's perceptions of ethnicity. Because Tutsi people live in Rwanda, Burundi and Congo, other Congolese tribes started defining themselves as somehow "other" and therefore close to Burundian and Rwandan Hutu; the true tribal pattern is much more complicated than that but this simplistic approach had gained ground. Conflict which had been regional became associated instead with ethnicity. I thought to myself that the world had become too small: clearly the

Congo/Zaire didn't want us but where else could we go? I still had traumatic memories of my own time in Burundi and this had been only the beginning of brutal killings there. As for Rwanda, it did not really appeal to me because it was only days since it had experienced the greatest genocide since the Second World War with somewhere between eight hundred thousand and a million deaths; the blood of its innocent victims was still flowing and the fighting had not stopped. People said that, despite the recent genocide, Rwanda was the safest place for Tutsi because the RPF had now taken control. It still didn't really appeal to me though and I started to wonder if I should go to Tanzania instead. I had said goodbye to my family in the village without telling them exactly where I planned to go and, as they knew no-one in either Tanzania or Rwanda and it was still unknown whether my cousin Samson Muzuri had survived the genocide, it would make no difference to them which I went to.

It didn't take me long to get to Bujumbura as it is only about twenty kilometres from Uvira but I didn't know where to spend the night when I arrived there. I went to find one of Kayitare's friends, a man called Butoyi who was the director of the Burundi Battery Industry (BBI); this was a bit presumptuous on my part since he didn't know me at all and our only connection was that we both knew Kayitare. When I arrived at his house, his wife called him from the little bistro where he had been relaxing and he was furious. He shouted at me that I had no right to go to his house without an invitation and that it was Kayitare who was his friend not me. I tried to take it philosophically, saying to myself that here was a man who had picked up the ways of the city and did not behave like traditional people in the villages. But then he took me to the bistro in his Mercedes Benz and apologised for having been so angry. He bought me a beer which I drank to be polite though I didn't normally drink alcohol. As we drank together he became very nice indeed. He found me a place to stay, sharing a bed with his neighbour, a bachelor. It was this man who dissuaded me from going into Tanzania, saying it was dangerous and I would be unlikely to survive.

Early the next day I set off to the bus station to take a bus to Rwanda. There, to my surprise, I bumped into someone I knew and he told me that Noah was in Bujumbura. Of course I immediately decided to visit my brother before leaving and, luckily for me, the man was able to take me to a district called Bwiza to see him. I was overjoyed at the thought of seeing someone from my close family at such an emotional time: I had left, perhaps for ever, my home country and all it meant for me – my family, my friends, my education and most of my possessions. Now at least before it was too late I would have a brother to talk to, a brother who was so much older than me that he was almost a father figure. When I saw him I was overjoyed and began to speak to him in the same happy way we had conversed the last time we were together, a year before. But his reaction was strangely quiet and unresponsive. He was different and hardly spoke at all. I chattered on to him, telling him I was very lucky to have got out of the Congo because the others were in danger of violent deportation but he hardly said anything at all. Never having seen him, or anyone else for that matter, in this state, I was confused. At that time I had no knowledge whatsoever of mental illness and it is not something recognised by my traditional society. In our language we do not have words for concepts such as "trauma", "psychological shock" "depression" or even "stress". These would be alien ideas to us. I was simply puzzled and hurt. I left him and went back to the bus station to continue my journey to Rwanda

My mind was not clear. With all the anxiety and sadness of leaving my country and family and then the shock of seeing Noah in that state, my sleep patterns were completely disturbed. With the rocking motion of the bus in the African heat, I nodded off to sleep and did not get off where I had planned. Ndamage's sister, who had survived the genocide, lived in Butare in the south and this is where I had intended to stop but, unfortunately, I slept so deeply that I went all the way to Kigali, a nine hour journey from Bujumbura.

CHAPTER 23

Arriving in Rwanda after genocide

IT WAS THE MIDDLE OF THE NIGHT when we arrived in Kigali (the capital of Rwanda) and the first thing that struck me about this war-devastated city was the continual yapping and barking of dogs. There were more strays than usual because so many had lost their owners; unfed, they wandered around fighting with each other and sniffing hungrily whenever they smelt dead bodies. Later, many of these animals had to be shot, particularly as they had developed a taste for human flesh but, for now, they were almost useful because it was the noise of dogs that often led to the discovery of corpses. Bodies that had been left in obvious places had mostly been taken away for burial and places such as churches, where many still lay, were guarded. But the dogs sniffed out the hidden horrors, including those bodies in graves that victims had been forced to dig themselves before being murdered.

War had destroyed the infrastructure of the city and there simply weren't the resources to deal with this huge catastrophe. There was still some danger too because there were pockets of fighting continuing throughout this war-torn country. Despite everything, though, there was something reassuring about Kigali because the military officers of the new regime were circulating and offering to help everyone. I had grown up with soldiers a fairly constant presence but until now they had been men I feared, aggressive men who spoke in harsh voices and made unreasonable demands. Now they were men I looked up to with great respect, the victorious soldiers of the RPF. They were perceived as saviours by the vast majority of the population and songs were sung in their praise. I knew they had been trained to be fair because I remembered my own training when I first became "Jimmy". It was constantly drilled into us all that Hutu were not the enemy: enemies were only the bad people amongst the Hutu, people who had been brainwashed to hate Tutsi. So these soldiers were young, idealistic men, still working for the good of their people without pay.

The driver called out to us, 'Anyone who hasn't got anywhere to sleep, stay on the bus!' That was a relief because I was wondering where I could go and didn't want to be at the mercy of the savage-sounding dogs. Eventually the driver took the remaining passengers to an RPF barracks where a military officer, who treated us with great respect, provided us with food and somewhere to sleep. Next day the driver offered to act as a taxi and take us to wherever we wanted to go in the city. The only person I could think of that I knew in Kigali was Kayitare, whose house I had looked after in Uvira. I didn't know where he lived but I knew that he was the director of Volta Super, a battery factory. Electricity and water were still cut off in the aftermath of the war and factories were not yet operational; even if things had been normal, it was a Sunday so there was no chance the factory would be open. Still, I insisted on going there anyway, not knowing what else I could do. The guard at the gate told me there was no-one on site and the telephones weren't working so the best thing I could do was to wait there; with a bit of luck someone might pass by and be able to tell me where Kayitare lived. It is difficult to describe how I felt. For a boy of my age, just wondering about the results of my final exams would perhaps be enough. But that, once so important to me, now seemed minor. Now it was a question of survival, not just for myself but also for my family, my clan and all of my people. I was confused and had not slept well so could not think clearly anyway. Overall, I could sense a sort of numbness creeping over me, as if my reactions were so confused that I could respond only by feeling nothing at all.

With this state of mind I waited the whole morning by the road in this industrial district and eventually, in the early afternoon, a small car driven by the factory owner's son, Kimoshori, came along. I told him my problem and he drove me to Kayitare's place. Kayitare and his family were just as I remembered them: very pleased to see me, warm and welcoming, down to earth and never giving themselves airs. What was different was that there were so many people, especially children. The children were orphans of the genocide because only months before two of Kayitare's sisters, a brother and the brother's wife had been killed. Some of them had lost all their family, including brothers and sisters. In the following weeks in Rwanda I was to find this was not an unusual situation because practically every family had been touched by the genocide in some way. Many families had been wiped out completely and it seemed every family had lost at least someone. As well as the children in Kayitare's house, there were also young wounded soldiers who had served in the RPF and fought for the liberation of Rwanda. These were either officially demobilised or deserters and some of them had serious wounds. There were also two young women who had been raped during the violence and three younger girls.

Consequently, though this house was large and modern, it was absolutely full of people. Because of the difficult times with many people homeless, Kayitare and his wife had welcomed all of these people in addition to a cousin who lived with them and their own family of five children – Guy, Aline, Adeline, Dennis and little Soubirou. Mamma Kayitare was a remarkable woman. She had brought her children up so well that the whole family were extremely good to all of us. She treated all of her "guests" as if we were her own children and she helped her children to understand which of us were particularly vulnerable and in need of special consideration. I was impressed to find the whole family so giving, to the extent that the children didn't object to sharing their beds. I shared the only double bed with the eldest son, Guy, and a child soldier, Floribert; sometimes we would have to make space for a visitor too. The Kayitares shared their bedroom with some of the younger girls while there was a boys' room for their son and some of the orphans. The two small bedrooms were allocated to Mamma Kayitare's niece and to someone who worked for them. Kayitare treated us like family and took responsibility for all of us. Having such a high-profile job, he was wealthy and he also had the support of relatives over the border so he could afford our upkeep financially but it is astonishing to find people so willing to set aside their own comfort. Mamma Kayitare remains vivid in my memory as an incredibly welcoming person who knew how to give while pretending not to give at all. 'Alex, please go into town and get me some *Canta* (a hair product in a very small, easy to carry carton). I'll give you enough to get your lunch and a drink too while you are there,' she might say. 'If you have any left, you can either keep it or just get some charcoal for me.' This was her way of giving me the opportunity I wanted to stroll around town chatting to friends with some pocket money to spend. She knew I would prefer to use the money on something for myself rather than on dirty charcoal which she did not really need, just as she knew also that I could never have asked her for money to go out with friends. 'This is transport money for all of the boys,' she might say, putting me in charge so that Guy and Floribert would have to ask me when they needed money; by making me an older brother in this way, she helped to build up my self-respect. Living with them, I started to feel normal and human again. The contrast between the cruelty of war and the generosity of families like this is difficult to comprehend.

This time in their home was a remarkable experience for other reasons too. I listened to many diverse stories from people who had suffered horrific problems and it began to seem to me that my own suffering was quite minor. My experiences of violence in the Congo paled into insignificance by comparison. I had begun to accept violence as something normal and to me it was now only the severity of that violence that was remarkable. As I listened to the stories of the other people in Kayitare's care and became aware of the chaos in that large city, I felt almost privileged that I had suffered so relatively little. One thing I learnt about for the first time was how rape was used as weapon of war. Having witnessed an individual rape as a small boy, I already knew what a horrific experience it was for the victim and I had always known the huge stigma it involved, affecting not only the victim herself but also the whole family. Now I learnt that rape had been used during the genocide as *kubohoza,* an ironical expression suggestion that the rape victim had been spared death so that she could suffer a worse fate, suffering pain and then bearing a child she did not want and that no-one else would want either. Of course, the girls did not talk directly to me or the other boys about their suffering but I saw them crying at times and in serious conversation with Mamma Kayitare. As is our custom, they had become sisters to me and the other boys so we felt anger for what they had suffered. Luckily, neither of them had become pregnant as a result of their ordeal. We had plenty of happy times together too; I remember how the other young people used to like to listen to my Kinyamulenge dialect and tease me about it.

Despite everything that had happened, there was a feeling of calm in the house and a great sense of solidarity as we all helped each other. Because the water supply in the city was cut off, one of our shared tasks was to fetch water from the United Nations (UN) camp in the Kicukiro area of Kigali. We all hated the UN troops, MINUAR (meaning UN Mission to Rwanda). In fact all the ordinary people of Rwanda hated them because they had been there during the genocide and had done nothing to stop it. They had the means to prevent the slaughter of innocents but did not. I was so angry that I would sometimes approach a UN soldier to ask him why he hadn't tried to save people but I never got a reply. They enjoyed a good life, driving around everywhere in their luxury vehicles, eating in Kigali's best restaurants and looking around the town for pretty girls who were willing to sell themselves. These girls were nicknamed MINUAR, a very negative stereotype, meaning that their bodies were cheap and affordable by the UN soldiers. It was difficult to believe that these were troops sent by the international community. Overall, people felt the world had done nothing to defend Rwandans. It was a bitter disappointment to me as I recalled my grandiose boyish dreams of becoming Secretary General of the UN so that I could bring hope to humanity, coming to the aid of the oppressed. Being young and naïve, I continued to turn over in my mind what I could do if I had a position of influence in this organisation. I had no understanding at all of how the UN operated through the influence of the international community and was disillusioned with their great promises of "never again" which seemed empty against repeated occurrences of genocide.

Kigali was in ruins. Almost all the buildings were damaged and some were completely destroyed; burnt out vehicles were still in the streets. It was estimated that for every ten square meters there would have been at least one atrocity; this meant that, as I walked around buildings, office blocks, bars and restaurants, I was aware that they had probably been places of horror just a few months previously. As someone who had arrived from outside, it was difficult to connect and fully believe but at the same time, I knew it was very real for the people who had lived there throughout. Their attitude was sometimes puzzling. Though some seemed traumatised, the majority seemed surprisingly normal as they searched for bodies and generally sorted out the belongings and inheritance of their dead relatives; I thought perhaps they were just numbed by the sheer scale of the horror.

In places there were still corpses around, particularly inside the churches because this is where people had fled to during the massacres. They had believed they would be safe there: their attackers would respect the holy places and God would protect them. Sadly, this had not been the case, and the insides of churches were horrific morgues packed with the bodies of men, women and children. *Imana Y'Urwanda* had been the Supreme Being for Rwandans even before the missionaries had brought Christianity with its one God. Some had now lost their faith though the majority relied even more on their faith to help them cope with the tragedy.

I couldn't avoid the awful scenes of carnage because, like many other people, I was involved in trying to identify corpses. In my case, I was helping Kayitare find members of his family. One very uncomfortable element of searching for the dead was that we needed to ask around to find out where they were likely to have been killed. As we asked people, we were aware that they might have been involved in some way with the killings or, at least, have done nothing to try to stop the slaughter or offer refuge. When we had some idea where we planned to look, we would go around the bodies, searching for familiar clothing because the bodies were partly decomposed. Then we searched pockets for the identity cards. My stomach churned as I did this and the memory will stay with me forever. We did have some success. We found the body of his brother, the father of the two orphans the Kayitares had taken in. It meant a lot to people to find a body because it is important in our culture to give a proper burial. Much better by far, there were some survivors too – his mother and the orphaned children of one of his sisters.

My overall impression was that there was a strange contrast of tragedy and triumph in the country. Amongst the people who had lived there through the atrocities, there was still shock and confusion, but alongside that was a sense of *Intsinzi*, victory. Rwandan Tutsi had been spread throughout the world, mostly in neighbouring countries, for the previous thirty-five years, unable to return. Now they were back in the country, part of the new power and, despite the extreme tragedy that had been witnessed, celebrating victory. Their numbers were growing every day as people who had fled the Hutu regime returned. The streets rang with joyful singing, the most popular song being : '*Intsinzi abana b'Urwanda, Intsinzi mubicye byose, Intsinzi nje ndayireba*' which means 'It's victory, dear children of Rwanda. It's victory everywhere, I can see victory everywhere!'

As well as returning exiles, there were thousands of Tutsi refugees who, like me, were escaping growing violence in their country of birth; they too felt liberated and free. With this emphasis on victory, there seemed to be a lack of opportunity for the people who had escaped genocide to lament the loss of their loved ones or to contemplate the murderous slaughter they had witnessed. Although they had been traumatised only weeks before, most of them acted as if nothing in particular had happened. Then there was the Hutu population who lived under the shadow of suspicion because any of them might be accused of taking part in the genocide. Indeed, with so many people having been slaughtered, it was highly likely that some were guilty. These kept quiet, afraid of being denounced by a survivor, and the innocent Hutu people were very quiet too, subdued and ashamed by what had happened in their name. There were fewer Hutu than there had been before the war because many had fled in fear of reprisals from the RPF. Thousands of Hutu refugees were crossing the borders, particularly into Goma in Congo.

With such a buoyant sense of hope emanating from the new government and the military, I felt renewed optimism growing within me. One piece of excellent news that made me happy was that my cousin Samson had survived the atrocities in Butare, the second city of Rwanda. I didn't know Samson well but he meant a lot to me as something of role model. He had left our village to go to university in

Lubumbashi when I was very small. Since then he had become a sort of legend amongst our people. Occasionally he had reappeared in the village, looking strangely smart in his Western clothes and we all knew his achievement was amazing. Not only had he gained a degree in history but he wrote a thesis that has since become standard reading for scholars wanting to know the background to the conflict in our area (*see references*). He was offered overseas scholarships when he left university in 1983 but he was refused a passport by the Congo authorities so could not access them. As a Tutsi, he was unable to find a teaching post in the Congo and went instead to Rwanda which, at that time, was a difficult place for Banyamulenge people to get into. He never married and he settled into teaching in Butare, becoming politically active too. Having seen television footage of the bodies in that area after the genocide, I had never really believed he could have survived. Now I learnt that, at the height of the atrocities when almost all the Tutsi population there were slaughtered, he had been smuggled into Burundi by priests. He had arrived in Burundi with nothing but the clothes he was wearing at the time but was then able to send a message to our village to ask for a cow to be sold to finance him until he could start a new life. Now he was back in Rwanda where, with his skills and experience both politically and in teaching, he would be sure to find a new life for himself.

Socially my life became quite interesting. Kayitare introduced me to important people in the town and I even had the honour of being invited to a wedding, the marriage of one of the high-ranking army officers that Kayitare knew, Major Birasa. This was a new and impressive experience for me because I had never been to a modern, official wedding. I felt quite comfortable amongst Rwandans now. It was good that I had learnt Kinyarwanda from Ndamage before I left Uvira; now I had improved my fluency and accent so that I was not very noticeably foreign and, in this city that was so swollen with new arrivals, I felt at home. In fact, having helped the RPF and knowing that I had lost friends and family in the fight for freedom, I felt that I had a complete right to be there. Rwanda had become a homeland for Tutsi who had been persecuted in other countries for their historic origins. If I was ever teased for my Congolese background, I would simply say 'I don't need to deny my Congolese background to affirm my Rwandan identity and I don't need to deny my Rwandan identity to prove that I am Congolese.'

I was worried about Kayitare but, like the other young people in the house, knew it was not my place to try to give advice to a man of such high standing and integrity. He said nothing about what he had suffered but it was obvious that he was deeply affected by the general tragedy and the killing of his brothers and sisters. He drank a lot, particularly *Uganda Waragi*, the Ugandan whisky. His silence and the way he seemed to retreat into himself reminded me of how Ndamage had reacted when he learnt of the massacre of his family. It also made me think of my brother Noah; he had not told about his experiences after I left him in Burundi but he had surely lost good friends there. Gradually I was becoming aware of how people are affected by tragedy and horror. I was starting to understand that some of the people I saw acting in a strangely calm way after the genocide were actually ill. However, it would not be until years later that I could analyse it in more depth and attempt to describe it in psychological terms.

CHAPTER 24

Reunions and losses

THE ORIGINS OF THE TUTSI/HUTU CONFLICT are very complicated. It has long been assumed that the Tutsi are descendants of pastoralist people who moved into the area centuries ago but other evidence suggests there was never really an ethnic divide between the two groups. Both speak Kinyarwanda, a language that is part of the Bantu language group, but still the Tutsi are often not considered as belonging to the Bantu "people". In any case, there has been a great deal of intermarriage and the physical distinction is not always clear. Traditionally though, there were hierarchical systems in this area with kings in overall control. People wielding power owned cattle and tended to look different – tall and slim with narrow faces and sometimes fairer skin than other ethnic groups. These physical attributes were generally perceived as being more "beautiful" and taken to represent a different tribal group known as Tutsi. A sort of caste system developed but it was not rigid. Many people did not closely resemble the stereotype and Hutu could become Tutsi merely by owning enough cattle. Unfortunately, the Tutsi/Hutu distinction was reinforced by the colonial powers. The original German colonisers of the area that is now Rwanda and Burundi, assumed that Hutu were Bantu whereas Tutsi were members of a "superior" race, probably arrived from further north. This misconception continued when the Belgians took over so Tutsi kings continued to rule with colonial support. Resentment amongst the Hutu increased until there was a violent revolution in 1959 and a Hutu regime took control in Rwanda. The identity card system, introduced by the Belgians and continued by this new regime, then took on a more sinister significance. Not only were those who resembled to stereotype marked out but people who did not look obviously of one "tribe" or the other were no longer safe. The card specified whether each individual Rwandan was Hutu, Tutsi or Twa (Pygmy), children of mixed parentage being given the same classification as their father. As a result, even people who did not look stereotypically Tutsi could be singled out and discriminated against.

It was against this historical background that the terrible events of 1994 took place and now, in its aftermath, there was turmoil in Kigali. Hundreds of Tutsi were returning after having lived for many years in exile. At the same time hundreds of thousands of Hutus, some but not most of them implicated in the massacres, were streaming out and heading for other places such as Goma in the Congo, fearful of reprisals. The Tutsi who had lived in the city until the genocide were decimated in number and starting to become a minority, most of them searching for lost loved ones. While some were more or less sure that the people they were looking for were dead, others were still hoping to find them alive, because many people had simply become separated during the atrocities. Others, like me, were trying to trace men who had signed up for the RPF.

I had become aware how often these enquiries ended in bad news; but bad news can be better than no news and so I decided it was time to try to find out what had happened to my relatives: my brother Oreni, my cousin Ndoli and Gadi, Ndabananiye, my second cousin, the son of my cousin Kenasi and my cousin, Anti-Choc. All of them had joined the RPF and we had received no news of them. On the first day I set off to Kacyiru, a south-eastern area of Kigali, accompanied by Kayitare's oldest son, Guy. He was a very quiet boy and only about thirteen years old so I was surprised when he tried to counsel me. He told me that the important thing was to think of the future rather than worry about whether these relatives were alive or not; everyone had lost so much that we should just get on with life and look ahead. I was amazed that someone so young could think like that. I was not going to forget my relatives anyway. Oreni was the brother I had always looked up to and admired and we had shared a great deal together. Ndoli and I were more like twin brothers than cousins; practically the same age, we had grown up together as the best possible friends. Ndabananiye was very young and had only joined the RPF the previous year. He said at the time that he knew it was hard for the family losing four of its young men to the army but that at least one or two of them would survive to return and defend the family. If any of them died, he insisted, they should be considered a necessary sacrifice in the fight for peace. He was an idealist – likeable and adored by all the family. Petero was an interesting character as he had become famous in sports such as football and boxing, a sport not generally accepted in our society. He was strong and energetic and this was the reason he was nicknamed Anti-Choc (meaning unbeatable). Gadi was at the centre of family attention because of his stomach illness.

On the second day I continued alone, again going to Kacyiru. Finally I met a military officer who was able to inform me that Ndoli was alive, working for the Rwanda Intelligence Agency. He even gave me the address where I could find him. I was overjoyed. On hearing the good news, I immediately hurried back to Kayitare's place to tell the others. On the third day I started to look for Ndoli. Guy again accompanied me but this time one of the former child soldiers who lived with us, Floribert, came too. We took the bus to Kacyiru through the derelict streets. The only vehicles apart from the occasional bus were those belonging to the military or the UN or Non-Government Agencies (NGOs) that were providing humanitarian aid. I was full of excitement and anticipation at the thought of meeting Ndoli but, at the same time, worried in case he would have bad news for me.

I told myself that, whatever he had to tell me, I must not cry. To cry would be to show unacceptable self-pity when I could clearly see so many others around me who had suffered much more. So I braced myself as we approached the entrance to the house where we had been told Ndoli lived. By coincidence, he was outside with his friend Masasu Nindaga, someone else I knew from the Congo. They were about to leave together on an official motorbike. Ndoli had grown a great deal and was now a very big, muscular man in smart modern, civilian clothing but I recognised him immediately and he recognised me too from quite a long way off. He immediately jumped off the motorbike and ran towards me shouting. We all broke into a traditional way of greeting – dancing, running, and embracing at least ten times. Masasu couldn't stop laughing and teasing me for being "Mvuka the civilian" meaning that I did not join them to fight and preferred to offer civilian support. Then Ndoli told his friend to go to work without him, saying he would go later. He took us all into the house where he gave us something to drink.

I noticed then that his mood had changed: he seemed to be sad and fighting back tears. I felt the same way myself but didn't want anyone to know what I was thinking and delayed asking about the others. Finally, Ndoli took me to a private place and said quietly that he was so sorry to tell me that Oreni, Gadi and Ndabananiye had been killed. I stayed calm and quiet though I was gripped with a terrible feeling in my chest. I thought of all the happy times I had spent with Oreni and how he had always protected me. He had been a massive influence in my life and was a very significant person in our family. Ndoli didn't volunteer any details of his death until I insisted. 'You have to tell me!' I said. Then he told me that Oreni had been a terrific soldier who had survived the whole war and then been killed during a ceasefire at the time of the peace process. I had to press him to continue and he was clearly sad and bitter about what had happened. 'A ceasefire is a ceasefire!' he said angrily. He wasn't there himself at the time but had heard what happened. A Hutu army rocket had been fired when there should have been no shooting; it landed by Oreni, ripping away one of his hands and part of his body. He died a few hours later after massive blood loss. Ndoli would tell me no more; if he knew anything else it would be something he didn't want me to know. As for Ndabananiye, he had been ill with malaria a lot of the time and so did not have the physical fitness to move out of danger quickly when under attack. Without medical help, he had grown weaker and weaker until he had been killed on the battlefront. Next, Ndoli starting talking about Anti-Choc. He held his breath battling to hide his tears before saying 'There's another unfortunate situation: Anti-Choc is alive but in military hospital because he has lost both legs.' Gadi was killed too, but he didn't know the details.

I was devastated. I knew that, like everyone else who had lost loved ones, I must "turn the page" and carry on into my future. But that future would be without Oreni or the others in my life. Also, I felt at a loss about how to tell my family – parents, brothers, sisters and all the extended family in the Congo. I had no contact with them and did not know what had happened to them. There was nothing I could do to help or prepare them for this bad news. I knew though, that they would want as many of our clan as possible to survive and I must carry on keeping myself alive for their sake as well as for mine.

Ndoli and Masasu came to visit me every evening after their work at the Intelligence Office. Kayitare really liked them and gradually, over a drink, we shared all our family news. It was from them that I learnt that my cousin Samson was now in Kigali and one evening they took me to see him where he was staying at the Caisse Social in Kacyiru. It had been a great relief to me to know that he had escaped the genocide but I had no idea how he might have been affected by it. However, it was clear he was doing his very best to stay the same positive character he had always been and look towards a better future. 'Now our individual lives depend on how the country survives the humanitarian phase,' he said. He did not speak in detail about what had happened to him but it was obvious that he was devastated by the suffering and death of so many of his friends because, if ever he mentioned one of their names, he would go silent and then make a comment about the cruelty of the killers. He had not seen me for years and so was surprised to see how I had grown up. He asked me for news from our Minembwe home and apologised for "abandoning" us, explaining that it had been dangerous working in Rwanda and travelling was extremely difficult.

I felt more secure knowing that at least two people from our family were in the area. Damacene was dead but Gakunzi was still alive, on active duty in the Nyungwe forest where there was still some fighting. He also gave me news of my friend Tokos. He was in the South and was a very well respected intelligence officer. It was unfortunate, though, that he was not in the more disciplined part of the army because he had started to drink too much strong alcohol, which was affecting his health. A few days later I went to visit Tokos and could see what Ndoli meant: my old friend didn't eat but drank continuously and was clearly not physically well. He was as entertaining as ever though, still joking whilst at the same time being introspective and philosophical. He gave me a great deal of analysis of the situation and plenty of words of wisdom. He said he was pleased that I had stayed in the Congo. 'In a revolution there are many roles to make the battle successful,' he told me, adding: 'Peace can only come at great cost. We have lost friends here but if Africa is not prepared to say no to injustice and wrongdoing then there will be even more victims.' He encouraged me to continue my studies so that I could play a non-fighting role in the movement towards peace. Then, with his usual wit, he told me that, in the University of Life, he was a highly qualified person too, *le professeur sans diplomes* (a professor without a degree).

Within a few days of my return to Kigali I was reminded that the war was not yet really over when Ndoli told me that Gakunzi had been severely wounded in the fighting in Nyungwe. There was still a lot of fighting all over the country, particularly in the North and South; often buses travelling between the towns suffered violent attacks. Indeed many people were killed after the genocide had officially ended. Gakunzi was taken to a military hospital in Kanombe and I was lucky enough to be able to visit him. This was the first time I had seen him since we had separated in Uvira. At that time we had been relatively innocent boys together so it seemed strange to see him now as a wounded soldier. He had been injured in the shoulder and hand but was fully conscious and still committed to the cause. 'The struggle must continue,' he told me. 'We must root out injustice completely.' Like Tokos, he tried to make sure that I didn't feel guilty about not having volunteered for active service with the RPF by assuring me that the role I had played in Uvira in raising awareness and encouraging mobilisation was just as important as the actual fighting. 'Apartheid in South Africa wasn't defeated by simple force,' he continued. 'There is also a peaceful route and political dialogue. Individuals can each play their own roles and make their own sacrifices in different ways.'

CHAPTER 25

Rushashi – an opportunity

A FEW MONTHS AFTER THE WAR, life began to return to normal in Rwanda. Despite all the problems, schools were open again and the government was encouraging everyone to work and set aside the need to rely on aid from elsewhere. In this same spirit, Mamma Kayitare told me that I should restart my studies. I was surprised because it had never been easy for me to find the money for my fees or transport and I assumed it would be even more impossible now I was alone in another country. 'Don't worry,' she reassured me, knowing full well what I was thinking, 'go and talk to someone at the Ministry of Education.'

I did as she suggested and went to the Ministry. By the entrance were some soldiers who asked me what I wanted so I explained that I wanted to register for an educational course. It amused me when one of them told me, somewhat apologetically, that I would have to go to the third floor and the lift wasn't working because there was still no electricity. 'I've never been in a lift in my life, so that won't worry me!' I said. I was then directed to the right office where a woman sat by a table. There was hardly anything you might expect to see in an office – just a simple table with an ordinary chair; no papers or books or other office necessities. 'The offices were ransacked in the war,' she explained. Then she went on to tell me that thousands of previously exiled Tutsis had returned to Rwanda from neighbouring countries and needed to access education or apply for jobs. However, they had studied under different systems and in some cases even in different languages so it was difficult to assess their qualifications or educational standards. As a consequence, the Ministry was setting up a special three-month course for people who had completed their secondary school; the course would culminate in a national examination which would give successful candidates the equivalent of the bac (*baccalaureate*) and, consequently, access to university.

In my case, I had just taken my bac in the Congo but the results normally took six months and, as I had fled the Congo, I was not at all sure whether I would be able to find out if I had been successful or if anyone would actually give me the written proof I needed; ethnic hatred had grown so much in the Uvira region that I feared my certificate, if it ever reached the school, could be torn up. So I told the woman that I would be very interested in taking part in this special programme. When I heard all the details I was even keener – it all seemed too good to be true! She told me there were no fees and the school would include accommodation. In the Congo, boarding schools were for the rich so this seemed a wonderful luxury to me, though apparently in Rwanda boarding schools were the norm, funded by the Government, and in no way luxurious. There were some things I would need to provide myself, such as a mattress, a blanket and eating utensils, and another disadvantage was that the school was being set up in Rushasi, an area that was not yet completely safe. I couldn't let these details put me off though because I saw education as an opportunity. The danger could not deter me because I was used to living with insecurity. Getting myself educated was the only way I could see that would enable me to make something of myself so that I could survive and make a better life for my family and myself.

As I left the Ministry I felt elated by the thought of a new beginning. At the same time I had serious misgivings. For one thing, I knew that the education system and syllabus here in Rwanda was different to the one I had grown up with though, fortunately, the official language in both countries was French. Another concern was the security situation because, although the war was officially over, the country was really still in a state of crisis. As a newcomer, I did not fully comprehend all that had happened; I had experienced plenty of inter-ethnic hatred and violence and yet, not having lived through that terrible genocide, I felt naïve and uncertain alongside the Rwandans. I did know, however, that the area around Rushashi was still experiencing violence from militia and infiltrators known as the *abachengenzi* and a bus had recently been attacked there. I had recently attended the funeral of Major John Birasa, the man whose beautiful wedding I had attended only a month before, and I was still in shock from his tragic death. He had been killed in this area as he led the battle to fight the infiltrators. Mamma Kayitare was very positive and supportive and immediately said, 'I'll see to everything you need.' She did indeed find me all the basic equipment and she also gave me a little money for a few necessities. Ndoli gave me a little too. Within a week I was ready to go. I was excited but anxious, knowing that the next three months could determine my future. I hoped desperately that the studies I had undertaken in Uvira would help me and that the syllabus here would not be so different that I couldn't cope with the studies. I took the cheapest transport available, a bus donated by the Japanese and known jokingly as the Rwanda Rwose, meaning it was cheap enough for anyone. It took me through the beautiful rolling hills that reminded me of why this tiny country of Rwanda was sometimes referred to in the tourist trade as *le pays des mille collines*, the land of a thousand hills. It had been popular with European travellers who called it the Switzerland of Africa and enjoyed its pleasant climate. Rwandans themselves often said '*Imana yirirwa ahandi igataha murwanda*,' meaning that God might go elsewhere during the day but he would always be so attached to Rwanda that he would return there to sleep. As I admired the scenery, it was hard to reconcile the natural beauty of the landscape with the genocide that had happened there, or to imagine that the clear mountain air had been made to stink with the rotting flesh of innocent human beings. I shuddered at the thought of anything like that happening in my own homeland. Looking up at the distant mountain tops made me think of home, wondering if I would ever return to that beautiful place and asking myself, as so many times before, how my family were coping with the ever-growing violence. I lived with constant anxiety about what was happening to them.

The bus took me only as far as a village called Bassin and from there I would have to walk to Rushashi. It was a very remote area with a rather forbidding landscape of dry, stony hills and I did not know the way to go. However, I wasn't the only person to get off the bus carrying a mattress; there were also two young Rwandans. I couldn't tell if they were Hutu or Tutsi but expected them to be friendly if they were going to the same place. I joined them but found them rather distant and uncommunicative. I was hesitant to speak much myself because I thought they might tease me about my accent which was distinctively Congolese. Still, they knew the area and the hills there so I was happy to have someone to follow. They spoke to each other about awful things but in a joking way. They were talking about the genocide. 'Where did they throw the bodies of the Deo family?' asked one cheerfully. The other replied in an equally relaxed way, describing how the daughters and mother had been raped before the family were all massacred in an extremely cruel way, giving some graphic details. Then they continued by discussing their friends who had been killed. At one point, in an area between two hills, they stopped and commented that the valleys of Bassin had not yet been completely "liberated" and we could be in danger. This made me ask if we should turn back but they answered scornfully, 'Are you afraid of dying? You had better not come at all then!' Of course I could not allow myself to be seen as a coward so we all three continued until we reached the school.

On arrival, my first big surprise was to find that I knew the deputy director of the school and he remembered me too: he was Mr Kamanayo, someone I had known in Uvira and who had lived in the Congo for many years. The next surprise was when I recognised my old friend from school in Uvira, Kayaya. Incredible but true – after years of not knowing what had happened to each other we met by chance in this rural area of another country! He was a little older than me and a solid, sensible kind of person so I felt more at home when I realised he was there too.

The school was almost new and had been built with French aid. It was an impressive building but had been abandoned in the last year of the war. The construction was still good and it was clear that it had once been very well maintained. Unfortunately, it had been pillaged so the laboratories and other rooms had lost a lot of valuable equipment. Some of the school class rooms had been used to store corpses and there were plenty of mass graves nearby so it was perhaps not surprising that local villagers did not seem friendly.

We were given a timetable, taken on a tour of the school and shown our dormitories and the canteen where we would eat. I was really looking forward to eating that evening but I was soon to be disappointed. It was the sort of food I had expected but it had a very unpleasant smell that turned my stomach and included lots of weevils because the ingredients were so old. The cooks explained to us that all the food supplies were not local fresh produce but had been donated by the World Food Programme; we could not refuse it when there was nothing else on offer. Students from richer families bought themselves bread, milk and butter in the little shop and made jokes saying that the weevils would act to supplement our diet. From then on I had difficulty eating and suffered a lot from vomiting. As Banyamulenge, Kayaya and I were more particular about our food than most people because of our people's traditional attitude toward what they ate. So we ate very little during those three months and, whenever possible, had just bread and tea.

Kayaya introduced me to his close friend, Severin, who was a very entertaining character. He had only recently arrived in Rwanda and he continued to speak Kinyamulenge, making the whole dormitory laugh with his jokes. Though they understood his way of speaking, the Rwandans found his language quite comical especially when, like a true Banyamulenge cattle herder, he recited cattle poems at six in the morning while we were getting ready for classes. Severin knew three young Tutsis from North Kivu: Wera, Runyota and one with a name that made everyone laugh. Unlike the rest of us, he hadn't chosen a new, westernised Christian name since Mobutu had repealed the authenticity law and it was almost as if he had two surnames. I "christened" him Dennis and he was known as that from then on. It wasn't really surprising that he didn't mind what people called him because he was a person who didn't mind what people thought about him in general. He was never upset about having no money or when the girls laughed at the way he spoke Kinyarwanda. He got on well with everyone. Of our friendship group, he was the only one who connected really well with Hutu students, even though in appearance he was the stereotype of a Tutsi – very tall and thin. Sometimes I felt he didn't take his studies seriously enough and I lectured him a little about this. He just looked at me in his usual affable way, as if I had every right to tell him off.

Kayaya, Severin, Dennis, Wera, Runyota and I were all in the same dormitory near to each other and together we formed a group of Congolese Tutsis so we felt more confident amongst the native Rwandans. Rwandans have a reputation for being less outgoing than the Congolese; our school fellows were quiet and more introspective than us, perhaps partly because of what they had been through. To us, it seemed as if they were hardened by their experiences, as if they had been through some sort of hideous initiation ceremony that gave them a maturity we did not have. Now we boosted our self-esteem by going round as a group, cracking jokes the others wouldn't understand and chatting together in Swahili, a language they didn't speak. Sometimes our schoolmates even seemed intimidated by our boisterous ways. The girls found us attractive though and we made friends with several of them, including Laurence and Furaha, two nice girls who had only narrowly escaped the genocide.

I found the classes were at the right level for me and soon got back into the habit of study. Our teachers were of Hutu and Tutsi ethnic groups of Rwanda and I found them all quite helpful so it was quite a shock to me when one or another of them disappeared. This happened several times during the three months and each time the director would come and explain to us that there had been strong evidence of complicity in the genocide so the teacher had been arrested. It was difficult for us to imagine an apparently nice teacher slaughtering innocent people and led us towards a general mistrust of anyone; it was impossible to know what people were really like. Perhaps it was this lack of confidence in other people that led me to stick to friends with a background similar to my own.

After two months at the school, we all went home for a week's holiday and to prepare for the final examinations. It was Christmas 1994 to New Year 1995 and Kayitare, who never missed an excuse to have a party to take his mind off things, organised a big family celebration. He had his usual whisky and danced to traditional music with his wife in front of a big audience of all the people who lived in his house. The music stopped at midnight for at least half an hour as gunfire could be heard throughout the town. At first the sound of guns frightened me but they were only a replacement for fireworks to mark the New Year and express the joy at the fact that war was officially over. So we all went outside to see the shooting.

I climbed onto the roof for a better view; in the excitement and happiness of celebrating liberation, we had totally forgotten the danger of stray bullets. Kayitare had the good sense to order us down again and, next day, we learnt that several people had been accidentally killed by this firing.

I travelled back to Rushashi with my Congolese friends and also two girls, Laurence and Furaha. They enjoyed having our company and protection for the journey; we were all good friends by the time we got back to the school. We sat our exams and waited for our results. I was thrilled to find I had passed with distinction amongst the top five students. It was great to go back to Kayitare's place with such good news and Mamma Kayitare put on a party to celebrate my success. Just as we were settling down at the table, I noticed a medical vehicle entering the compound with Runyota, in it. I was surprised to see him there and even more surprised at the bad news he brought. 'Laurence is dead!' he announced. He had come to tell me that one of the two girls we were friendly with, Laurence, was dead. Apparently there had been a traffic accident. She had been on the back of a truck and had been thrown off, dying instantly when she hit the tarmac. It was tragic. Like the rest of us, Laurence was celebrating having passed her baccalaureate; she had told us that it would enable her to have a scholarship to study in Switzerland. Runyota had come to tell me because he didn't know what else to do and he thought I would help him find Laurence's family. We immediately set off to find Wera and then the three of us went together to the hospital; it was a shock to us all to see her body but Wera was particularly affected because he was very fond of her and had asked her out. It seemed bitterly ironic to all of us that this lovely young girl who had survived the genocide should die in this way. It was so pointless. We had come to understand that hate and killing happen but could not see why a minor accident and a natural cause could take Laurence away from us at such a happy time. There was simply no explanation for it.

We then found ourselves in the position of being responsible for her body. The police and public services followed the principle of *'Que les morts soient enterrées par les leurs'* (the dead should be buried by their own friends or families) and in this case there was only us.

In our attempt to trace her family we went first to find another friend from Rushashi, a genocide survivor. We found him at a party at the Diplomat Hotel, drinking and dancing. Much to our surprise, he showed no emotion when we told him about Laurence. 'That's life!' he said. Clearly, the loss of all his family in the genocide had given him a different outlook. He was able to tell us that her family lived in Rwamagana in Kibungo Province and also that there was a member of the family in Kigali. So we went off hunting for this man and a soldier in the street told us that he was at his own marriage ceremony in the Hotel Meridien. It was considered that we should not interrupt his important day in this way so there was nothing for it but to go to her home ourselves to tell the parents. We were given a lift in a medical aid vehicle to Rwamagana, where we found the little sister at home and learnt that the family were organising a party to celebrate Laurence's certificate. We told them what had happened and then went back to Kigali with the intention of returning the next day with the body.

When we arrived, we helped with digging the grave and washing the body. At the actual funeral we were still dressed in the same clothes we had worn while doing all this work; to us Congolese it is a sign of respect to the dead to be present at a funeral dressed in a way that shows we have given hands-on help to the family and share their grief. However, most of the guests were smartly dressed and took us to be servants rather than Laurence's friends mourning her death. We were a bit offended by this. Another thing that struck me was the way people accepted death without a great deal of grief. The people of that area, who had suffered the horrors of genocide, did not seem to recognise the amplitude of this tragedy, this young and promising life cut short. Death had become something rather routine and unremarkable to them and they didn't think much about it. Of all the students we had been with at Rushashi, only three joined us at the funeral. This didn't mean that they had no sympathy. It just meant that they had learnt to accept death as something natural; they simply intended to carry on surviving themselves for as long as they could. There was even a sense in which they didn't care about living any more.

CHAPTER 26

A new challenge

ONE OF THE FIRST THINGS the new government did when it came into power in 1994 was to ban the identity card. Then it set about getting the country's infrastructure working. It was felt that one of the first institutions that should be normalised was the University. The Ministry for Higher Education made a public announcement by radio that it would be opening again in January 1995 and selection for places would be by examination. Obviously this was an ideal opportunity for me. The University of Rwanda, situated in Butare, had been established years before and had an excellent reputation. Tragically, when the 1994 genocide began, the university itself and the city of Butare were among the first places affected. This was because, in addition to the usual tension between the two groups, there was the added perception that here many Tutsi were in comfortable professional or academic positions. Being highly educated, they were westernised and sophisticated, reinforcing the sense that they were somehow "other". Many "elite" people were eliminated in the massacres there.

Although I knew Butare was scarred from the brutality that had happened so recently, it still had such a reputation as a beautiful place that I was looking forward to seeing it. I knew I would have no problem with accommodation when I went to take the entrance examination because my cousin Samson was there and so was Ndamage's sister; before I came to Rwanda I had planned to stay with her.

I bought a ticket and took the minibus with high hopes of passing the entrance exam. On the bus I sat next to a young student who had survived the massacres and was now returning to his studies. He told me a lot about the university, the city and the places we passed. The scenery we passed through was breath-taking and I could see that why this area was often referred to as the land of fruit and greenery. We passed interesting sites such as the modern farm of Songa and the Institute of Scientific Research. One thing that surprised me as I looked through the window was that I could see political posters proclaiming friendship and solidarity with the Belgians and French. I found this ironic considering the tragedies the country had just gone through and the resentment people felt that there had been so little help from the international community.

There were several stops on the way and one was at Rubona, a tragic place because there were many mass graves of Tutsi workers. Another time we stopped to buy fruit, a customary thing to do in this area renowned for fruit-growing.

As we approached Butare, which the Belgians had called Astrida in honour of their queen, we passed many impressive buildings from the colonial era. On the outskirts of the city, my companion pointed out the famous National Museum that was a gift of the Belgium King Bauduin. This Museum hosts some of the most beautiful ethnological collections and records of the Rwandan Kingdom dating back to the early 19th century.

When we reached the Governor's official building, the driver stopped there for a while. Nearby was the Queen's house and I walked up to it to look through the gate. Now abandoned, it was a very beautiful and large house with a massive garden. It had belonged to Queen Gicyanda Rosarie, the widow of King Mutara III who had died in mysterious circumstances in 1959. The monarchy was destroyed two years later by the new Hutu regime. Queen Rosarie continued to live in Butare along with her mother and several ladies-in-waiting until, during the genocide, she was kidnapped by military officials. Later she was shot along with the other women behind the National Museum; only one young girl survived to tell the story. Two days later, the queen's mother was also murdered.

This was just one of the hundreds of tragic stories of the genocide in Butare (*see timeline*). The majority of the Tutsi population had been slaughtered and Ndamage's sister, Mamma Clement, was one of the few survivors. She had hidden with two of her children in a stretch of water, dipping under the surface when the killers approached. When the most dangerous time had passed she and the children were hidden by a Hutu friend.

I found her house easily enough and she welcomed me warmly as her brother's friend. To my surprise and joy, I found Ndamage there too. He had finally made his escape from the Congo. We had a lot of stories to exchange and he told me that things in the Congo had gone from bad to worse – even my dogs Milou and Leopard had been shot. He was, of course, delighted to hear that I had gained my certificate and was hoping to get into the university but, beneath his and his sister's warm congratulations, there was deep sadness and our conversation inevitably turned to the terrible losses they had endured. They had lost their brother Damas with his wife and children and Mamma Clement had lost two of her sons and two daughters as well as her husband. These four children were studying at the university while her husband had been a very important man, a director at the National Institute of Research. Their elderly father was also killed. Lovingly, she went through her photograph albums, which had somehow been spared in the looting and killings, showing me photographs of these people that had been taken away from her so suddenly and cruelly.

'*N'Umututsi cyane*', which means 'he is worryingly too Tutsi' was a common saying, meaning that someone was marked out because he or she was stereotypically Tutsi – tall, slim, and well educated. Such people were particular targets during the genocide and Ndamage's brother and his family came into this category. Grief for them was increased by the thought that their only wrong-doing was to be "beautiful". Coincidentally, it turned out that my cousin Samson was a close friend of Damas, the brother; he told me many times what a lovely family they had been.

Most of Ndamage's family had been highly educated people who lived in Butare but the traditional family home was in the village of Huye. Mamma Clement was physically and emotionally exhausted from searching for bodies of her relatives, and had waited for Ndamage's arrival to look for their father's body. I volunteered to go with him as soon as I had taken the entrance examination. When our search began, it quickly became apparent that this innocent, respectable, elderly man had not died quickly but, like many others, had been hacked to pieces.

Mamma Clement had already found the bodies of their mother and immediate family, husband and children, and they were planning to have a special day for the burial and funeral service for them all, including the brother, Damas, and his family, whose bodies had not been located but were presumably in a mass grave somewhere. What had happened to this innocent family was so horrific that I felt myself slip into deep depression and I started to ask myself if I really wanted to continue with my studies when my concentration had evaporated in the face of these terrible happenings. It was unbearable to see the suffering of my old friend and his sister and I couldn't think of anything to say to console them. Mamma Clement could talk of nothing but her lost family and how she and the other three children had managed to survive as if by a miracle.

Her oldest surviving child was Georgette and she, like me, was planning to go to the university. She told me the entrance exam would be extremely difficult and unlike anything I was used to in the Congo since the education system here was so different. I assured her that I would be fine, having spent three months gaining my certificate, but I was certainly worried all the same. One week after we had taken the exam, the results were pinned up on a wall in the administration block and I went anxiously to see them. The list was long and I had to scan down it for a while before I found my name but then I was overjoyed. I had succeeded! I would at last be able to get higher education and make something of myself. My happiness was dampened a little though by seeing the disappointment of the students who had not made it.

My results were strong enough to give me a choice of faculties so I selected my preferred subjects, Social Science and Economics. However, a week later my cousin Samson was appointed assistant professor at the university and, much as I looked forward to having his company, I realised that he would put pressure on me to change my mind. Sure enough, he proceeded to tell me that there was much more chance of good employment if I studied science; education was about securing a good future rather than just choosing what I enjoyed doing, he insisted. In our society we always respect our elders and I soon bowed to his wishes; I knew he was a very experienced man who had my best interests at heart and trusted his judgement. He organised my transfer to the science faculty where I began the core course: pharmacy, medicine, biology and agronomy.

The main buildings of the University of Butare are located just outside the city on a small plateau near a large forest of Ruhande. Just nearby was the place where one of Kayitare's brothers had been killed, the father of two of the orphans I had grown fond of in Kigali. In the university surroundings there were plenty of mass graves whilst bones and skulls were still sometimes seen in various places around the University campus. The oldest building (Batiment Central) is striking and dates back to Belgian rule. Its historic atmosphere made it seem special to me and I could sense how prestigious it was to be a student from local people's attitudes towards us. I found most of the university buildings dark and depressing, as if they could not shake off the aura of the horrors that had taken place within those walls. Only six months previously, practically all the Tutsi students had been targeted. Because Tutsi women are perceived as being generally more beautiful than other women, they received particularly venomous treatment. Hutu extremists perceived them as the image and symbol of their ethnicity and treated them as sexual objects. By humiliating, degrading, and ultimately destroying Tutsi women, the extremists could inflict pain not only on those women themselves but, symbolically, on their relatives and community. Using sharp objects, they inflicted hideous pain on their victims to dishonour them, their relatives and their tribe whilst at the same time destroying the reproductive ability of that group. Thus, women were extremely vulnerable. Some were "spared" and received *kubohoza* (rape) instead of mutilation or death. Others were killed along with the vast majority of male Tutsi students. Amongst the victims were two sons and two daughters of Mamma Clement, Ndamage's nephews and nieces.

The large Tutsi population in Butare had included many students and thousands had been killed. It was under this shadow of genocide that we were expected to "forget" and settle down to our studies. One constant reminder of the atrocities was the large number of students who were pregnant because they had suffered kubohoza. It was difficult to see how they felt about their situation; to me it seemed as if they were trying to disconnect from the stigma and get on with life, not planning ahead too much. Perhaps they felt cheered by the fact that they were still at least alive and, having come so close to death, happy just to continue one way or another. It was sad to see it, knowing that here was another long-term tragedy: many unwanted babies would be born because the community would not tolerate a child of another ethnicity that had been forced on them by an enemy perpetrating genocide.

There were only five thousand students from various backgrounds at the university including those taking higher degrees and those returning to complete courses. Our expenses were covered with the help of a United Nations development grant and we were even given a small government loan so that we could have some pocket money each month. As at Rushashi, we were expected to provide some of the basic things like eating utensils and blankets. First year students were not given anywhere to stay but were expected to find friends at a higher level willing to share a room. There was an equal number of Hutu students and we Tutsis felt uncomfortable at times, asking ourselves if they had taken part in or encouraged the massacres. It was a relief for me when I found someone who was not only from the Minembwe area of the Congo but who was actually of my clan. He treated me like a little brother and I benefited from his advice and opinions as he was a very sensible young man.

Socially the University wasn't at all bad: it was a meeting point for students from all sorts of backgrounds with many different cultures and languages. Students, particularly males, tended to associate with certain groups according to type. One prominent group was the *conards* (jokers). They were known for their jokes and for not bothering much about how they dressed. They were rather sexist in that they cracked a lot of jokes about girls but didn't really take much of an interest in the opposite sex. Most of their spare time was spent drinking. Another group was known as the "dogs". These young men were keen on fashion and took a lot of care with their appearance so that they could impress the girls. They were polite in their manner, speaking French a lot of the time, and enjoyed being with girls. I was classified as a "dog". This derogatory word was one given to us by the conards simply because, according to their principles, a true man should not run after females like a dog runs after people it wants things from. Really though, there was not a lot of bad feeling between the groups: it was just youthful high spirits and the need to justify the way an individual behaves.

So my social life was quite pleasant, especially as I had found some of my old friends from Uvira. Within the first week I came across my best friend from Uvira, Budagu, who now liked to be known as George. We became inseparable as we were in the same faculty and were both "dogs". We balanced each other well: I was able to introduce him to a lot of friends and he was a stabilising influence for me, helping me to control my emotions. We discussed interesting things, including the future of the region and our people; we talked about eradicating poverty and conflict, promoting education as a tool to fight ethnic hatred. We both took part in establishing a University drama group and acted in the first play which was attended by national authorities and local NGO representatives.

I also came across my old friend Isaac Rumenge who had trained with me for our work with the RPF. We liked to talk about the liberation of Africa, knowing that our mission to improve our country was far from finished.

Butare National University being the main and official university in country, students there were considered as future leaders. We had the privilege of being visited by most of the government officials who gave talks and encouraged discussions. This included various topics, such as debates on issues of reconciliation, security, economy and leadership. Government leaders also visited the university to interact with students socially. On one occasion, as I was a referee for a friendly tennis match, I was surprised to find myself talking to a man whose image was familiar through TV. He suddenly appeared in the tennis hall and came to me to ask whether he could join the match. Speechless and wondering whether I was dreaming, I said yes without even consulting my fellow players. This was the President, Paul Kagame! He was considered a hero in Rwanda and most African countries because he had been leader of the RPF when they stopped the genocide. He was incredibly respected for his integrity and vision.

I was so surprised that, to confirm that I was not dreaming, I looked through the windows around the tennis hall and realised that we were surrounded by soldiers (the president's bodyguards) and hundreds of students trying to see him. 'Wait a minute,' I said to the president. He smiled as he saw me shaking in an attitude of shock attitude and said '*Ntakibazo*' meaning 'no worries'. He was in Reebok sport clothes and looked like a very ordinary person. When time arrived, I asked him to join the match. '*Murakoze*', he said meaning respectfully 'thank you'.

After the match, he asked one of his bodyguards to bring us drinks and then sat on the floor and discussed with us how we were getting on with our studies. He kept asking basic questions such as 'What sort of facilities do you have? Are there enough books? Is the laboratory equipment back to normal?', 'Do you have electricity?' which made us even more reassured that he was a supportive and accessible person. Around the building, I could see that the crowd of students was growing more and more and the President's guards were putting barriers around to ensure that he would not get pushed when he made his exit. I could not believe that I was actually sitting next to him and answering some of his enquiries around student life. He reminded us: 'The country is still in a very difficult situation financially and we expect everyone to take part in re-building every institution'.

Following this unusual encounter, I enjoyed meeting some of the most respected African leaders such as the Pan-Africanist and former Tanzanian president, Mwalimu Julius Nyerere. I was amazed to see his modesty and hear his wise ideas of promoting peace and harmony among African societies.

Academically, as the year progressed I became less and less motivated in my studies. I had always believed and told my friends that success results from a combination of hard work and enthusiasm. It is possible to work hard but without enthusiasm or motivation. This is what happened to me after having been persuaded by my cousin to study subjects that didn't interest me. As the exams approached I began to worry that I wouldn't get all the grades I needed to continue and the idea of failure worried me as I had never before failed. In fact, I passed all the exams except Maths and Chemistry, but decided to change faculty in the second year to avoid taking those subjects. They had five credits each so could affect my overall results significantly. So by the second year I was in the faculty of Social Science and a great deal happier there. I was well-motivated again and enjoying my studies. Once more, my future seemed bright and hopeful.

CHAPTER 27

Expulsions

I STARTED THE ACADEMIC YEAR 1995 to 1996 full of optimism. I was finally on the course I preferred and my ambition, to one day be a well-educated man who could help his people in a positive way, seemed to be within my reach. At the same time, I was constantly worried about my family and friends who were still in danger. Ndoli kept in touch as much as he could so I knew that the situation in the Congo was getting steadily worse. Many people who had the means to get out had already done so, as I had myself, but now the situation was so desperate that even people who had nowhere to go were fleeing. Then the extermination of Tutsi in North Kivu began and there was a mass exodus from that area. Some reached safety by going over the frontier into Uganda while others headed for the refugee camps just inside Rwanda, Gisenyi and Ruhengeri. It was not a safe journey because the *Interhamwe*, the violent militia that had been responsible for the 1994 genocide, was still active and thirsting for Tutsi blood almost two years after the genocide of 1994. It made no difference to them if these Tutsi were Congolese or Rwandan – all were vermin to be exterminated. As a result, between seven hundred and a thousand destitute men, women and children were massacred on their way to the Rwandan refugee camps. Hearing about all this was a terrible shock to my friends and me. We were safe at the University but we knew the many thousands of Tutsi still in the Congo were in grave danger.

In March 1996 ethnic prejudice was made official when the Congolese (Zairean) government declared that all Tutsi were foreigners and began to exert pressure on them to leave the country. Many of the Interahamwe responsible for the 1994 genocide were hiding out over the border in the Congolese jungles. These violent groups threatened not just our people but the stability of Rwanda itself. From there, as well as posing a threat to the Congolese Tutsi, they were able to make murderous incursions back into Rwanda, especially as the Congolese government was doing very little to protect the border. It was at this point that my cousin Ndoli was contacted by superior officers in the RPF to see how he could work with them on DRC issue. The RPF, now the official Rwandan army, were in agreement with Ndoli over the need to enter the Congo. Ndoli wanted to take advantage of the fact that we shared a mutual interest in dealing with them. The official stance of the Rwandan government was that, if neither the Congolese government nor the United Nations would disarm these dangerous thugs, the RPF must do it. Though Ndoli's main object was to save his own people, it was clear to him that the best way to go about it was by engaging the superior members of the RPF to work with them. So they worked together and Ndoli was given the task of coordinating secret operations to gather information on the position of Mobutu's armed forces in the Congo. Ndoli confided in me about this, telling me that it gave him the opportunity to warn various clans when they were in particular danger, giving them the opportunity to get out before matters escalated. He also started to identify other Rwandophones (Banyamulenge or others from North Kivu) who were already working within the RPF. Among them was Nicola Kibinda (the highest ranked among those from the Banyamulenge community). Although he could not share all his secret information with them, he wanted to know where they were. Amongst the superior officers of the RPF, a small team was set up to support his work.

In May, Ndoli met two men for the first time who would go on to be extremely significant in the Congo. These were Laurent Desire Kabila and his son Joseph Kabila. They were not Tutsi but they were against Mobutu's dictatorship. The older Kabila had a history of involvement with various groups who had fought against Mobutu in the 1960s and had gone on to play a significant part in the Mulelist rebellion (*see timeline*). Che Guevara, that idealistic South American who had led this rebellion, had not considered Kabila to be a man of integrity but, nevertheless, that was how Kabila made a reputation for himself. When the rebellion failed, he fled to Tanzania and later went to Uganda. In the 1980s he linked up with the underground movement fighting to install Yoweri Museveni as

Ugandan president, a post he still holds today. While he was in East Africa, Kabila became known to the RPF. Now he was back in the Congo with his son, ostensibly trading in gold but actually hoping to become involved at a high level in the fighting there.

In June, Ndoli was invited to a hotel in Cyangugu for a meeting with superior officers of the RPF so that he could explain his plan to them. He was asked many questions about the possibility of conducting war in the Congo. He explained to them about the networks he had established and assured them that a successful revolution was definitely possible. After the meeting, he was taken to meet Laurent Kabila again but this time they were introduced to each other in a way that established their roles.

Meanwhile, Kengo wa Dondo, the prime minister of the Congo (Zaire) went to Kigali to discuss the huge numbers of Tutsi refugees in Rwanda. Shockingly, he declared that it would be difficult to reintegrate Tutsi Congolese back into his country. 'Even if the Congolese government were to recognise them as having a right to citizenship, the hostility of the indigenous population would complicate any attempt at reintegration,' he declared, implying that we were not "indigenous". For Ndoli, this amounted to a confirmation that the only way forward was through force within the Congo itself. If Mobutu's government would not accept the Congolese Tutsi and did nothing to stop the killings, we absolutely must do something.

In June, Laurent Kabila told Ndoli that he had a military force at his disposal in the Fizi area. Meaning to take advantage of this offer, Ndoli came again to Butare, particularly keen to work with Isaac Rumenge, who was an exceptional young man. Strong, brave, confident and determined, Isaac had no hesitation in helping my cousin with his plans. They also recruited two other Banyamulenge university students, young men of high integrity. Then the four of them went on a spying mission to make contact with Kabila's men in Fizi. This was not really successful though because it turned out that those military men had been abandoned by Kabila in the 1960s and were no longer his faithful supporters. In fact they had joined a Burundian anti-Tutsi militia group.

Now problems began to escalate in South Kivu. On the Ruzizi plain, fifteen Banyamulenge, including key religious leaders were tortured to death by Mobutu's soldiers, including the special death squad unit. Amongst our people, there was grief and panic but also anger. We felt it was time for retaliation, time to tell all the young Banyumalenge who had joined the RPF and survived the fighting in Rwanda that now they must save their own people from the terrible genocide they had seen in Rwanda. Many other young Banyamulenge were also keen to join a military infiltration back into the Congo, seeing it as a chance to save their relatives. Ndoli reassured that there was no doubt whatsoever that they would receive full support from Rwandan soldiers in the RPF because they wanted to confront the Interahamwe once and for all. He was confident of this because superior officers in the Rwandan Secret Service continued to work with him.

Ndoli and another senior officer visited the University to start the movement. Some elites in Butare, such as Jonas Mugabe, Charles Mukeha and my cousin Samson Muzuri, were contacted and a meeting with them was set up. Almost all the students with a Congolese Tutsi background became involved in raising awareness and Ndoli recognised them as people who could understand the situation and who one day might be influential leaders. During these meetings I met a young Munyamulenge called Charles Murama, who did not say much but was very motivated to help his people.

All of this was happening at a time when I was supposed to be a student working towards a degree. Obviously, my mind was not really on that. Instead of getting on with written assignments or socialising in the way students normally would, I regularly met my friend Budagu George to talk about what was going on and how the new rescue arrangements were progressing. We supported each other because we shared the same anxieties. We then joined other Banyamulenge students to listen to the news on the radio and discuss what could potentially happen.

By July 1996, the first military group led by Ndoli had been chosen to go into the Congo and their mission had been a success. This was followed by another mission, led by Nicola Kibinda, which was also successful. Though the operations were extremely difficult, no-one was killed, hurt or captured. Unfortunately, by the third mission, which included Gakunzi, Mobutu's Intelligence officers had become aware of the infiltrations so the Congolese army were forewarned and, as a result, about a third of the sixty soldiers were killed. It had become open warfare rather than a secret movement. Those involved in the secret meetings carried on but now we also had to mobilise people willing to be new recruits to the action in the Congo.

By September 1996 there was a tense atmosphere at the University campus amongst the Tutsi of South and North Kivu because they were on the alert and closely following all the latest events. Then the regional governor of South Kivu, Shweka Mutabazi, released an official announcement over the radio that all the Banyamulenge should leave the Congo within a day. That is to say, a population of more than 250,000 were told to abandon their homes and leave the country within twenty-four hours! The following day the national government also gave out a deportation order. It was like giving enemy tribes permission to attack our people: in North Kivu and the Uvira area there were unprovoked attacks on innocent people; many were murdered in a deliberately slow and painful way. The luckier ones who were merely deported were stripped of their belongings and loaded into lorries to be dumped at the frontier.

At the University we reacted to this shocking news by organising a meeting to raise funds and collect anything that could help the deportees who had lost everything. These destitute survivors were arriving mainly at Bugarama by the Ruzizi bridge on the frontier between Rwanda and the Congo. United Nations aid workers had set up a makeshift camp about three kilometres from the border crossing. A group of us arranged to travel to Bugarama by bus, a three to four hour journey, to look for friends and relatives and see what we could do to help.

As we travelled there, we were all worrying about people we knew, my biggest concern being Noah's family who had been in the Uvira region trying to find a way to cross over to Rwanda the last time I heard from them. My friend Freddy was one of the most anxious of our group because rumours had been circulating about what had happened to his father, Mahota. Some reports said he had escaped to Burundi whilst others said he had died with other deportees. Mahota was a religious man who had spent his life trying to strengthen friendship between the various ethnicities. He was second in charge of the Methodist church throughout the South Kivu region and had set up his own home in a Babembe area where his children grew up completely integrated with other tribes. I remember smiling when I visited them and heard how fluently Freddy's young brothers spoke Kibembe. As Freddy's friends, we tried to shield him from the rumours until we knew the truth for sure.

Another of my friends who was worried about close relatives was Amani. His family had experienced tragedy the previous year when his father, a very influential Banyamulenge leader, had died in Rwanda, where he had gone to find a safer home for his family. Amani had already received a message to say that three of his siblings had escaped and were in another refugee camp in Rwanda but their story was alarming and left him very anxious for the rest of the family. With the ever-increasing threat against Tutsi people, a family friend from the Bafulero tribe had run to their house offering to save the children by smuggling them across the border at a safer crossing than Bugarama hidden under cargo in a lorry. Thirteen-year-old Esther and eleven-year-old Papy, were sent immediately; in such a hurry that Esther was still in the bathrobe she had slipped on as she came out of the shower. Fifteen-year-old Douglas had refused to go, saying he would die with his mother, grandmother and baby sister rather than leave them without any men for protection. So the two younger ones travelled alone but, the next day, the Bafulero woman returned and insisted until he too was smuggled out by lorry. This friend and the lorry drivers took severe risks to help their Tutsi friends, as did many good people of other tribes. The three children all crossed, terrified but securely hidden, at the safer frontier crossing in Bukavu. They were reunited at a Kibuye refugee camp, from where they were able to send a message to their older brother at the university.

When the four hour bus ride to Bugarama ended, we walked straight to the bridge where the refugees crossed. The two countries are separated by the River Ruzizi and the refugees had to come over the bridge to find safety in Rwanda. It was a lovely day, warm as usual but with the fresh mountain air so typical of Rwanda, and the physical beauty of the area was remarkable. Here the Ruzizi river sparkled in the sunlight as it meandered peacefully through the lush, green valley. Over in the east stood the high mountains of Crete Congo Nil while in the west the mountain chain of Mitumba marked out the Uvira and Walungu territories. But against this spectacular natural beauty, a scene of utmost horror was taking place. On the Congolese side of the river there were military men from various factions: the Interahamwe who had perpetrated the genocide in Rwanda, Mobutu's Presidential Guard known as the death squads, and Hutu militia from Burundi, all supposedly under the supervision of the regional governor, Shweka Mutabazi and Bernard Nyangoma, the Burundian rebel leader. As the lorry loads of deportees arrived, they were greeted by these military who robbed them of any possessions they still had, saying they had no right to leave the Congo with anything that belonged to the country. Sometimes this included forcing them to strip off all their clothes. We witnessed women and children being threatened that they would be shot if they turned round while crossing the bridge. Some of the men were even less fortunate. They were held back and tortured before being thrown into the river to drown.

It was one of the worst experiences of my life to watch all of this whilst being totally unable to help. Our side of the frontier was guarded by RPF soldiers who tried to keep us calm, warning us that there was nothing we could do; it was apparent that they were frustrated too but their role was to maintain peace on the Rwandan side and they could not start an international confrontation. We knew, though, that our relatives and friends were amongst those people suffering so horribly. At one point, we witnessed a young man being kicked and beaten and pulled from one attacker to another; apparently he had annoyed them by refusing to be submissive. After finishing him off by jumping on him and shooting him, they dragged the body away to one of the small buildings nearby. This is an incident I can never forget because I had recognised the young man as a friend of mine, Kanga Sebugorore, a friend who had always impressed me with his strength and courage; though younger than me, he was always quick to defend himself against insults. It was just after this incident that we learnt the true story of what had happened to Freddy's father. He had spent three days under arrest when he was beaten and tortured. Eventually he had been allowed to join other deportees with his three young sons but he and two of the boys were killed at the border. We tried to break this news as best we could to Freddy but it was devastating.

As night began to fall, despair set in. We felt as if our people had been abandoned by the rest of the world, just as the Rwandan Tutsis had been abandoned in 1994. When the RPF soldiers asked us to leave for the night, we pleaded again for help, asking them to cross over and do something to avenge Kanga and protect the others who might later face the same fate. They simply repeated that they could only take military action if the militia attacked Rwanda itself. We walked the three or four kilometres to the refugee camp, numbed and hardly speaking, not knowing what to say about this world where violence is just a normal state of affairs. Having seen how people arrived over the bridge, we could imagine how the people at the camp would feel and we were desperately hoping many of the people we knew would already be safely there.

At the camp we started to search for people. I could not find Noah's family but found other people I knew. Amani was overjoyed to find the rest of his family. It was a wonderful moment when he was able to tell them the good news that the other three had arrived safely. At the time, I had no way of knowing their escape was a blessing for me too as, nine years later, Esther became my wife. Being in the refugee camp was a very moving experience. People who had once enjoyed comfortable homes and loving families were living in the most basic conditions, often not knowing what had happened to many of their loved-ones or, worse still, knowing they had been tortured and killed. Tents had been set up where people could shelter or sleep on the bare earth. Women slept in different tents to the men but we all met together in one large tent to pray and sing together. Temporary water tanks had been set up and basic food was given out but people were still hungry and small children cried continuously. There was no real sanitation, so we were concerned about cholera and other diseases and gave advice to people about how they could move on. They told us if they knew anyone at all in Rwanda and then we liaised with the aid workers to get them transported to these places

We spent that night and the following day at the refugee camp, returning to the border again the day after that. We knew many of the families still arriving, always in a state of great distress because their stories were horrific. Amongst them were the wife and children of Simeon Rukenurwa, the leader of our Uvira community. They had been forced to leave without him, knowing he was in the process of being tortured to death. The wife had witnessed them hacking at his legs to give him multiple fractures and induce a slow, painful death; she was completely distraught. Freddy's mother arrived at this time too. She had a newborn baby and had been forced to leave the hospital where she had recently given birth by caesarean section. She had no idea at this point what had happened to the rest of the family; the terrible news would be broken to her later after she left the camp for medical treatment.

Gradually, more and more people arrived at the refugee camp. There was still no sign of Noah's family but I found Mamma Musirimu with her sisters and children. Musirimu was not with them because he had been away in Shaba on business when the deportations started. It was hoped that, as an influential businessman with useful contacts, he would be safe.

After spending five days in this tragic atmosphere, I felt even more determined to do something to help my people so I was happy when Isaac told me that we were to meet a highly-ranked officer in the Rwandan army who was supporting the operations in the Congo. Apparently the Banyamulenge who had infiltrated the Highlands of South Kivu, under the leadership of Gakunzi, Rugazura, Ndoli and Nicola Kibinda, had succeeded in restoring security to our clansmen's area but the war was carrying on elsewhere. In October the crisis escalated and started to affect Banyamulenge in other areas of the Congo. Twelve thousand people were deported from the Shaba region. From Lubumbashi (in the Shaba region) the Banyamulenge fled to Zambia. Those who were living in the central parts of the country such as the capital, Kinshasa, found it more difficult to escape. Some fled over the river Congo to Brazzaville but others were burnt alive.

CHAPTER 28

Escalation in the Congo

I WENT BACK TO THE UNIVERSITY but found I simply had no heart for my studies and could not concentrate on learning while these terrible things were happening. I was at a loss. I felt helpless but did not want to abandon my people. I didn't even know if my family were still alive. Though I did eventually learn that Noah's wife and children had finally arrived at the camp, I had no news of many other people. We continued holding meetings every night to discuss what could be done to support our troops in the Congo who were trying to protect our families and communities. By now, the violence was starting to be noticed in the international media and it was being referred to as "a liberation movement". What had begun simply as Banyamulenge self-defence had become outright war and later it would be referred to as "The first Congolese War".

Soon, the name "Banyamulenge" had become very famous. However, the term was not well understood and became a catch-all term in the international media to refer to all the different and heterogeneous groupings of Congolese Tutsi. Journalists wrote their stories without understanding the history of the area and with no knowledge of how people had been persecuted. When the Banyamulenge were mentioned by the BBC, this was the first time the world heard about a community that had been struggling for many years to survive ethnic exclusion. Even today, there is still total confusion amongst journalists and specialists of the region who find difficulty in understanding the difference between Banyamulenge and other Congolese Tutsi. They tend to think that Banyamulenge problems began only as a result of the Rwandan genocide. This was and is still based on a lack of understanding of the true causes of the conflict. The international community have never recognised that the Congolese Tutsi are an endangered minority who needed protection of their fundamental rights. This basic misunderstanding led the UN to believe, during peace agreement in 2001–03, that the problem could be resolved by integrating a few Tutsi elite into posts of responsibility within the Congo, whereas the real issue has always been how to offer protection for the rural Banyamulenge against violent hatred and racism.

By November 1996, in Eastern Congo (Zaire), the major towns started falling to what was referred to by the international media as a 'mysterious movement' called the Alliance of Democratic Forces for the Liberation of Congo (AFDL), with Laurent Kabila, a forgotten revolutionary of the 1960s, as spokesperson. Isaac had been away from the University much of the time, busy with his recruiting work but he had always returned to continue his studies. Then suddenly one day he said goodbye and went off to join the troops, telling me that this time he would not be coming back. He wasn't the only one: plenty of my friends, including Dennis and Matani, went off to fight in defence of their people. My cousin, Samson Muzuri, joined too as one of the political leaders of the movement, giving up his post as professor at the University. My decision whether to become a fighter or not became extremely difficult as I felt I should support my friends. I considered joining the AFDL but there was the issue of how many sacrifices our family should make and who should look after the rest of the family, especially Noah's wife and children who had just arrived at the refugee camp and had not yet found a more permanent place to live. I started counting the losses within my family: Oreni, Gadi and Ndabananiye were dead, Antichoc had lost both legs while fighting, Ndoli was still heavily involved and leading the movement, Samson Muzuri was actively involved in the movement, my nephew Butoto had recently joined, and we still had no idea what had happened to Noah in Burundi. So, joining the AFDL became an extremely difficult decision. On the one hand, I felt that if I didn't volunteer to fight I would be letting down friends who had volunteered, particularly as I had encouraged them to go through my mobilisation and awareness raising. On the other hand it was going to be extremely difficult for the family who needed some survivors in the younger generation to support them in their old age and to continue the clan.

I finally decided not to join the fighting but, like the others, I no longer felt that study at the university was worthwhile or important.

It felt like time to leave and, when I was called by Ndoli to meet him in Kigali, I packed up my things and left. At this meeting, I saw Laurent Kabila, now a well-known person to me because, as well as having heard about him from Ndoli, he had been interviewed on the BBC World Service. He was at this time just the official spokesperson for the movement. When I saw him I was not hugely impressed. He did not offer an opinion of his own and gave the impression of being rather shy; I wondered why he was there and what we could achieve through him. I thought he had lost touch with the new developments and was not ideally suited to the task but had agreed to be involved because of his own ambitions.

However, in November, as the rebellion was becoming successful and starting to gain control of the East, two senior officers in RPF went to Uvira and had a brief meeting with Ndoli and Isaac to ask him if he would agree to making Kabila the head of rebellion rather than just spokesperson. They made it clear that it had to be a careful choice. Ndoli agreed. He felt he was the right person to lead the movement considering his vast experience and the way they had worked together so far. Kabila was not only a military man. He was also a very competent politician and incredibly eloquent in several languages including Swahili, French and English.

By this time Isaac Rumenge had become the military operations secretary. He was asked to draw up a written document of this agreement which they all then signed. In this way history was made. Though no-one could know it at the time, Kabila would go on to become the president of the Democratic Republic of the Congo (DRC) though at that time he was a little-known exile who had fled to Tanzania in the 1960s. He had been contacted by the small RPF group that headed the operation in the Congo and brought back to head the liberation movement because we needed to avoid the misconception that our fight for freedom was an attack by outside forces from Rwanda or Burundi. We wanted it to be clear that our struggle was about defending our own people in our own country rather than an attempt by our tribe to dominate the others. Kabila was not from our tribe but he had a history of opposition to the dictatorial Mobutu regime and so could symbolise unity for other

Congolese people besides Banyamulenge. In him we hoped we had a leader who would be perceived as "really Congolese" and therefore a legitimate figurehead for a national movement towards freedom from dictatorship. In years to come we would realise we had made a terrible mistake in giving him our trust.

Meanwhile, Mobutu's troops continued to commit atrocities. Not content with the expulsion of Banyamulenge from South Kivu, they then started on the Bibogobogo area. They massacred thousands, including women, children and old people. Villages were burnt and cattle stolen. Though I did not get news of my close family, who were in a different area, I heard that my mother's brother, Pastor Rabani Mushapa, had been stabbed to death while looking after his cattle in Nemba, a very isolated area. His body had not been recovered which for my people is even more serious than death itself: the person continues to be in a state of dying until his body has been laid to rest. He was a man respected by everyone in our community as a wise man full of goodness and compassion, someone the whole family and community looked up to, always the person they relied on in difficult times. This was precisely why he was targeted: in removing him, they had removed a pillar of our Banyamulenge society. I felt heartbroken by the news of his death and knew that it would be a terrible blow for my mother. I so wanted to comfort her and share her loss but I had no way of communicating with her.

Uncle Rabani's family were amongst the deportees who were treated the most cruelly. Violently attacked and forced to flee their hamlets, this group of people from the Bibogobogo area had no choice but to walk down the mountains towards Lake Tanganyika. On the way, they were attacked, beaten and tortured again. On reaching the village of Kabela on the shores of the lake, some were killed while others were forced to board an old boat, hoping to reach Burundi. In the middle of the lake it sank, drowning all on board. Those who had stayed on shore, including my cousins, Uncle Rabani's children, were packed like sardines into an old lorry and taken to Uvira. Many died before getting there but the few survivors were deported via the Ruzizi Bridge.

By this time I was in despair. It seemed to me now that there was simply no point in living this way, without freedom. Freedom was something worth dying for. At one point, despite the earlier decision I had made to remain a support for my family, I decided to return to the Congo to join the fighters. I was actually on the list of new recruits to be taken to the training camp. At this stage there had been some good progress: the southern part of South Kivu had started to become much more secure. This was all thanks to the efforts of our troops who had become aware that Mobutu's murderous regime was corrupt and consequently weak and unable to put up great resistance. So for a time we were optimistic.

Unfortunately, differences between RPF officers and the Banyamulenge leaders arose. RPF officials intended to relocate all the Banyamulenge community to Rwanda so that the operations could continue without more causalities or victims. This was shocking news for Banyamulenge commandants like Ndoli. At this point, he regretted not having been clearer about his intentions earlier. He realised that at the beginning he had never clearly stated to the Rwandans that for the young Banyamulenge who joined RPF, their priority in returning in Congo was to save their community and preserve their way of life. Maybe if he had communicated this initially, disagreements could have been clarified before. RPF senior officers simply did not understand our culture and our philosophy of *Iwacu* – how our lives, home, families and land are intricately bound together. We could not abandon the land where our cattle had thrived, where we had planted our *Umuvumu* trees to represent our spiritual relationship with a particular area that had supported us and witnessed the birth of our children.

When Ndoli informed the RPF leaders that it was not possible to relocate the Banyamulenge, there was friction. The Rwandan leaders felt that their authority was being undermined by young people they had trained. With this reaction, we didn't seem to have the numbers to maintain our current military advantage and we began to realise that we could no longer rely on our Rwandan friends for support. A disappointing political fact was becoming more and more obvious. The new Rwandan government was willing to offer a safe haven for refugees but it did not want to be involved in protecting communities over its border. Now they were no longer rebels fighting for justice but an internationally accepted government, they could not be seen to be supporting groups in other countries just because of their ethnicity. Their main concern was the regional security issue and potential threat to the new Rwandan government. It seemed like a betrayal to us because thousands of young Banyamulenge had helped to liberate Rwanda and stop the genocide there, some even sacrificing their lives in this fight for freedom. In the process, they had come to think of Rwanda as their nation, a homeland for an ethnic identity that had been divided by artificial borders. The Rwandan government, on the other hand, could not see itself as a tribal homeland along ethnic lines. Having just experienced horrific divisions and even genocide, it was being rebuilt as a modern state that encouraged integration and friendship between all its citizens. As a modern state, it must respect its borders; where there was injustice in neighbouring countries, that should be for those countries themselves or for the international community to deal with.

The Banyamulenge felt let down when Rwandan support was withdrawn: we had fought for justice for people in a country that was not officially our own and we now expected them and the international community to help us in our time of great need. People were being persecuted and murdered simply because of their ethnicity. In places, especially in North Kivu, this had expanded to include other races who had become "Rwandophones", speaking one of the dialects that together formed a language family originating in the Rwandan area. We Banyamulenge felt that, quite clearly, this was an injustice that should be recognised and stopped by all nations, including the Rwandan government.

In this disagreement with the RPF, Ndoli, Gakunzi, Rugazura and Nicola Kibinda, head of operations, tried to continue. They took their men to fight for the town of Fizi where my uncle Rabani Mushapa had been murdered. They did not have enough troops and, as they surrounded the town, Nicola was shot and killed. After this, morale was low and we began to lose a lot of our troops.

Following the death of Nicola, Ndoli ran into difficulties working with Kabila who had been told, falsely of course, that Ndoli was planning to get rid of him. Ndoli reassured him, saying that there had been some differences with RPF senior leaders and that the rumour must have grown from that. To sort matters out, Kabila invited Ndoli to visit him where he was based in Goma. This involved my cousin taking a journey that could make him vulnerable to senior officers of the RPF who were not happy with him. A close friend in the RPF advised him that the best route to take would be via Rwanda rather than by boat through Lake Kivu and he took this advice. Unfortunately he was arrested anyway and put into prison.

When I heard about this, I was devastated. Ndoli was like a brother to me and I felt for his suffering but it was more than that. He was also the leader in defending our people against attack. Now it felt as if security and peace were further away than ever. Laurent Kabila carried on the fight and made gains in Eastern Congo. He was no longer the quiet man I had met in Kigali. He spoke to the media about the movement as if he had initiated it and his confidence as leader grew when many areas fell to our troops. He was very sorry to have lost Ndoli and, on one of his short trips to Kigali, unsuccessfully requested his release.

Under Kabila, the fighting lost some of its Banyamulenge focus and came to be seen more as a general rebellion against Mobutu. The international media remained unaware of what were the initial causes of the conflict. For us, having lived through all that had happened, some of the interpretations were ludicrous. It was particularly disturbing when we heard reports that seemed to interpret the massacres as simply "tribes killing each other".

A final blow to my morale came with the sad news of the death of my good friend Tokos. This young man, who had always been so inventive and full of fun, had effectively drunk himself to death out of depression.

CHAPTER 29

Uganda

I WAS VERY WORRIED ABOUT NDOLI but had no way of contacting him, not knowing exactly where he had been taken. His loss was a blow for our forces and, on top of that, there was the doubt about how much support we were getting from our former allies and it no longer seemed to me that we were winning the war.

As a result, I changed my mind about volunteering to fight in the Congo. Tokos and Gakunzi had both stressed to me that there were other ways to help my community to survive, other routes towards peace. I was very concerned that my people might remain the voiceless oppressed because the international media was in many ways misinformed and superficial; misrepresentation by the media could mean the UN would never get to understand that the root cause of the conflict in the Congo was the historic and on-going oppression and persecution of the Banyamulenge. My fear was also that we had reached a point where we simply could not continue to stick our necks out for our heads to be chopped off. We had an army that would continue to defend us but the war was causing suffering to everyone, the innocent as well as the perpetrators. I felt this cycle of violence should and must stop somehow for sustainable peace. I concluded that I could do more good by publicising what was happening and how it had all begun rather than by going back to the Congo. The Banyamulenge needed international recognition before they could succeed.

I contacted a friend, Charles Murama, who had been a law student in his second year at university until, like me, he found he could no longer concentrate while atrocities were being committed against our people. Together we decided to leave the relative comfort of Rwanda and go to Uganda, to get away completely from the war zone to a place where we could find another approach to the international media. We knew it would not be easy as we had no money and did not speak English, the language of the educated elite there; we knew we would arrive as just two more asylum seekers amongst thousands. Still we hoped we might achieve something. We set about selling as much as we could of what we owned to raise some money and were soon on a bus for Kampala with all that was left of our possessions and around $400 between us.

Not knowing anyone there, we were obliged to sleep in the streets but this seemed like a minor discomfort compared to the suffering of our people as they fled their homes in the face of war. Our money was used as sparingly as possible to buy food and, not liking the traditional Ugandan food, (Banyamulenge being notoriously discriminating in their eating habits), lived on a diet of mainly chips with ketchup that we bought from takeaway stalls. We could not bring ourselves to join the queues of refugees, mostly people from Darfur and Sudan, who waited patiently for hand-outs. Our money kept us going in this way for about a month and when it ran out we went to report to the United Nations High Commission for Refugees. Instead of being protected we were handed over to the police who promptly arrested us. We then became asylum seekers in prison. However, being in a police cell meant we had shelter and that wasn't as bad as sleeping rough on the streets. Having experienced the violent and extremely aggressive Congolese police, we were very pleased to find the Ugandan police less hostile and even willing to engage in conversation. At that time I didn't speak English, the official language of Uganda, but, like us, they knew Swahili as well as their own tribal language. Unfortunately, we continued to dislike the local food (though I have since come to like it) so when we were given meals we just picked at the beans even though we were very hungry. As a result, Charles became ill. A week later we were released and found ourselves back on the streets.

One of the policemen had given us a few Ugandan shillings out of kindness and he wasn't the only person who helped us. When we went to the Kampala Pentecostal church we met a Rwandan woman who was working with a project to help refugees. As soon as we told her we were Banyamulenge she took pity on us and let us stay in her home; within a week of our leaving the prison, she had become Mamma Odette to us and treated us as if we were family. She had four children of her own but her husband was away on business. There was another woman who helped us too; I believe she had Burundian origins though she now had Ugandan nationality. Strangely enough, she never told us her name, presumably because she wanted to distance herself a little and not become too involved. She had an administrative job working for someone of high status in the post office and she let us use a telephone to make international calls without charge. She had been able to tell by our appearance and our accents that we were Banyamulenge and, knowing what horrific things had been happening to the Tutsi, helped us as much as she could. These weekly phone calls were very important to us, our only link with our friends in Kigali who kept us up to date as much as they could with all that was happening.

One Sunday, when I was at a local church without Charles, I met a young man of twenty-six called Amar who worked for an organisation called Overseas Development Institute. He was an interesting, highly educated man, having taken his degree at Oxford University. We got on well together because he was a fluent French speaker, a Swiss citizen. We had many deep conversations and discussed politics together. I told him about the situation in Congo and he, being Sri Lankan, told me all about the Tamils and the civil war in his country. As our friendship developed, he invited me to move in with him, even though he had been warned by Ugandan colleagues, where he worked in the Ministry of Finance, that people from the Congo are thieves and he should never entrust his key to a Congolese refugee. I thought a great deal about this stereotyping. I didn't see how people could generalise about the inhabitants of a country that has more than sixty million people, more than four hundred ethnic groups and so little infrastructure that the various communities have little contact with each other. There is such diversity within the Congo that it could even be argued that some people are more like Europeans than other Africans. So it seemed illogical to me to think that all Congolese could be thieves or any other particular type of person. Anyway, my friend took no notice of their warnings and was keen to have me share his home.

Charles didn't mind me leaving him because we were both starting to feel guilty about how much we had taken from Mamma Odette and this move would make one less mouth for her to feed. My new home was a comfortable, two bedroomed modern house in a compound with four other expatriate homes. I hardly saw Amar during the day because he was busy at work. Having more time myself, I volunteered to help with the housework but he refused, saying I was there as a guest and he had someone else to do the work. In the evenings he would cook and then we ate together. As well as discussing politics and serious things we shared jokes; he was a good mimic and made me laugh imitating famous people we knew. He had good taste in music and introduced me to a lot. Though he didn't like pop music, he helped me get up to date with the modern world by telling me about groups such as the Beatles, Abba and Queen. It was good for me to have this chance to be updated because I was not in touch with the news of popular culture in the western world. For example, I was a bit embarrassed when I knew nothing about Princess Diana's car crash, something that shocked the others so much that they gathered in the compound to talk about it. Uganda is in the Commonwealth so there is a lot of English influence there but I knew very little about the United Kingdom and the Royal Family.

Perhaps the most memorable experience I had with Amar was when he paid for me to go camping with him in a national park called Mburo. I felt completely at home camping because of my lifestyle as a boy and nothing was new to me in terms of the many animals we saw. What was totally new for me was seeing how the expatriates, mostly Europeans, reacted to this situation. I could not speak their languages but it was interesting to watch how they behaved. Their timetable was full of things that just seemed like everyday life to me, like waking up early to watch the sunrise or spending the evening looking at the moon and stars. Didn't they see the sky all the time where they came from? How could something so ordinary be so fascinating? Then they would organise meals where everyone brought something to share, which seemed odd to me as this was something that just happened in my community without any organising. It was a bit more understandable that they wanted to go and see the lovely scenery and animals but I was puzzled why they then had to write down their experiences as if they were in some way remarkable. My impression of these European tourists was that they had a child-like, wondering outlook on the world.

Overall, Amar was an inspiration for me. I was impressed that he had risen from a humble background and taken his studies so far that he now had a worthwhile and influential job. I felt I should follow his example and take my education as far as possible. I knew I must get back to my studies and was making steps in this direction: I had even taken an examination through a French Canadian charity in the hope of being selected for a scholarship in Canada.

Every week I went to the Kampala post office to phone contacts in Rwanda to keep us updated with the news. I was always hoping that somehow someone might have found out what was happening to my parents and friends but there was never any word of them; there was absolutely no way of communicating with a village as remote as that other than by actually walking there. With what we learnt through the phone calls and with our intimate knowledge of the history of the conflict in the Congo, Charles and I took every opportunity we found to publicise what we knew. Whenever we could, we explained to international agencies about the Banyamulenge people and how ethnicity was the root cause of this war in Congo. Then, one Friday, Charles and I went to the French Cultural Centre to speak to a journalist we had met. We started to tell him about the massacre of Banyamulenge at Bibogobogo but he wanted details on something more recent that he had picked up vaguely on Gahuza Miryango, a BBC radio channel broadcasting in Kirundi and Kiryarwanda; he wanted to know about the massacre at Kalemie in Shaba. I felt panic grip my heart because I knew this was where Musirimu went on business and I had heard nothing at all about it. I raced as quickly as possible to the post office. Our friend could see how distressed I was and immediately gave me the phone.

I managed to reach one of my contacts in Rwanda and she confirmed that terrible things had indeed happened but it was old news, these terrible things had happened months before. I was trembling and could feel my heart thumping as I waited for her to give me details. And then the blow came: Musirimu had been killed at Kalemie and his body had never been recovered. He had just signed a large business contract there and intended to continue to Lubumbashi and Kinshasa to join his son, Jean Jacques. His high status had not saved him: he had actually been arrested on the plane and taken away. After being tortured, he was tied up, put still alive in a large bag and then thrown into the river Lualaba. The news was particularly shocking because I had always believed that the extremists would never attack a man of Musirimu's standing. He was not only a kind and wise man – he was someone who would stand up for the rights of anyone, whatever their ethnicity, and he had always campaigned for peace and understanding between the different ethnic groups. Like his father before him, he had promoted education and civil rights for the highlands of Itombwe, hoping that one day we could be integrated into society as a whole. He had rare qualities of leadership that our people could not afford to lose. Because he had opened his home to me and been a father figure for me, I grieved Musirimu's cruel death and the complete disregard for his dignity in death more than the others I had heard about, but he was only one of many. By now, most of our outstanding leaders had been wiped out; these were the men who had tried to combat hatred and promote friendship. In addition, many ordinary people, including some of my friends, had been killed and Ndoli was still in prison in Rwanda.

This terrible state of affairs left both Charles and me in deep despair and we also felt guilt: guilt that we were not fighting in the Congo to defend our people as so many of our friends were. Charles could stand it no more and decided to return whatever the risk. He had been feeling for some time that he should no longer continue to depend on Odette for support and this was now the last straw. In my case, I was still hopeful that I could achieve more by staying out of the Congo. By this time I had learnt that I had passed the examination I took through the Canadian charity and was hoping to get a university place in Canada. So we decided to separate after so many shared times together. We had been really close, as our personalities seemed to complement each other. Where I tended to make contacts with people who could help us, he had a way of making friends with people who might otherwise be hostile. In this way we were a partnership and survived quite well. As our clothes became more and more worn, we shared them between the two of us. 'You stay here because you have the promise of a grant for your education,' he said. 'You can continue the campaign through the media but it doesn't need two of us. I'm going back.' He was gone within hours. I remained, though it wasn't easy to set my mind to anything other than the dreadful events in the Congo; I was tortured by anxiety for my family.

I needed something to set me on another path and I found it in an American I met, a man called Charles Evans. As my friendship with him grew, I found myself inspired by his lifestyle. He was over sixty and had lived in Africa for twenty years, the first fifteen as a volunteer working with Food for the Hungry and teaching vulnerable children, and the last five years as a missionary and aid worker. His family in South Carolina supported him financially and he lived frugally. His house, in Kampala, was reasonably comfortable with three bedrooms but he shared it with all sorts of needy people, victims of various extreme situations, such as orphans and refugees. Charles was the very opposite of the corrupt international aid agencies I had become so disillusioned with – those corporations that seemed to pour their wealth in directions far from the people truly in need. He simply helped everyone he could and shared all he had.

This gave me a new way of thinking. I realised that pleading for the rights of my people was not the only non-violent approach I could take. My people had been victims, but victims too have a role to play in promoting the rights of the downtrodden of all ethnicities. Through our lifestyle we should show the world that every individual has the right to a decent standard of living. I wanted to live like this man, crossing racial barriers and helping anyone in need, in this way showing the world that my people are good and can be part of a better world.

I had another reason for thinking positively at this time. There was wonderful news from the Congo! In April 1997 my cousin-brother Ndoli was released from prison and by May 1997 our troops had advanced the full 2000 kilometres to Kinshasa and overthrown Mobutu, who fled to Togo. The country was renamed the Democratic Republic of the Congo (DRC) and Laurent Kabila became the new president. This heralded for us a new age of peace and freedom and there was joy everywhere, not only in the new DRC itself but all over Africa. Mobutu had been one of Africa's greatest dictators and his downfall symbolised hope for a better future. Suddenly the name "Banyamulenge" took on new meaning and became famous all over the continent as a symbol of strength, courage and endurance. In East Africa there were buses (*motogari*) given that name. In Malawi it was now the name of a football team to signify victory throughout the season. In Kenya, not only was there a hip-hop song but, in Nairobi, many shops put up signs to warn thieves and burglars, 'These premises are guarded by Banyamulenge'.

On a personal level, I was absolutely overjoyed that Mobutu's thirty-two year reign had come to an end. Throughout my whole life I had lived under his tyranny and oppression, aware that danger from his militia might be lurking anywhere in my country. Now my cousin Samson Muzuri was part of the new government. I was convinced that a new age of peace and development was about to start for my people.

In this positive state of mind, I started to think of heading back to Rwanda. I was confident I would find some kind of humanitarian work there and then perhaps later I might get the opportunity to go back to University and finish my degree. Also, I wanted to help my sister-in-law, Anna, who was in Kigali struggling to bring up her four children without my brother Noah. When it became clear that the Canadian scheme had come to nothing, I made my plans. Charles Evans and Amar gave me money for transport and I went back to Rwanda.

CHAPTER 30

Back to Rwanda, the country of a thousand hills

MY BROTHER NOAH REMAINED a bit of a mystery to me. In retrospect, I realise he had become mentally unstable but at that time I was rather puzzled. I still didn't know what atrocities he had witnessed in Burundi and I was only just beginning to suspect that his strange silence at our last meeting was somehow connected with what he had suffered. The whole family lost touch with him completely for about two years and then, quite unexpectedly, he appeared in Kigali in 1996. Apparently he had stayed some time in Bujumbura, the capital of Burundi, and had managed to save enough money to set up a business in Kigali, importing construction materials. He had sufficient money to organise a comfortable house and good schools for the children; all seemed well until he announced that he had business in the Congo to attend to. His destination was exactly where the war was at its bloodiest, in North Kivu. It was as if he were attracted to danger and unable to accept his responsibilities to his wife and seven children. His wife, Anna, who had always been such a good sister to me, struggled to cope alone but, without a regular income, the money soon ran out. She moved in with distant relatives who had a ramshackle place in the bidonville (shanty town) and it was to here that I headed when I left my comfortable home with Amar in Uganda.

Going back to Rwanda felt almost like going home. Congolese Rwandophones like me, rejected by the country where they were born, sensed the pre-colonial links and cultural and linguistic similarities we shared with the Rwandans and felt at ease amongst them. Unlike in the modern Rwanda, the Banyamulenge maintain a strong family system based on clans and, knowing my ancestors had come from the area that is now known as Rwanda between two hundred and fifty years ago, I spent some time tracing my roots there. I was particularly interested in the name of one of the hills in Kigali city: Kukarugira, meaning Rugira's hill. Rugira is my brother Noah's surname, given to him in respect for my grandfather's grandfather. Rugira's son, Kayira, had led his people away from drought and famine to the Kakamba area of what would later be known as the Congo, searching for good pastures. He became their king but his kingdom remained attached to that of Rwanda even after the borders had been established. This historical closeness, along with the fact that we had fought so hard to end the discrimination and genocide of 1994, made Banyamulenge people like me feel part of the new Rwanda. Unlike in many African countries, there was no great issue here over citizenship. The new ideology was to reject tribalism and rights based on ethnicity; the official policy of the new Rwanda was inclusion for all who considered themselves Rwandans or from a Rwandan background historically.

In this new Rwanda, thousands of young Banyamulenge went to university and began the reconstruction of a new nation. They did this with great enthusiasm and commitment because, before the 1996 war, they had never had the opportunity to help much with development in the Congo where they had faced constant discrimination. Aware that they were part of an "under-developed" part of the world they had felt the urgent need for change and made tremendous efforts to gain education and contribute in lifting Rwanda and DRC out of poverty. They constantly found their way barred and, wherever they tried to go, doors were closed. The small number who had succeeded in advancing themselves had generally achieved this through a few well-placed bribes or by being on friendly terms with an influential person. The result was that by 1994 the total of Banyamulenge graduates from the Universities in the Congo was less than 250 and very few of these had found work in their own country.

My brother Noah was one of the many who left his homeland to find a teaching post. My cousin Samson was another example. He gained a degree in the Congo in 1983 but could find no work there and, instead, went to Rwanda where he became a teacher. He taught for eleven years there and, having been very active politically throughout, had expected to play a significant role after the RPF victory. This did not happen because, even though inclusion was the official policy and security was given to all, integrating the Congolese to posts of responsibility was politically sensitive. Though they recognised a clear moral obligation to provide safety and citizenship for Rwandaphones rejected by the Congo, Rwanda's leadership structure was developing fast and the government was trying to accommodate "international leadership standards". To recognise a strong bond because of ethnicity with people who had arrived from another country would put them in an embarrassing position. As a result, people with cross-border identities were not often offered posts of responsibility.

Still, this was a minor problem compared to what was happening in the Congo and we understood that not everyone could be part of the leadership of the country. Many people were needed to operate at a professional and technical level so the Banyamulenge came into their strength in Rwanda. For example, in the aftermath of the genocide, Banyamulenge played a big role in establishing justice systems and supported the country in promoting unity and reconciliation. On a cultural and artistic level they were noticeable too, particularly through our love of song; the African music heard in Rwanda now became influenced by our melodies and we gained a reputation for being good musicians.

Though I felt at home as soon as I reached Rwanda, I was also apprehensive because I knew this time I would not be able to live in comfort but would be staying with my struggling sister-in-law. As soon as I reached Kigali, I headed for the big bidonville (shanty town) where I knew the family was living. What a depressing place! It was a neighbourhood of makeshift homes, put together with any available materials, things people had managed to salvage from rubbish tips or derelict buildings. Many of them were joined, propping each other up, and all were vulnerable to heavy rain. Practically everyone who lived in this area of town was without work and, consequently, without an income. They lived hand to mouth, each day a struggle for survival, a search for the basic things they needed, like food. Some sold charcoal to make a little money. Children were half-dressed and always hungry. Very few children could go to school because there was no question of being able to pay the small fees that were always necessary for school enrolment. With no health care yet available and malnutrition widespread, many people looked ill, especially the children.

Seeing all of this made me even more concerned for Anna and her children. I asked after her until I found a child who knew her and was happy to lead me to her home. The family were overjoyed to see me and it was a very emotional meeting; I soon became Papa Mudogo a title often given to a young man who has taken on fatherly responsibilities, as uncles often do. It was a relief to find that the depressing neighbourhood had not destroyed their positive outlook on life. As before, I found Anna to be a remarkably resilient person, always bright and smiling. 'Don't worry,' she would say, 'we will get by somehow! We didn't survive all that suffering in the Congo to die of hunger here. We have known worse than this!' The children had been close enough to the atrocities to know exactly what she meant. There was consensus too on the issue of school: even if it meant going without food, Anna would find the money for school fees. It was a priority because education was the way to escape this dead-end way of life. Previously, when he had his business in Kigali, Noah had paid for very good schools, but now they were reduced to the cheapest in a poor neighbourhood, a school that could offer only very basic facilities and teaching. This hit Felix, the eldest, particularly hard because he was a bright boy hoping to excel. Still, the children were always well behaved and polite, understanding without complaint why they had so little. 'It's not like it was before,' Anna would tell them. 'We are almost like refugees now. We can't expect a high standard of living. But one day it will be alright again!' At times she worked days on end at a coffee factory for just a few dollars but she wouldn't allow the children to beg. 'Poverty is in the heart, not in pockets!' was another of her sayings. The children understood and were discreet to the point of making sure that they were always home at meal times, even if there was no food; they had to make sure that neighbours would not suspect they were not eating.

I knew I could go and live with Kayitare in the South, but there was really no question of leaving my brother's family while they were living like this. I thought of a few ways of helping. I had an electric piano, a very unusual asset in Kigali, that Charles Evans had given me. I rented it out a few times and then sold it. This kept us in food for a while as we only ate once a day. To cover the school fees, I kept approaching Noah's friends. On one occasion I noticed a rich man who needed to transport a lot of wood from his compound but who couldn't find a lorry driver. I told him I knew someone who could do the job and said I would find him for a little commission. In reality, of course, I didn't know any lorry drivers but I was determined to find one and eventually succeeded. It wasn't easy because most of them didn't trust me because there were so many people who, like me, were trying to find money. Anyway, I succeeded in getting some commission both from the lorry driver and the rich man. Later, after I had become friendly with a vet called Jean Paul, I did a little work with him in butchers' shops testing meat; my work wasn't at a very professional standard but it helped the financial situation. Still there were times when there was simply no food. If the children had gone without a meal for two days, I would take the younger ones to a restaurant owner I knew. He was a sympathetic man and would come over to me away from other people, to save my embarrassment. 'I'll pay you next week,' I would promise, showing him the hungry faces. I always managed to keep my word so he trusted me and helped me in this way whenever I asked.

The depressing life of the *bidonville* was made a little better by the thought that at least the war was over in the Congo. Mobutu was no longer the dictator and we had a government, which included some Congolese Rwandophone people. My cousin Samson was one of these and he was soon to be made ambassador to Canada. Some Congolese in Canada challenged this nomination of a Tutsi to such a prestigious post but President Kabila's decision was firm. It gave us hope because it demonstrated his willingness to include capable members of our community in the leadership of the country.

But then something terrible happened. On 12 September 1997 there was an aeroplane accident that cost the lives of twenty-five religious leaders who had been on their way to organise a big conference on unity and reconciliation, reuniting various groups after the conflict that had gone on for so long. This tragedy was an enormous blow to our community. To us, these leaders were our "eyes" who would lead us in the right direction through this difficult time of crisis. We had already lost so many of our important people but now these twenty-five men of peace were all killed at the same time. The tragedy of their death was amplified by the fact that there were no bodies to bury because they had been totally destroyed in the crash. This meant the relatives and other mourners could not "wash their hands" together after the burial in the customary way. Instead we could only join together in groups, gathering especially around any relatives of the deceased. We still held a washing hands ceremony but it was sad that there had not really been any dirt to wash away. Our grief was beyond words and the traditional mourning period, usually just over one week, was extended to two. Throughout this time, people of our community gathered together to console each other and joined together in song to pour out their feelings: *Mwami wacyu waturemye uturinda umujinya wa satani, uturindira muriy'isi ishaje. Nubgo twahuye nibigeragezo, n'ibibazo byo mw'isi, wagaragaje ukuboko kwawe. Ishimwe niryawe ishimwe niryawe yesu*, which means, 'God of creation, you have spared us from the devil's anger, you have always protected us in time of darkness in this old and cruel world. Even when we have encountered extreme struggles, you have shown your hand to us your people. Praise be to you, praise be to you!' On the final day of mourning, we dressed in our best clothes, which for some people meant our traditional way of dressing. Then the streets and churches rang out with our singing.

Budagu came to stay with me during this time, as he often did. He was still living at the university in the south of the country because he had continued with his studies there. Being a naturally quiet person, he had missed me and felt rather isolated when most of us left so he was always happy to see me again. For my part, I had a lot of things on my mind that I wanted to share with my friend: I felt guilty that I had not helped physically in the fighting in the Congo, I was upset that I had interrupted my academic career by leaving my studies and I was constantly worried about money and the state of poverty I lived in. Budagu cheered me up, assuring me that I had lost nothing and that I still had a great deal of potential. Budagu had a high regard for me and wanted to protect me; like Tokos, he encouraged my self-esteem by reminding me that I had my baccalaureate certificate and telling me to take pride in having chosen an alternative route towards searching for better life. Together, we talked about our friends, such as Busoka, and wondered what had happened to them since they returned to the Congo – whether they had survived the war and, if so, what they were doing now. We dreamt of a better world and how we could play our part in creating it. He was always an inspiration to me, especially with his opinion that the basic cause of all the violence and social conflict we had experienced was the result of poverty; as individuals we should work towards getting ourselves out of this trap and working towards change. We did not agree about everything but we always enjoyed our discussions.

Being with Budagu made me feel so much better too because he reminded me of my Banyamulenge home and our traditions there. Amongst our people, status was earned by the number of cattle owned, level of integrity, wisdom, honesty, sincerity and respect for elders and moral values but this did not really create a different social class: we all lived under the same conditions, eating the same food and dressing in similar ways. We were proud of our ancestors and culture and never felt divided by social class. Here in Rwanda though, there were marked divisions and living in the bidonville made me feel like the lowest of the low because status depended on wealth in the modern sense, the ability to live a westernised life style. This could change with an improvement in financial opportunities, like a good, steady job or good business transactions or access to higher education. To some extent this sense of social class was based on traditional attitudes because there had always been a king and a system of leadership.

Generally speaking, the current sense of social class had more to do with the tendency in all African societies for people to disassociate themselves from "bush" life. With the arrival of the colonialists, towns with modern homes and facilities grew up and people who lived this new lifestyle employed servants to do the manual work. Educated, successful Africans came to share this European kind of lifestyle, where prestigious jobs are distanced from manual labour and respect for hard physical work is lost. Traditional values are then forgotten and village Africans seen as a lower class. When I lived with Kayitare, none of this had affected me because I had been a part of his family and benefited from his position in society. Now however, I had no stable family connections in town, no financial support, no job, I came from a remote village in the Congo and I lived in the bidonville.

I knew that my only way out of my hardship and depression was to find a job. This meant living a double life: I had to keep myself reasonably well dressed and presentable and keep my address a secret; I could not search for professional work as a virtually homeless person. My dream was still to find work where I could help other people and, at the same time, earn enough to support Noah's family and myself. Rwanda still faced enormous problems with thousands of street children, orphans of the genocide. It was clear that there was a lot of humanitarian work to be done and I set about finding work for myself but it was not easy. With no money I couldn't even pay for public transport while I went looking. Having to walk everywhere was hard because it made me even hungrier and I had no money for food. I spent most days walking long distances without food, hoping Anna would have enough when I got home.

As usual, I had certain survival strategies I used, particularly in making useful contacts. One person I made friends with was Vincent, a high level Information Technology (IT) technician who had been responsible for setting up the first internet system in Rwanda just the year before. The web was not widely available: only in his office of "Rwandatel". He introduced me to it and gave me my own internet address. Having been trained by him in this way, I used the Internet regularly in his office. About a month later another internet connection was set up in Kigali Institute of Technology (KIST). As I walked around Kigali looking for work with the United Nations and other aid agencies, I would call in at KIST to check my emails. Only students and lecturers were allowed to do this but I managed to get past security.

Being able to do this was important to me as it was my only means of communication. I was able to keep up to date with news on the Internet and send emails. There was still no Internet in the Congo but I kept in touch with Gakunzi in Uvira through his satellite phone. I was still trying to spread the news about the growing threat of a human disaster in the Congo, hoping to help avert it. While it was generally considered that most territories of the country were liberated from Mobutu's regime and a new leadership was in place, there were still many pockets of anti-Banyamulenge militia groups in the eastern part of the country. They continued their ambushes and attacks on many innocent civilians. Kabila's regime seemed to be trying its best to restore security and peace but I was still very concerned about what was happening.

Seeing I knew how to access the Internet, students would often ask me to help them open their email or show them how to surf the Net. I was more than happy to help because I shouldn't really have been there but making myself useful made my presence seem legitimate. Most of the lecturers were Indian expatriates so did not recognise me as an outsider but assumed I was either a student or a local employee. The students obviously thought I was a technician. In fact I was so welcomed by everyone that the security guards did not ask to see my identity card and I could go and access the Internet whenever I wanted. Even better, I was invited to eat with the staff, on the assumption that I was one of them. I couldn't have wished for more: I was no longer hungry and I had everything I needed to access the information I needed to apply for humanitarian work.

It was while I was doing this unofficial work at KIST that I became close to my new young veterinary friend, Jean Paul; we liked to talk about the world situation and our hopes for the future. I didn't tell even him, though, where I was living and just how poor I was. Eventually I got a job with an Italian Non-Government Organisation (NGO) called Cooperation Italienne Nord-Sud. It meant leaving Kigali but their base was not far away and I would be able to return at weekends to help Anna. Most importantly, I would be earning and would get enough to cover my accommodation as well as to give some to Anna.

CHAPTER 31

Becoming a humanitarian worker

A HUGE CHALLENGE FACED RWANDA as it tried to move on after the genocide. The numbers involved in the tragedy were so great that the usual process of justice was not practical. Thousands of people had been accused of being implicated in the murders and more than 120,000 had been arrested, accused of genocide. An international tribunal was established but could not be the only solution to the problem: it was estimated that, using this system, it could take 160 years to judge 450 cases of genocide. Obviously another approach was necessary, an approach that would coordinate the various organisations involved – governmental and non-governmental, international and local. For the government, the priority was to eradicate the system of impunity, the idea that atrocities could be committed without individuals being blamed. Impunity had been endemic since the 1950s under the previous government but now it had to be eradicated once and for all, otherwise the cycle of violence, which had its roots in recent history, would continue.

To counteract it, a new approach was taken, an approach that was innovative but had its roots in Rwandan culture. Called by its traditional name, Gacaca, it was based within the community rather than just in higher, western-type courts. Traditionally, Gacaca had meant that victim and accused would "walk the green path" to a neutral place where a group of elders would judge their case in front of the whole community. Often the issue would be resolved on the journey because it facilitated dialogue. The modern approach recognised the value of dialogue between victim and accused and kept the main format. There were some changes; for example now there were twelve respected people (including women) and a chairman to organise the procedure but it all remained at community level. It was important to facilitate dialogue amongst ordinary village people to promote unity and to recognise traditional values and customs that could be involved in the process. Prisoners were encouraged to openly confess their crimes and ask pardon for them in front of the whole village and community. Those who did so were eligible for dramatically reduced prison sentences and the victims who pardoned them found their sorrowing and suffering greatly relieved.

The job I was given through the Italian Non-Government Organisation (NGO) was work of this nature in the Kibungo and Umutara regions, an area that had been severely affected by the genocide. At first our office was based at Gahini, a two-hour drive away from Kigali. Previously it had been the headquarters of the Anglican Church, a base for missionaries working in the country. There was a large hospital and an orphanage set up by Swiss people. Now it had become the main headquarters for the humanitarian efforts in the region. It was one of the most beautiful areas of Rwanda, on top of a hill overlooking Lake Muhazi and right by Akagera Park. Our water was pumped up from the lake as the main water supply had not yet been reinstalled after the violence. It was an idyllically lovely setting and I felt very lucky to have been given accommodation of my own here for the time of my short contract. Being on the border of Kibingo and Mutara provinces, I was centrally placed for projects in both areas and not too far away from Kigali to attend meetings there and visit Anna when I had a chance.

Very little of my work was in the office. It was mostly out working with villagers. I had two drivers who took me to various places. Cesar took me to Kigali when I needed to attend official meetings or conferences involving NGOs and government agencies, but Alfonse preferred trips into the bush. He liked to chat to villagers while he waited for me to do my job. Sometimes I had to go to places that were inaccessible even to four-wheel drive trucks and for that I was provided with a large Honda motorbike. Considering that I was visiting places where the Tutsi had been massacred, this was a risky thing to do but I didn't really think about it at the time. Perhaps that was because the danger I was in seemed so much smaller than what my friends in the RPF faced, or perhaps I was just so carried away with the thrill of driving a motorbike in this amazing landscape. I knew some aid workers on motorbikes had been ambushed; trip cords could easily be set up over the track.

The hours were not set and very often I worked through the evenings. It was important to respect local customs and fit in with what would suit the villagers. This was not difficult for me because, coming from an isolated rural community myself, I could readily accept their traditions though some were a little different to my own.

I learnt a great deal myself and gained an insight into the huge social problems that enveloped the country in the aftermath of the tragic genocide. My responsibility was to coordinate humanitarian efforts in the area, included promoting reconciliation between various ethnic groups, helping refugees and survivors to integrate back into normal life, and encouraging socio-economic enterprises that would allow the vulnerable survivors to become self-sufficient as regards providing for themselves and their families. It was hoped there would be long-term benefits in improving agricultural methods through advice and financial support or loans. At the same time, I was involved in meeting with the local communities that had been in conflict to debate the sensitive subject of reconciliation along the lines of Gacaca. A future for the community needed to be outlined, a way for the various groups to continue to live and work alongside each other.

One specific project I was involved in was helping widows' associations by giving them the means to reach a little social and economic stability. Another project was to introduce a new breed of milking goats to the region. The goats were of an Alpine Chamois species and the idea was that their milk would provide valuable nutrition. Unfortunately, the people who thought of this project hadn't realised that traditionally goats are not highly regarded in that area and could be seen as an insult to local people, despite their nutritional value. I had a hard time convincing my Italian colleagues of the social implications because it was so clear to them that goats were an ideal solution to the food shortage. Eventually, I managed to convince them that, for the project to succeed, we needed to lobby the government to publicise the benefits of goats' milk. We invited a high-ranking government official and the regional governor to come to a public ceremony where they would drink some of the milk publicly and show their enthusiasm for it. From there we publicised it more to raise awareness of its value. The people began to accept the idea of drinking it but only under certain conditions, in particular that it was just for children. The adults refused categorically to try it, not only for cultural reasons but also because the goats had come from France, a country that was considered to have contributed towards the genocide by having given arms to the Hutu, the declared aim being defence against the insurgent RPF. Consequently, milk from French animals was seen to be in some way impure. But at least we managed to help the nutrition of orphans in this way because the orphanages accepted the idea. To get over the cultural problems, we also began to consider crossing the alpine goats with a local breed: this could produce animals better suited to the terrain and climate as well as causing fewer objections from the elders.

We also used the new goats as part of the reconciliation project. Five were given to each family on the condition that the first three offspring would be given to other families with different social problems or ethnic backgrounds. By promoting this sort of interaction, we hoped to encourage dialogue between various groups, leading to cooperation and mutual assistance. It was an initiative that took into account Rwandan tradition where the gift of an animal, whether a goat or a cow, was a symbol of offering help in unity and friendship. At the ceremony when the gift was given, the people assembled would share the customary drink of *Urugwagwa*, while one of the elders gave a speech reminding everyone that the customs of the ancestors were based on such friendship.

It gave me a lot of personal satisfaction to be able to work on such worthwhile projects; helping people in this way diverted my mind to some extent from all my personal problems. Being in the invigorating mountain atmosphere made me think of my home and sometimes, as I tried to help the local people, it felt almost as if I were helping my own village. It certainly gave me plenty of ideas about how life at home could be improved.

CHAPTER 32

Genocide in the Congo

THERE IS AN AFRICAN SAYING, 'If you can't defeat your adversary, treat him as a brother'. It was known that Kabila had been brutal during the Mulelist rebellion of the 1960s; in fact many Banyamulenge had been victims of this, so perhaps we should have known we could not trust him. Still, we treated him as the leader because it was generally assumed that he had changed during his 36 years of absence from the country and we saw him as someone who could unite the various tribes of the Congo. He undoubtedly owed his success and power to the Banyamulenge so we thought he would be loyal to us. Once he became President, however, his secret hatred became obvious. Using us to win his position was one thing but protecting our interests after his success was totally different: we had only been his brothers for as long as he needed us and now his previously-hidden hatred was out in the open. It began with an announcement that all RPF officers who were still in Kinshasa after the victory of May 1997 should leave the country and go back to Rwanda. The Rwandan RPF officers left the city but Congolese Tutsi officers assumed the order did not apply to them. So a small number of Congolese Tutsi troops that fought alongside the RPF stayed in Kinshasa along with a considerable Tutsi civilian population. Then a sort of media campaign began, led by one of Kabila's leading cabinet ministers, Abdoulaye Yerodia Ndombasi. Radio and television began to pour out xenophobic ideology encouraging hatred of Tutsi and urging people to hunt and exterminate them throughout the country.

As a result, the violence began again and throughout the whole country the hunt was on for Banyamulenge. By the end of July 1998 there were savage massacres. In Kinshasa, Tutsi were rounded up by Kabila's soldiers and then locked up, burnt alive or starved and threatened with death in the Kokolo military camp. Through phone calls with Ndoli I learnt that many high-ranking people who had been given posts of responsibility in the new government had been murdered. The Minister of State, Déogratias Bugera, a Tutsi from North Kivu was missing assumed dead. Others had escaped but my cousin Samson was not one of them: he was still in Kinshasa and his residence had been surrounded by Kabila's soldiers.

Kabila's most faithful followers were his military from Shaba (Katanga), his own area. Confrontations between these soldiers and Banyamulenge soldiers were becoming routine. In addition, Kabila was encouraging tribalism, creating a general hatred towards Tutsi to the extent that ordinary civilians could be attacked, robbed and murdered and soldiers could be targeted by their own colleagues. Watching television reports and listening to the radio, I was plunged into extreme anxiety. I heard Abdulaye Yerodia, the then Minister of Foreign Affairs, describe all Tutsi as "vermin". Mwenze Kongolo, one of Kabila's associates who had previously been the Minister of Justice, said Tutsi should suffer the same fate as the Jews in the Second World War. These outbursts brought back to me the sort of thing I had heard with Ndamage when we listened to Rwandan news before the genocide of 1994.

On Saturday 2 August 1998, as an act of self-defence, a group of Congolese Tutsi soldiers regrouped in Goma with the intention of attacking Kabila's murderous regime. From Ndoli I learnt that the Uvira region was unsettled too but that, so far, things seemed to be under control there. The leader of the defence force there was Gakunzi and he seemed to be in a strong position.

Also on 2 August, there was an attempt at resistance by a group of Banyamulenge soldiers who had stayed in Kinshasa. At Tchatchi, a few kilometres from the city centre, they built a barricade of tyres and then set fire to it in an attempt to protect themselves and the Tutsi civilian population. It was a drop in the ocean. There were only 200 Tutsi soldiers against thousands of Kabila's loyalists. Their attempt lasted only a few hours before, out of ammunition, they were forced to make their escape into the bush and along the River Congo. Their act of defiance led to further orders to hunt and kill Tutsi "snakes" and so resulted in further atrocities. More Tutsi were "exterminated" by various armed groups who allied themselves to Kabila's loyalists.

Television showed images of corpses dragged through the streets as the killers sang and danced in jubilation. It was just like what had happened four years previously in Rwanda.

Who could stop all this savagery? Who could bring light to this huge country whose inhabitants seemed to be condemned to an endless cycle of violence? Victims of a history that was full of hatred and atrocities? It seemed to me that the Congolese people were the victims of history, condemned to hatred and oppression first by the colonials and now by their own leaders.

On 3 August, I went to the office to use the phone there. There I found one of my bosses, a UN expatriate from Mali, Dr Marko Ousmane, who was surprised to see me and asked why I had come. My excuse was that I needed to finish off a report on one of the humanitarian projects and he took my word for it. As soon as he left me alone, I tried to contact Kinshasa for news of my cousin Samson and managed to get through to someone who was able to tell me that, though many Tutsi in Kinshasa were missing and assumed dead, Samson had managed to leave his house and find shelter in one of the hotels in the city, the Intercontinental. This was something of a relief but there was still plenty to worry about.

While keeping the report on my desk in case anyone came in, I was listening to the news from Kinshasa on the radio. Towards midday, I learnt that President Kabila was continuing his murderous policies. Through the Ministry of Information he had given the order to exterminate 20,000 Banyamulenge who lived in Vyura in the Shaba province. Two mass graves had been discovered at Kisangani. In Lubumbashi, Tutsi corpses lay scattered along the main roads of the city. My heart was beating fast as my panic grew. My head ached from lack of sleep and I felt as if I were living in a nightmare.

At about two in the afternoon I tried to contact Uvira. The only way of doing this was by satellite phone but my cousin Ndoli in Uvira had one. He didn't answer and, very worried, I also tried Gakunzi but I couldn't get him either. I knew my old friend Isaac Rumenge was now a superior officer in Uvira but, as far as I knew, he had no phone. For a while I was stuck, not knowing what to do. I thought of Busoka who was also still in Uvira, never having left it. In order to survive, he had joined the defence movement and, because he knew the city so well, had gone on to play an important role both in gathering information and in the general development of the war of liberation. Unfortunately, I couldn't reach him either. Because I had heard about all the victimisation of Tutsi elsewhere, I knew there must be something wrong so I kept on trying to make contact with people. Eventually I managed to get hold of someone I knew – he had been a businessman in Uvira – in the refugee camp at Bujumbura and was told the worst. 'There's been outright, violent war in Uvira', he told me but he had no details.

At this point, my anxiety and frustration reached such a point that I slumped onto the desk in front of me, banging my fists repeatedly on it in an attempt to relieve my pent-up feelings and hold back my tears. Dr Marko rushed in to see what the noise was all about but I said as innocently as I could, 'Nothing, nothing at all – it's just that I accidentally knocked a few things over and I'm picking them up.' He accepted my excuse and left suspecting nothing.

But my feelings at that point were nothing compared to what I was about to experience a few minutes later when, trying again to reach Uvira, I finally managed to contact Ndoli. He was struggling to speak through his grief and anger but he gave a brief summary of events, probably feeling some relief at being able to share the burden with me. Apparently, Gakunzi, as leader of the military operations in the Uvira region, had been rather too trusting. Being by nature more of a peacemaker than a man of aggression, he had remained confident that what was happening elsewhere in the country could not happen in the region he controlled; he was sure he would handle the situation. He had a good relationship with his second in command, Herode, who, like Kabila himself, came from Shaba province. When Herode was ordered by Kabila to get rid of all his Tutsi mililtary, Gakunzi went to visit him with some of his officers, including Rujo, Isaac and Ndoli to sort the matter out amicably. Herode was perplexed. He couldn't see any reason for attacking this friendly minority and found himself in the tricky position of needing to choose whether to obey orders from Kinshasa and organise the non-Tutsi tribes to kill Banyamulenge or whether to work with his friend Gakunzi to bring peace to the area. He chose the latter, at least while he was in the presence of his friend but it was probably a case of *uzapfire mumaboko yabandi n'amaraso yawe ntakambeho*, meaning 'better your blood should be on someone else's hands than on mine'. He probably accepted that he would have to obey the President but would rather leave the job for someone else to do so that he wasn't personally responsible.

As the Banyamulenge officers left the house thinking they had sorted out the problem, they came under fire and Gakunzi's two bodyguards were killed, one of them a young Bigurumwami that he was very fond of. It was unbelievably horrifying to see these two young men killed just a minute or so after a peace agreement had been made. Isaac made a quick escape over the fence surrounding the house but the others were captured. At this point Herode intervened, still torn between his promise to maintain the peace and his orders from Kabila, so the officers were released. This was very lucky for them and quite probably a case of "not yet the worst day" – that is to say, a fearsome beast let them pass this time knowing there were other dangerous beasts ahead.

Gakunzi ordered commander Rujo to evacuate the civilian population as soon as possible while he and Isaac took military control of the centre of the city and its main road. He put Ndoli in command of the lakeshore right into the centre of Uvira, a distance of about five kilometres. All of this defence strategy was with only seventy Banyamulenge against hundreds of soldiers from other tribes loyal to Kabila and suddenly converted to anti-Tutsi extremists.

Rujo gathered together the endangered Banyamulenge community and did all he could to protect them. Amongst them were my uncle Zakaria and his wife who were both ill and had come to Uvira to be with their son, Ndoli, and to get treatment. My aunt was still unable to move and was also suffering from memory loss and difficulty in communicating. Sometimes in extreme conditions of war, people who could not save themselves were simply abandoned but Rujo organised men to carry my aunt. She herself was in great pain and begged them to leave her to die but Rujo insisted on helping her for Ndoli's sake.

Some Tutsi civilians met by the River Kalyamabenge to head off towards the mountains. Another group from the Catholic area of the city were ambushed and slaughtered. Gakunzi had been alerted to this ambush but could do nothing as he was busy leading the fighting for the main road. It is almost impossible to imagine such an atrocity happening in a big city right by the football stadium and a primary school but it did happen. Among the hundreds killed there was Gerevazi who had taught me how to strengthen myself to endure discrimination and hardship; without his informal lessons I might not have survived those early years in Uvira.

Ndoli managed to maintain his area and eventually reached a place close to Gakunzi and Isaac. Between them they managed to hold half the city despite being so greatly outnumbered. When they had advanced as far as the General Hospital, just opposite the Societe Muafrica, an enemy soldier hidden in a drainage ditch shot Gakunzi. He died on the spot and Isaac, who had already advanced towards Kakungwe, returned to make sure that the enemy wouldn't take the body. He also phoned Ndoli, asking him to come as quickly as possible. It was a terrible shock for them both to see their companion and fellow fighter lying in a pool of blood after so many years of struggle together. It was also demoralising for them all to lose their commander in this way but they knew they must carry on to defend themselves and to defend innocent citizens. They were back in action in less than twenty minutes, having organised the removal of their friend's body.

Ndoli had taken the satellite phone from Gakunzi's body to see if he could contact Banyamulenge military elsewhere and ask them for support but unfortunately it was encoded so he couldn't use it. There was nothing they could do but return to the fighting. Then, about 400 metres from the hospital, Isaac found himself surrounded by soldiers who were hidden in various places. He was shot in the legs so could not move to get away. Severely wounded, when he saw the enemy approach, he shot himself in the head to avoid being tortured or taken hostage.

As he told me all this, Ndoli's voice was broken and at times he had to stop to compose himself; as I listened, I could feel my throat tighten and the tears well up in my eyes. Isaac was a fantastic young man of great integrity. As well as being extremely intelligent, he was so tall, muscular and handsome that when I stood by him I felt like a little boy. Everyone looked up to him literally as well as metaphorically and girls adored him. I had first met him when I became "Jimmy". We had shared ideas of how the future should be and he had always been willing to fight for justice. Along with Ndoli, he had been at the heart of the struggle for peace and the rights of our people and now he had been killed at almost the same time as that other great champion, Gakunzi. Their loss would be severe not just for their families and friends but for all of our people.

With all this terrible news I could no longer hold back my tears and I was glad that Dr Marko had left. I didn't feel I could tell him or anyone else I knew. My head was thumping by this time and I felt empty inside. I just stayed in the office and then went to a bar at the Dereva Hotel in Rwamagana. As usual, I travelled on my large Honda motorbike with its UN number plate marking me out as someone important to be treated with great respect. One of the waitresses approached me immediately, asking if I would like to sit inside or outside. I didn't answer but I stayed in the garden. Another waitress came and asked '*Murafata iki*' meaning 'What would you like to drink?' In my grief I felt oblivious to all that was going on around me, alone with my eyes red. I felt I should be there with my friends, Jean Michel, Myriam and Jean Paul, but at the same time I knew I couldn't tell them what had happened. I found myself becoming preoccupied, reflecting on why I was perceived to be important and consequently treated so politely by the waitresses. I thought about the huge gap between the "haves" and the "have nots" and how that flashy UN motorbike had earned me such respect. It wasn't me personally that people respected but my image and their perception of me as someone important enough to work for the United Nations. When the day came that I had no work and no motor bike, I would get the same slow service as everyone else.

Next day I went to work as usual. The terrible news was something very private and I could not share it with my boss; I made no mention at all of events in the Congo. Nevertheless, though I was physically present in Rwanda, my heart and mind were in the Congo, all my thoughts on what was happening there. I did my job mechanically, going to Kibungo in the morning to visit a water purification project. In the evening I went to a big party hosted by expatriates in one of the wealthier suburbs of Kigali. It was an important affair with many influential people invited, including international journalists, so I really wanted to go. I went with Jean Claude and Myriam as arranged and found everything was beautifully done with delicious food and vibrant music. My friends did not know why I could not find the enthusiasm to dance and I tried hard to be sociable and act normally. However, I could think of nothing but catching up on news from the Congo and I left very early to get in touch with Ndoli, to see if he were still alive.

I couldn't reach him but I managed to get a lot of news from other people. The majority of Banyamulenge people from Uvira had managed to escape into the mountains and they had kept with them the bodies of Gerevazi, Gakunzi and Isaac. This was a great relief to me, not only that most people had escaped but that my three dead friends would be given a traditional funeral: for my people, to lose the body is a double death. I also learnt that in Kinshasa a lot of Tutsi had managed to find refuge in the Belgian Embassy which was close to where most of them lived. Those who hadn't managed to reach it were being stripped of all their belongings, beaten, arrested, interrogated and then tortured to death in one of the military camps in the capital. I could get no more news of Samson.

Not returning to the party, I kept all of this within myself and told none of my friends. Life carried on as normal. On 6 August, I had planned to meet with Jean Michel, Jean Paul and Jean Claude for a Swiss fondue breakfast; later Jean Paul was going to take us to eat *maini* (cow kidneys) near the Magerwa bidonville for lunch. However, I had heard that there was a refugee who had escaped the Congo and was now living in Kichuru near to Kamina. As his home had been in Kamina, I hoped to get news of some of my friends in the military academy there. These were Dennis and Severin, close friends from the course at Rushashi and two others, Mattieu and Matani. All four had left university to enrol in the military because they felt that this way they could help to bring stability to their homeland. Because they were university students, they had been selected to attend the military academy at Kamina.

I met the man and the news he had for me was horrific. At the Kamina Academy, the Tutsi had been singled out and herded into one building that was packed with explosives. Once they were all in there, the building was blown up and not a single person survived the explosion. My four friends had all perished this way. I couldn't stop thinking about how I remembered them. Matani had protected me like an older brother, particularly that time when we were ambushed at Nundu. Severin had made us laugh throughout our time at Rushashi with his constant jokes. Dennis was always so affable and friendly, getting on well with everyone and befriending Hutu students too. Mattieu, quiet and steady, was one of the older students at the university and had nearly finished his degree in economics when he volunteered. All were gifted young people with a bright future ahead of them.

I learnt later that this act of genocide, which never became recognised internationally, was instigated by Laurent Kabila himself. His own personal, presidential unit, the *Forces Spéciales d'Intervention Rapide* (FSIR) was stationed in Kamina and had been ordered to do it. They then continued by arresting any Tutsi military officers and some of their associates in the nearby town of Kamina. The President knew well that, in eliminating these trainee soldiers and other Tutsi military, he was cutting off the "head" of the Tutsi defence.

From this time onwards, like other Banyamulenge activists, I did all I could to alert our community and also the international community to the strong probability of a forthcoming systematic genocide. The signs were evident but what to do about it was not so obvious. Consequently, those of us who spoke of it were dismissed as complaining alarmists. Yet what had happened in Kamina and elsewhere over the previous six days represented the start of a planned and well-organised genocide.

The international community remained deaf to our calls for help and neighbouring countries such as Angola, Namibia, Uganda, Rwanda, Zimbabwe decided to protect their own home security and financial interests in this mineral-rich area. Within weeks, the international media was viewing the conflict as a second African war rather than recognising the underlying cause as the victimisation of a particular ethnic group that had itself been brought about by the historical mismanagement of cross-border identities by successive governments. To the world, it became a war involving six nations and the genocide was allowed to continue. The western countries had taken the conflict out of its historical context. Their response failed to understand the historical injustice that had created the dehumanisation of one group of people.

The tragic consequences continue until this day. "Cross-border" people have repeatedly found themselves at the epicentre of violent conflicts arising from the unresolved questions of cultural and ethnic identity. All of these problems have their roots in the superimposed borders, an issue which continues to plague Africa.

CHAPTER 33

My family experiences "Africa's World War"

THE LAST TIME I HAD HEARD anything of my brother Noah, he had been in one of the most dangerous zones of Lubutu. This is a very remote area, extremely difficult to reach and, as a result, almost totally beyond government control. Rich in gold, diamonds and coltan, a mineral much sought after for its use in electronic devices such as laptops and mobile phones, the region had now become a battlefield for its mineral resources. There were at least three distinct groups of militia fighting there – the Mai Mai, the Simba and thousands of Interahamwe, the militia who had committed the genocide in Rwanda – and all of them wanted to control the area so they could exploit its mineral wealth. Each of the factions was autonomous and imposed its own laws, far from any central government control. They inflicted unimaginable atrocities on the local population with impunity. Along with torture, pillaging and extortion, other horrors were on the increase, such as the systematic use of rape as a form of warfare. Every day the insecurity seemed to grow worse.

Knowing how dangerous this area was and not having heard from Noah for a while, it seemed highly probable that he was dead. Then dramatic news came that someone had seen his body. There was no way of confirming this information because we couldn't go into the Lubutu forests to find him ourselves and there could be no official identification when so many bodies were concerned. A few weeks later, we were told that, though the body resembled Noah, it was not definitely his. As he had been missing for a considerable time and had been inside the danger zone, we were mentally prepared for the worst. Still, I didn't want to pass this sad news on to Anna and the children.

To try to find out more, I went to Goma and stayed there for two weeks. From my university days, I knew someone who worked with an Iranian transport company that conducted a lot of business between Kisangani, Bunia and Lubutu. I managed to get a place to stay while my friend arranged for me to spend my days in the radio communication centre to hunt for news of my brother. By sheer coincidence, one of the employees there told me he knew Noah and he was in the middle of the Kisangani forest near to the River Congo. I could find out no more though and returned to Kigali.

The news about my cousin Samson Muzuri was better. I heard from an undisclosed source that he had managed to escape to the French Embassy where, as a diplomat, he had been given sanctuary. Knowing he was on Kabila's death list, the French were perplexed about how to get him out and kept him there for ten months. Obviously they could not take him to the airport or by any of the normal routes out of the country so he simply stayed with them. Of course I was extremely relieved to hear he was still alive but I could not be completely reassured knowing that he was still in Kinshasa. Furthermore, I couldn't really make a lot of enquiries through my NGO contacts because that might attract attention and alert Kabila's regime to his whereabouts, which had to remain secret.

I could not get my cousin off my mind and had great difficulty sleeping: I seemed to be counting every minute and every hour until I could get reassuring news of him. Then, after a few days of anxious waiting, I heard that he had been smuggled out of the country by the French Embassy and had reached Brazzaville, the capital of the neighbouring Republic of Congo. Finally I was able to talk to him on the telephone. His voice was low and he sounded desperate after his experiences. He had abandoned all his possessions and had no money to get himself out of Brazzaville, which is so close to Kinshasa that he would never be safe there because a death squad could easily reach him. He had to have the money to get out and asked me to get it for him. Obviously, I had nothing like enough to pay his travel costs but I contacted some of his previous colleagues who had managed to escape the massacres. Having been in similar danger themselves, they identified immediately with his problem and sent me the money but, by the time I had managed to raise it, Samson had made other contacts and managed to escape to Goma.

It was by now December 1998 and I had no idea what was happening in the village with my family. When I had spoken on the phone to Ndoli in Uvira, I learnt that my father, my brother Bonfils and my cousin Kenasi were all in the Lulenge jungle looking for pasture for the cattle, as usual in the dry season. This was worrying because, since the outbreak of the second war in August 1998, the number of nationalist Mai Mai militia in the east of the region had multiplied dramatically. They took advantage of the remote jungle areas to attack the civilian population. Now the conflict had escalated to the extent that it involved six African nations and more than a dozen rebel groups. The country had become a battleground for all sorts of conflicting business interests because of its mineral wealth. Angola, Zimbabwe, Namibia, Uganda, Rwanda and Burundi were ostensibly involved to establish security in the region but for some it was actually to defend their financial interests. Some had signed financial agreements with Laurent Kabila and were afraid that, if the war continued, they might lose their investments. Therefore they felt bound to be involved, whether for or against Kabila.

The Mai Mai militia consisted mostly of Babembe, Bafulero, Bavira, Bahunde and Banande men and boys. Their initial aim was to exterminate all the Rwandophones and specifically the Congolese Tutsi as well as to resist incursions from any Rwandan armed forces or rebel Congolese groups perceived to be allied to the Rwandans. Sometimes, though, they acted just as brigands, pillaging and stealing. In the main, they were directed by warlords, traditional tribal chiefs, village chiefs and local political leaders. They lacked cohesion and political ideology and were largely invisible to the outside world. Some groups were allied to government forces. They were, in effect, a localised defence force supported by the Congolese government so that they could oppose any armed conflict from Rwanda, Uganda or other hostile groups.

Kabila had armed them but had very little control over them because this area of the country was so inaccessible. Virtually unchecked, they continued to commit violent atrocities: sexual violence, pillaging, arbitrary killings and targeted killings at quite an advanced level. There was a high incidence of forced recruitment of children to help commit the violence and attack Banyamulenge villages and herders. These vicious militia groups became and still are terrorists who circulate freely but, because they have never attacked white people, as with El Shabab in Somalia, the international community shows no interest in them.

For this reason I was constantly worried about my family and friends herding in that remote area. There was no way of communicating with them and the only way of getting news would have been to go there myself in person. Some time after Ndoli had told me about them being in this dangerous area, I then heard from someone else that my father and his group, along with other men from our village, were in a place called Mugisanga and that this zone had been attacked. Various reports were confused and unclear and it was difficult to know what had actually happened so I went to Bujumbura in Burundi to get the details.

There I received terrible news. On 3 September 1998 in the early hours of the morning they had been attacked by the Mai Mai, one of the worst militia groups whose main purpose was to exterminate the Congolese Tutsi. My father, always the one who slept lightest and awoke first when there was danger, heard distant noises and woke up all the other men. Within minutes they were being fired on with machine guns and the little huts where the calves sheltered were alight. Trying to get the animals out, my father was aware of bullets whistling all around him. With everything ablaze, the men had no choice but to run into the forest, not even having time to get dressed first. Some were killed but others hid in the forest, still naked. My father was confused. No longer a fit young man and with blood pouring from his head, he assumed he had been shot because he had difficulty moving. Kenasi, who shared a very close relationship with my father because he was the eldest son of my uncle Zakaria and there was not much difference in their ages, was desperately trying to help him. Telling him to lie down and keep out of the way, Kenasi used his old rifle and tried to fight back. This ancient weapon was of little use against so many enemies using AK-47s. As dawn approached, Kenasi uttered his last cry and fell dead.

With Kenasi's rifle now silenced, the Mai Mai thought they had killed everyone and turned their attention to the cattle. They left, taking all the animals with them: 3,700 in total and including 103 belonging to my family. Sebatunzi and Elisha, our neighbours, and my brother Bonfils had survived unscathed as they had all managed to hide in the forest. Luckily also, my father's wound was not as bad as feared: it was caused by a tree branch and not a bullet. However, he still could not really move and he was completely devastated by the loss of Kenasi who was the closest person to him in the family. The two of them had been almost inseparable. Bonfils and the other two men then decided to follow the Mai Mai to try to get back some of the animals, leaving my father to do his best to look after the dead. Though he had very little strength left, he managed to find the men who had been killed and covered their naked bodies.

It wasn't long before the three who had followed the Mai Mai were forced to retreat. They had come under fire again and it would have been suicidal to try to do any more so they were forced to accept the loss of all the herds. The priority then was to look after the dead. The death of their clansmen in this way was a loss beyond reckoning. Though older people like my father still remembered the rebellion of 1965, my clan had never suffered such a huge loss as this. Being in the middle of nowhere, they had no tools to dig a grave and no way of taking the bodies back to the village. The best they could do was to cover their dead comrades with whatever they could find and then offer prayers for them. Then they left them on the edge of the forest in this lovely setting where they had spent so much of their lives. They made the long, lonely walk back to the village in silence.

Not only was it terrible to have left their fallen comrades there, but it was also strange to be returning without the cattle. These herders live their lives in symbiosis with their cows. For my father it was the first time in his life he was without any. His cows were not just animals but also his companions. They were almost like people with their own family history, personalities with cultural and psychological differences. This on top of the death of his nephew was such a terrible blow that he said, if it were not for his Christian faith, he would have had to kill himself because he could see no point in living. His strong faith gave him comfort in the thought of a life after death.

When they arrived back in the village the following day, there was shock and despair. My soldier nephew, Butoto, the son of Kenasi, simply could not accept his father's death and the theft of our cattle and decided to go back with Bonfils. My father did all he could to make them give up the idea, saying that he didn't want another tragedy in the family but they were so fired with anger that they ignored him and went to find the cattle. They set off on their long journey but were caught in an ambush at a place called Kwakagembe. Butoto died instantly, meaning that in just a few days my family had lost both Kenasi and his son Butoto!

The whole family fell into a state of deep despair. Most affected was Kenasi's wife. She had lost her son Ndabananiye during the war in Rwanda and now she had lost her husband and their son Butoto. My mother, who still didn't know if Noah was alive or not, found her thoughts of what had happened to Oreni and her brother Rabani flooding back, and was in such despair that she could hardly speak. She still had vivid memories of the violent attacks of 1966 when many men were decapitated in Kugatongo village. Now, with so many of the family scattered to different places, her main anxiety was whether this was finally the worst or if more deaths would follow. Like my father, she wished that they were no longer alive to witness these terrible events.

But even this was not the end of the horrors. A few months later, just after the funeral and mourning ceremonies for Kenasi and Butoto, my lovely cousin Nyakanyambo was murdered. Though I remember her best as a little girl, a younger female relative that I felt naturally protective towards, she was by that time a married woman with three children. She had gone to get food in the market at Mumikarati and, on the way back, had the bad fortune to meet Mai Mai. Other women heard her frantic cries from a distance but there was no-one who could help her. She pleaded with her attackers, telling them she had a baby that needed her, but they showed no mercy. In their eyes, she deserved to suffer and die and they wanted to insult our family. After they had raped her, they inflicted a long, painful and humiliating death by thrusting knives into her vagina, knowing that to attack the body of a Banyamulenge woman is to symbolically reflect that suffering on to the family and community, inflicting pain and humiliation on everyone.

Thus, of all the tragedies my family had endured up to that point, this particular one involved a shock and reaction that is beyond description. The passage of time has given me the ability to live with the memory of many tragic deaths amongst my family and friends, but this is the one that I find the most difficult to come to terms with. Her name, Nyakanyambo, means pleasant, just and beautiful, and that is how she was. I remember her as a little girl when I was a slightly older boy and we met during those happy times when the children were listening to stories from "grandparents". Even now, I simply cannot bear to think about the sexual humiliation and slow death of this innocent young woman. Whenever I read reports of sexual violence being used as a weapon of war, I ask myself if the world understands what lies behind these cold statistics – real, innocent victims like my pretty cousin Nyakanyambo. She should not be just a number, one small addition to the total: she was a real, vibrant person, full of life and very much loved.

Time passed and there was still no news of Noah, though I returned to Goma again to try to find news. I wondered whether, if he was still alive, he knew what had happened in the family. One story I heard from my friend who worked in Goma was that someone who had known Noah in 1998 said he was supplying food and sundry items to the military camps but that they had refused to pay him because of his ethnicity. It was also said that Noah had suffered such great psychological shocks during the Burundi massacres and the Congolese wars that he was not mentally stable. I continued to wonder and hope.

CHAPTER 34
Child victims

DEVASTATED BY THE FAMILY ISSUES and the on-going violence, I felt that I needed to do something positive. I felt that, having experienced social injustice and violence from childhood, I had three options: either let my problems define me, let them destroy me, or let them strengthen me. Also, I knew I needed to forgive myself and release myself from the constant guilt I felt about not having done more to protect my family or take part physically in their defence. I needed to forgive myself in order to be able to forgive others. I made a conscious decision to use my hardships and terrible experiences as a foundation to give me strength. I knew that I was fortunate to be still alive but also recognised from European friends that the basic right to life is something that is taken for granted in other parts of the world. I decided that my being alive had a meaning and purpose. I was determined that, even if only in a small way, I would make a difference.

Rwanda gave me opportunities for that, especially through my contacts with the orphanages. The genocide of 1994, an atrocity of such amplitude that there had been nothing like it since the Holocaust of World War II, had left an estimated one million orphans. Many of them were traumatised by having seen other members of their family tortured and slaughtered; also, thousands of the young girls had been raped. Throughout the country there were abandoned, orphaned children, some of them trying to care for younger siblings as well as themselves. Through my work with the Italian NGO distributing goats' milk, I came into contact with some of the orphanages that had been set up. In particular, I got to know two very idealistic Swiss people: Jean Louis and his wife Eliane. They had left their home immediately after the Rwandan genocide and invested all their money in a centre for helping young orphans. They began a big campaign to raise awareness of the terrible situation in Rwanda and gained the support of humanitarian aid agencies in Switzerland, managing to convince them to offer financial support to their efforts to help orphans of the genocide. I was very impressed by these people who had given up their comfortable homes and regular jobs to create something of real value for the innocent child victims of the genocide. Their idea was not just about giving temporary shelter and food. They also wanted to establish a vocational centre where the young people could study worthwhile crafts that could lead to longer-term opportunities and economic benefits, thus offering refuge in the short term but also a future of hope. This was unusual for an orphanage.

All age groups were represented. Some were only babies who had been found beside their mother's bodies but, sadly, there was not a good survival rate for such tiny victims and thirteen had died since the centre was established. I remember one healthy baby who really appealed to me because of his unusual character. We nicknamed him Bobo as we did not know his real name. Interestingly, his pale skin suggested that his father was white and I wondered if the father had been rescued as more "deserving of protection". In total, at least 124 children and young adolescents were being supported and each had a tragic tale to tell. They included children who had been soldiers and young girls who had been raped.

Having established the orphanage, Jean Louis and Eliane tried to organise the construction of a big vocational centre but unfortunately they suffered a severe setback. While they were on a trip back to Switzerland, they had left the director in charge but, in collaboration with the construction company, he stole all the funding so that the building work could not continue. At this point they engaged a volunteer from Geneva, Jean Michel, to be the director instead. Other problems also arose, especially in their negotiations with local authorities. It seemed to me that, in their enthusiasm and idealism, they expected Rwanda not only to recognise their efforts but also to react as a European country would, operating in a similar ways. They didn't seem to realise that this was an African country trying to establish itself after the devastation and it would move forward in an African way rather than with Swiss efficiency.

Ironically, the sincere way in which they lived so simply without the comforts other Europeans and NGO workers expected, did nothing to help their cause. Instead, it aroused suspicion and resentment from people less altruistic, who used funds to rent comfortable houses while they worked in the area. Even the Swiss ambassador felt they "brought shame on the Swiss". With so many orphans to support, they needed cooperation from other organisations so this was a problem. I tried to advise them about their public image and how to relate to important people but they didn't take on board what I said. We were soon firm friends and I became very interested in their work, continuing to worry about how their approach was affecting the sustainability of the orphan centre. I tried to make them more culturally aware when initiating contacts with government agencies or local NGOs. They did not really act on this though; instead, it became Jean Michel's responsibility to make the necessary contacts and to manage the centre as best he could.

I became involved in doing some voluntary work for the orphan centre while I was still employed by the Italian NGO and, working together, we all became great friends. Their work really inspired me and we enjoyed many happy times together. These pleasant social times were in contrast to the heartbreaking stories that came from so many of the young people we worked with. Some of them had horrific experiences, such as being involved in the fighting themselves or even of having seen their entire families killed. One such person was Hakizimana, a boy from the Hutu ethnic group, and I heard his whole story as I tried to support him.

Like many other Hutu villages, his was moderate and its innocent inhabitants were therefore seen by the Interahamwe as Tutsi sympathisers who deserved to die. All the other members of his family had been killed by this vicious militia group but he was only taken hostage. As the RPF approached the retreating Interahamwe, they had spotted the boy in the cross-fire and rescued him, keeping him with them until they could find somewhere to leave him. It was a month before they found a temporary place for him and by then the war was over. Like most boys, Hakizimana loved football and it was while he was on his way to play a game with other children that he stepped on a land mine that took off both his legs. It was in this terrible condition that he was first brought to Eliane and Jean Louis;

they took him to Gahini Hospital where he went through various surgical operations over the course of two years.

By the time I met him and was asked to support him, he was about fourteen years old and in the recovery process. He told me that he would like to become a mechanical engineer. This was not an easy career option considering the status of disabled people in the local community and the fact that there was no formal mechanical engineering centre in the surrounding area. Because the area was still officially in a state of emergency, local garages were being used either as military barracks or as bases for UN agencies and were almost impossible for ordinary people to access. I made contact with a military commandant called Rashid who was a senior mechanic engineer in Rwamagana Barrack. I told him about young Hakizimana and at first he was very discouraging. 'Even if it looks like we are at peace, we are actually still at war and anyone who is not a member of the military staff may be suspected as spy, no matter how old he or she is.' I pleaded with him, insisting that Hakizimana had been rescued by RPF soldiers and had nothing in his background that could possibly link him to the enemy. I also reassured him that I would be the guarantor for anything that might happen.

Finally he said, 'I'll take him but please never mention that we have had this conversation!' Then I told him that Hakizimana was disabled and had artificial legs. I was nervous that he might change his mind, but Rashid was so used to seeing such causalities that he only asked whether he would be able to carry out his training in mechanics without disability facilities. Hakizimana completed his practical skills training after few months and went on to start formal training.

CHAPTER 35
Child soldiers

WHILE I WAS AT THE SWISS ORPHAN CENTRE, I had become even more concerned about the plight of child soldiers and decided to move on to campaigning against the forced recruitment of children into armed forces. The practice of *Kadogo* (forced recruitment of children) had been eradicated in Rwanda but I knew that it remained a real problem in the Congo. There they were brainwashed into believing that they could wash themselves in "magic water" and become immune to bullets. The traditional healer or sorcerer would prepare a magic potion and then the new Mai Mai recruits would be tattooed on different parts of the body, especially on parts that were believed to protect sensitive organs such as the heart and brains. Finally, they would drink "magically blessed" water. Those who went through these rituals then believed themselves to be invisible to bullets and other arms such as machetes or spears. It was believed that bullets would just flow down and over the body like water, hence *Mai Mai* which means 'water water' in Swahili. Magic power would, it was believed, destroy the power of bullets and other arms. Other conditions that must be met so that everything could work successfully included maintaining high morale, staying awake and covering themselves with leaves. Many died as a result of their blind faith in magic but the myth continued, especially in the east of the country.

It was with this in mind that, with my friend Jean Paul's support, I set up an organisation called "*Campagne Pour la Defense de Droits des Enfants*" (CADDEORG), which means Campaign for Children's Rights. From the start I realised that the work of the organisation would be extremely difficult, the most important reason being that children and young people are involved in armed conflict not always because they have been forcibly recruited but often because of the environment they were born into.

Most of the children involved in the fighting grew up in extreme poverty whether in rural areas or in the socially divided bidonvilles (shanty towns) of cities. Though some have loving parents waiting for their return, many are orphaned "street kids". While some may have known peace, most grew up with war and violence all around them. In the DRC (Congo), many children grow up as I did, surviving tragic and traumatizing events with many of their basic human needs not met.

With all normally accepted doors towards the future shut, many young people see an alternative way forward through "employment" as sex slaves or fighters with local militia groups. Another option is to get involved in extreme hard labour for exploiting mineral resources. In this work they get paid less than a dollar per day and become part of a long chain of mineral trading that involves corporations. Sometimes it is the parents themselves that send their own children to work in these mines.

Knowing I had nothing to offer these young people as a viable alternative, I decided to work with children before they had been recruited to such degrading work. I was inspired to use sporting activities as a distraction from child soldiering, hoping it could lead to some interesting activities that might enable integration into "normal" life. Sports seem affordable and possible. I had experienced a case where, with only one ball, hundreds of street children came forward and it was an opportunity to pass a on a message of hope. I made contacts with some organisations and a friend called Augustin who worked in the Ministry of Youth and Sports. Augustin assured me that such a project could be supported and gave me some useful contacts to help make this happen.

One of my family, my nephew Butoto, had become a child soldier and had just been killed. Deciding that I did not want this to happen to anyone else from my village, I went to the Eastern Congo to make contact with children in the army. At this time, the East was under the control of a rebel movement that grew up after the second war of 1998 and the Tutsi killings. Having spent time in Rwanda, I was immediately struck by the extent of the devastation that war had brought to Eastern Congo but, at the same time, my experience in the orphanage run by Eliane and Jean Louis had inspired me to question the violence that I had previously always taken as "normal". Like other

Congolese children, I had been born into a system where there was no state institution set up to protect young people. We relied entirely on our family and the church for protection, support and education. Not every child had this support though because the devastation of war had made so many orphans.

It was inevitable that some of them would, for the sake of survival, view warfare as a way of finding a job. Many had little choice but to profit from what was happening in this war for mineral wealth. "Jobs" available included not only being fighters but also being sex slaves to the various militia such as Mai Mai and the Interahamwe, the group that had committed the genocide in Rwanda

Thousands of children had been recruited by various militia groups to terrorise the population, protect the mineral resources and sometimes just to help in the violent struggles between the various groups. Though mostly boys, some were girls, raped and then used as slaves or sexual hostages. Some of the children had witnessed terrible atrocities, even being forced to witness the killing of members of their own families. Their sole means of survival was to make themselves useful to these violent groups to the point of becoming enemy targets themselves and committing vile acts.

I stayed in Bukavu, in eastern Congo where I was lucky enough to meet with some senior military commandants that I knew and who trusted me enough to let me stay with them for a week. Being high-ranking military leaders, they all had about fifteen bodyguards each, including child soldiers. In staying with them, I realised how difficult it was for me as a Munyamulenge and a Tutsi, to work with militia in the bush so I reminded myself that, as they say, charity begins at home, and decided that I should start with contacts and young people that I knew from my village.

While staying with those commandants, I had managed to make contact with some *Kadogo* (child solders) and met up with a Munyamulenge man I knew. One of the commandants offered me his military four-by-four Toyota Land Cruiser and said that I could use one whatever business I was involved in. I was sure that, had he known what I was trying to investigate, not only would he be less helpful but I would have been arrested. As it was, I drove into

Nyawera with his bodyguards and then we sat together in one of the local bars. Here, I got the opportunity to talk to one of the *Kadogos* called Ngarukiye. I was careful because I sensed that, if he did not like my "preaching", he would report our discussion and leave me in a position of mistrust. As I tried to persuade him that his current lifestyle had no future, Ngarukiye challenged me. If he survived the war, he said, his main problem would be whether he could make a living for himself in the Congo where the only source of employment is either in government leadership or within Non-Government Organisations/agencies. 'I am here to find peace, I was not forcibly recruited and as long as there is no alternative I will continue to search for peace,' he added.

After a long conversation with Ngarukiye, I met with another Munyamulenge senior commandant. His name was Serukiza (nicknamed Tambwe) and I had grown up with him in my village of Runundu. As direct neighbours, we had been childhood friends and shared many happy times together. He had first become involved in the violence when he joined the rebellion to defend the community and I had not met him since. When I saw him again, he was just as I remembered him – always laughing and joking. When he was not busy with his radio sorting out his orders, he was keen to spend time with me and talk about our happy days as children back in the village. When I told him about my concern for the *Kadogos*, he laughed and said everyone wished the children could escape this violence but that they had not been conscripted by force. Like me when I was "Jimmy", they had joined of their own free will. I could see that this was not only a difficult subject for Commandant Tambwe but he actually seemed to consider my opinion as impossibly idealistic. He kept interrupting the discussion by checking whether we were safe in the area. When we settled to talk, he was very critical of the idea of disarming young soldiers when there is no other solution for their poverty or ensuring their security in the villages.

Hearing Tambwe and Ngarukiye's comments left me thinking about how all these children had grown up with oppression and extreme social injustice and, when the opportunity arose, they had decided to join the rebels. The process of getting these young people back into a normal society could not really begin until there was a strong government in place that could create a stable, peaceful infrastructure and environment for them. In this context, it would not be straightforward trying to convince individual children that what they were doing was wrong. I managed to persuade some that, contrary to what they had believed, the future did not lie with violence but I always met with the question 'What shall I do if I leave?' Only those who knew they had access to education or another good alternative could really believe there was another way of living.

I went back to Kigali and explained to Jean Paul, who was still trying to get his brother out of the armed conflict, how complex our work was. I decided to go to Uvira in South Kivu via Burundi and, after that, to continue to Luberizi Plain to see a commander called Mututsi but generally called by his nickname, Motomoto. Previously he had been one of my best friends and I had grown up with him. He had been at primary and the first part of the secondary school with me in Minembwe until he was about fourteen and then he joined the RPF. When the war in Rwanda ended, he came back to the Congo to protect his people and he had been with the rebels ever since. He was currently heading military operations in Luberizi.

Luberizi is an incredibly beautiful stretch of land along the river Ruzizi to the north of Lake Tanganyika. Because of its proximity to Rwanda, it was implicated in the war there, particularly in being an area that Hutu refugees fled to. These were accompanied by the Interahamwe, the militia responsible for the genocide. Apart from this, the area had also been affected by the political crisis in Burundi after the assassination of President Ndadaye in 1993. Later it became a notorious killing ground because so many Tutsi were slaughtered there in 1996 and then it was affected by the successive wars of 1996 and 1998

I paid someone to drive me through the Ruzizi plateau towards Ruberizi. The last time I had used this road was back in 1993 when I was Jimmy. Since then the zone had been a battlefield and looked different. The road was now barely visible because, not having been maintained, the vegetation that should have been only on either side of it had now grown all over it. As we travelled, the driver pointed out to me places where there had been recent violence. He also told me that he was afraid the old vehicle wouldn't make the whole journey because many of its parts weren't working properly and it could break down at any time. Suddenly, the engine began to overheat and the driver began to breathe heavily – a sign that he was anxious and afraid that the vehicle might stop altogether. At one point it did stop but we managed to push it and restart it and finally managed to get through the most dangerous part of the journey.

We reached Ruberizi and were greeted by some of Motomoto's rebels, many of whom were young boys of about fourteen or fifteen from my village and very pleased to see me. One of his bodyguards went to find Motomoto and tell him of my arrival but meanwhile I took advantage of the opportunity to talk to these boys. I felt very emotional when I spoke to them because their whole manner and way of expressing themselves indicated that they had lost their childhood prematurely and were addressing me as if they were men. I felt torn as I told them they could get out of this armed conflict whilst at the same time knowing that I had no way of guaranteeing that I could find them an alternative occupation. One of the young men, Rukema, assured me that Motomoto was a man of considerable charisma and determination who was always kind and responsible and never mistreated them. They would all like to see an end to the conflict but first wanted to finish off the *adui* (Swahili for "enemy"). Rukema reminded me of other young people I knew who had died on the battlefield. He reminded me that, if he and the others left, they would have nothing else to do. His father was dead and one of his brothers had just died also. His other brothers did not have the means to pay for his education, the only way he could have access to work in Rwanda or Burundi. While Rukema and fellow Kadogos were convinced by my arguments about quitting, they remained loyal to Motomoto. Rukema kept challenging me with questions such as: 'Why are there so many so-called aid and humanitarian initiatives but not much change?' How can education come before peace? It wouldn't be so expensive to fix the poverty problem or stop the war so why the endless song?'

Our discussions were interrupted by the arrival of Motomoto himself. As he emerged from the bush, he had a frighteningly wild look about him but his smile was sincere and honest and he gave the impression of being a man of determination. He proceeded to assure me that his wild appearance was due to the fact that he lived in a zone of military action and spent his life on the active front. He reminded me that his group were in constant active combat with other militia.

Motomoto suggested to me that we should find a safer place to sit and chat. 'We could be attacked at any time,' he told me. As we walked, he went on to say that the Mai Mai were spreading desolation and attacking the population everywhere. Though it was the Banyamulenge they hated most and wanted to destroy, these were not their only target. 'We can never let them do what they want,' he insisted. Then he went on to tell me that it was not only Mai Mai he had to oppose. The Interahamwe were also in the area operating as three distinct groups: the ALIR (Alliance de Libération pour le Rwanda), the FDLR (Forces Démocratiques pour la Libération du Rwanda) and the *Rasta* (a local word that meant "free to do anything"), a group that opposed the other two.

The place we finally found to sit and discuss was just like that place on the border between Rwanda and the Congo where I had witnessed atrocities. It brought back to me those nightmare memories of that terrible day in September 1996 after Mobutu's government had decided to expel the Tutsi. Then I had watched helplessly as hundreds of people were cruelly maltreated and some even killed, including my friend Kanga. At the same time we had received news of many other killings, including those of Simeon Rukenurwa and the family of my friend Freddy.

Here in this place of tragic memories Motomoto reminded me of why he was at war with the nationalist militia. 'They want to wipe all Tutsi off the map!' he said and then went on to remind me that he had three little daughters and would much rather be busy supporting his family than fighting but he had abandoned his children to follow this chosen path. 'Someone has to make the sacrifice,' he told me, tears streaming down his face. As I discussed the issue of child soldiers, he openly reminded me of the realities in these boys' villages: 'We are protecting them. Their lives could be much more dangerous if they became involved in revenge for their families, like your nephew

Butoto.' he said. He then looked back and brought up the subject of how he had first joined the army during the RPF movement, 'I was a good boy at home, wasn't I?' he asked. As I nodded, he lowered his voice saying 'We were brought into this because of injustice.' Then he took my hand: 'We are separated by war,' he went on. 'I could be killed at any moment but you have a strong chance of living for a long time. Please, if I never return to them, see that my little girls are looked after!' Sadly, a year or so later, he was killed.

Following this, I travelled back to Bukavu again, feeling I needed to know more what had happened with Ngarukiye and his fellow Kadogos. I was relieved to learn that some of the boys had deserted the rebel movement and tried to make contact with relatives.

I went back to Rwanda with a heavy heart, knowing that the situation for child soldiers was even more complicated than I had thought.

CHAPTER 36
Inside NGO work

OTHER SWISS VOLUNTEERS, such as Flavien, Fabrizio, Christian and Michel, joined Eliane, Jean Louis and Jean Michael later, three of them moving on to work in Kigali shortly afterwards. There were other European charity workers too, such as Myriam who worked for a Presbyterian orphanage. I introduced some of my friends to them, Jean Paul and Jean Claude, my old friend from Rushashi, and in this way our friendship group grew.

After my contract with the Italian agency finished in October 1998, I began another job through a community development project founded by the United Nations Development Programme (UNDP). This work was in the same area of the country working with rural and vulnerable communities, trying to encourage modern agricultural techniques and set up centres for the maintenance of animal health services. I was excited about this new posting because it so suited not only my education in agronomy but also my family background. I came from a community of subsistence farmers who had no access to modern agricultural machinery or commodities such as fertiliser, people who worked simply to support themselves and rarely had enough to sell on for profit.

These limitations are one reason why poor countries are unable to escape crises that hit them. One of the Italians I previously worked for had told me in a brief discussion about Europe that farmers there are given subsidies and encouraged by the government so they are able to work many hectares and achieve high production, their crops enhanced by the use of mineral fertilisers that they were able to buy. I felt very strongly that we should be using a similar model so that the country could work towards self-reliance. The World Food Programme supplied seeds and imported food, often in a very poor condition by the time it reached the people it was meant to feed. I wanted a different emphasis with people being given the means and knowledge to get the best possible yields from their farming so that the country could produce fresh food of its own. I felt that funds should be used to help local farmers produce more.

Soon, I found myself in dispute with my Malian boss on the issue of sustainable aid: he seemed happy to continue the current system which encouraged dependence on hand-outs rather than helping people towards an enhanced method of farming that could transform their lives in the future as well as simply help them feed their families in the short term. It seemed to me that the current system was unsustainable. The Rwandan farmers I met often told me that packaging standards put huge restrictions on them, making it impossible for them to access markets outside Rwanda. Also, their work was all done manually, cultivating small areas that could not feed many people. Even if they managed to produce more than they consumed themselves, this relatively small surplus could not compete with the massive industrial production of the developed nations.

Agriculturists in poor countries such as Rwanda will always be outpriced by imported products that were produced cheaply either because the farmers were subsidised or because of mass production. Even more frustrating for me was to learn that my bosses were paid enormous salaries without really trying to find long term solutions to Rwanda's problems: they just wanted to complete the task they had been told to do by the providers of the funds with as little inconvenience to themselves as possible. Furthermore, the project management was frustratingly bureaucratic; for example, a large part of their budget was spent on roadside posters advertising the presence of UNDP; this seemed to me a terrible waste of money. It quickly became obvious to me why these aid organisations were not succeeding in making much difference to the lives of ordinary people and I became disillusioned with my posting.

The project ended after twelve months but I handed in my notice rather earlier to make my protest. Though I felt I had achieved very little during this time, at least I was lucky enough to have the opportunity to take part in the international conference set up to develop a strategic ten year plan for livestock and food security.

No longer having a paid job, I lived most of the time in the bidonville in Kigali. I started to spend a lot of time with my volunteer friends and found work to do whenever I could. Within myself I was becoming more and more confused. I felt torn between various identities to the point where I hardly knew who I was myself. My traditional upbringing meant that I should take pride in myself and who I was, not hiding anything of my past. But I couldn't escape the Rwandan social divisions which, as in other countries, are based on a strong class system.

The public image I cultivated was of a well-educated young man who worked for humanitarian Non-Government Organisations (NGOs) and in this capacity I had links with people in high positions of considerable responsibility as well as friends who were highly educated and westernised, even expatriates. I had to attend important meetings and look the part while, at the back of my mind, was the knowledge that I lived in the slums and was responsible for supporting Anna and the children, On top of this, I was constantly worrying about my family, knowing that the situation in the Congo was continuously worsening.

Intellectually I felt at home with my new friends but privately I suffered depression; I felt tired and angry to be pulled in so many directions. What I earned was not enough to allow me to keep up my social life as well as support Noah's family. Both for work and socialising, I needed to be able to dress in a modern way and to be always smart and presentable. More than that, like most young people, I felt under pressure to present to the world an image of myself that was "cool", to live that life that depended so much on appearances and would keep me seeming "normal" in the eyes of the people I liked and admired. I couldn't let them know my secret life. I never invited any of them to where I lived. This made it difficult for me to have a deep relationship; there was no question, for example, of having a girlfriend. Whenever I was socialising with my friends, I would hide my worries, pretend I was fully at ease with my companions and try to make sure no sign of my private life was visible. To do this, I had to carry myself with confidence, trying to look relaxed while secretly worrying about how I was going to survive and how I could help Anna and the children survive.

I did succeed in keeping up appearances and I shared many happy times with my group of friends, notably Jean Paul, Jean Michel, Jean Claude and Myriam. Myriam worked in a centre for orphans and she was a very caring person, a good listener. Talking to her became a sort of therapy for me as she showed a real interest in and concern for my personal life. She also told me a lot about her background and her hopes for the future back in Switzerland where she came from. Still, even though she was a good and sincere friend and I told her many things, I never told her my closest kept secret about my living conditions and concerns for my brother's family. Perhaps it was because, as we talked about life's problems in general, all that was wrong with the world, my own problems seemed too small to mention; basically, though, I simply couldn't admit to my double life.

One day when I came home from my usual meeting with these four friends, an intolerable smell hit me as soon as I approached our "house". Apparently, our one and only lavatory had broken down completely. These pit toilets are basic constructions but serve to keep disease at bay when they are in a good condition. They are pits dug deep into the ground outside the house and shielded for privacy with banana tree leaves. Branches are used to reinforce the sides and stop them caving in, a simple wooden cover is used over the hole to keep out smells and from time to time something is dropped down to speed the decomposition of the waste. Many of these pit toilets had been damaged during the genocide when bodies were thrown into them and the recent heavy rain had been the final blow for ours. The part that covered the hole had fallen into the cesspit and there was nothing left covering it.

To me this seemed like the final straw. Now, not only did we have trouble finding enough to eat but also we couldn't even go to the toilet! To mend it would need money that I wouldn't have until I had been paid at the end of the month. I was at a loss. I simply didn't know what to do. For me it wasn't too bad because I went out every day but for the rest of them it was intolerable. The smell was unbearable and there was no question of moving anywhere else for at least a few weeks. 'You said everything is temporary!' Felix said to me. He always looked up to me as someone who would know the answer to his problems but this time I could find nothing to comfort him with. At this moment I was devastated by the conviction that Noah's children, so well behaved and intelligent, were losing their childhood. Instead of experiencing in stages the transition to adulthood, they would be obliged to struggle and work simply for the survival of their family.

I finally found someone to confide in when an old university friend, Bienvenu, arrived in Kigali and lived not far from the bidonville. He had given up his studies to go and fight in the Congo but now he had left the army and had work in Kigali as an assistant civil engineer. We connected immediately because he knew all about my background and there was no need to hide anything. 'You should never live a life that is not really yours,' he advised me. 'You should always be yourself. There is nothing to be ashamed of in being a young person who has to struggle to get by!' I knew what he meant because it reflected exactly the integrity and pride that is part of our Banyamulenge tradition but I could not fully agree with him. I told him that, though I agreed with him in principle, I simply wouldn't be accepted by my social circle if they knew about the squalor I lived in. 'Be yourself' is not necessarily good advice to people in my position.

I did some consultancy work for a Dutch aid agency that was working on a development project in the Changungu area and also helped my Swiss friends at their orphanage who, unfortunately, were running into difficulties. On the one hand, the Swiss Embassy did not prioritise the support of orphans and, on the other, the Rwandan government was trying to improve the image of the country by challenging outside perception of the country based on its history and throwing off its reputation as a place swamped with humanitarian problems; it was considered that the existence of orphanages would give a bad impression to the outside world. They were trying to find a rapid solution to humanitarian issues and move on to reconstruction phase; while this was very good it required a slow process. With no support from either the government or the Swiss ambassador, The Swiss-Rwanda project of Jean Louis and Eliane was forced to close down and all the projects already under construction were simply abandoned.

It was heart breaking to see. I tried to make contact with government agencies that would help and we managed to get a brief extension but, basically, everyone concerned lost heart and decided to leave Rwanda. Jean Michel had already left as his volunteering term had ended. Jean Louis, not wanting to face the closure of the centre, had gone back to Geneva with no intention of returning. Eliane had fallen very ill in September 1999 and needed to return to Switzerland temporarily for treatment. She returned a few weeks later with a new young volunteer, Joelle Bucher, to help for two months with the final arrangements, but they both had to leave permanently in December 1999.

As an interim measure, I took over the running of the centre, trying to liaise with the Ministry of Family and Social Affairs and International NGOs, in search of host families for the children. Two of the children were particularly difficult to find suitable homes for because they had become very westernised. During the genocide they had been part of a group of 88 children who were taken to Italy where they had been fostered, sent to school, learnt the language and so on. However, the process of adoption was so involved that finally the Red Cross and the Italian authorities felt obliged to return them to Rwanda. After three years of living as Europeans in supportive homes, it was heart breaking for them to become African orphans again. It was a strange learning experience for me to discover that, in the developed countries, procedural policies to protect children within the law sometimes went beyond common sense. Another example of such bureaucracy happened during the genocide in Kigali. A group of children were stopped from boarding a plane because French soldiers could not accept children without a passport. These children consequently died. I found it difficult to comprehend how such things could happen. In an extreme humanitarian disaster, is it really necessary to ask if a desperately vulnerable child has the correct papers or a valid passport? In my opinion compromise is sometimes needed to take the best possible option even if it is not perfect.

It was a sad day when I had to officially turn the centre over to government authorities and surrender the vehicles, the lorry and the Nissan. My greatest worry, though, was in liaising with other humanitarian agencies trying to find families for all the children. Many had nowhere to go. It was terrible watching them leave the centre to go and look for somewhere to stay.

As they left, I felt it was time for me to leave too. First I went to Bujumbura in Burundi and stayed with a relative who was involved in peace-building work; then I went back to the Congo for a few weeks, hoping to find out all I could about my family. Unfortunately, it was too dangerous to go back to Minembwe so I could not actually meet them. At this time the country was divided into two with the main rebel movement occupying half of the country from the east to the centre. Peace deals were being initiated with the aim of forming a transition government that would control the whole country but meanwhile the East, ungoverned, was in a situation of statelessness and issues were worse than ever.

By this time, I had become convinced that the root cause of all the problems in the area was a combination of the mismanagement of regional and cross-border identities and extreme poverty. On the one hand the DRC (Congolese) authorities failed to recognise the country's diversity in culture and languages and the fact that these overlapped its borders; on the other hand poverty limits children's opportunities and pushes families towards doing anything simply to survive. These twin difficulties are exacerbated when ill-judged measures are taken to address them. Current initiatives tend to address conflict and poverty and deal with its consequences without getting to the root cause. The complexity of the real situation has remained unrecognised or undermined by aid policy makers so the efficacy of the measures they take has always been limited. As a consequence, countries like the DRC (Congo) continue to endure political and social turmoil.

All across the Great Lakes region, political tensions were becoming extremely violent and dangerous with Rwanda still very involved to protect its own security and survival. There seemed to be nothing I could do to help on a non-violent level. As a result, I decided that I could achieve more by leaving Africa and promoting human rights from outside this troubled area. I travelled from the DRC to Uganda, where I was helped by friends from a humanitarian agency to seek a new life elsewhere. Wherever that would be, I planned to campaign from there to raise awareness of human rights and search for solutions to the problems I know so well.

What I did not realise is how extremely difficult this journey was going to be for me personally. I had not fully considered that it would take me even further away from my parents for many years and I would not be able to even get news of them. On-going wars and conflicts meant I had not seen them for almost six years but now, with this new departure and not knowing where I would finally settle, it would be even longer before I could see them again. In my head I could still hear the voice of my mother in tears six years before as she asked if I really had no choice but to go. Louder and more persistent, though, was the voice of my father who had said: 'Genda aho uzagirira amahoro niho ubuturo buri'.

This means: 'Just go to somewhere, anywhere, that you will have peace and be able to survive. Then call that place home!'

As Desmond Tutu said, "If you are neutral in situations of injustice, you have chosen the side of the oppressor. If an elephant has its foot on the tail of a mouse and you say that you are neutral, the mouse will not appreciate your neutrality".

Epilogue

I HAVE NOW FOUND THAT SAFE PLACE in a quiet English town on the south coast of England. Here I live in peace with my wife and two small daughters who, I hope, will grow up enjoying full human rights and automatic access to education. Arriving in Hastings as an asylum seeker in 2000, I was hopeful but had no idea how well things would turn out for me. At that time, I spoke hardly any English and could not communicate with many people, including my fellow refugees who were from various war-torn regions. I was given a work permit after three months and, though my first jobs were not really what I wanted, I eventually found satisfying work within the voluntary sector. I attended the local College of Further Education where I learnt English and took other mainstream courses and then completed my Higher Education studies through Brighton University and a Masters degree through Sussex University.

I now have an MA in the Anthropology of Conflict, Violence and Conciliation and I have occupied different responsibilities in voluntary and public organisations. My studies involved me in a wide range of international research and advisory work which has helped me to realise my boyhood dream of being able to influence policies towards peace and sustainable development in Africa. In 2005, two years before I completed my Masters degree, I married Esther, the young girl mentioned in chapter 27. To win her was one thing but I had also to follow our tribal traditions, negotiating with my future in-laws and winning over the clans' elders through a series of traditional ceremonies, including offering a symbolic 'bride price' in the form of cattle to celebrate the new ties between the two families concerned. My happiness was complete when, in 2006, I finally managed to get news of my parents and learnt that they were still alive. Having left them thirteen years before, I was finally reunited with them. My parents' happiness was not about seeing me again but knowing that I live in a safe place and being reassured that I have

My wedding to Esther, 2005

Graduation, 2008

Our daughters, Abigail and Keziah, 2012

Reunited with my father after thirteen years, 2006

Left: In the name of Peace
– shaking hands with the
leader of the killers of my
family members, 2010

found a completely different world. This reminded me that, unlike in the modern world where achievement is measured by success, my first fifteen years of life were in a world that is more like how life must have been hundreds of years ago here – simply a question of survival.

Minembwe remains the focus of my greatest and happiest childhood memories but today life there is more difficult than ever. Not only do conditions for my parents and their fellow villagers remain harsh, but violence has continued to plague the region since 1996. In October 2011 there was a terrible incident involving the selective and cruel killing of seven people, among them some relatives, simply because of their Tutsi ethnicity; they were travelling towards my village in Minembwe. Health care in the region is almost non-existent and people still need to travel as far as 200km if they suffer from a serious condition. My parents are very elderly now and both ailing but, having such a high respect for his people's traditions, my father is resisting my attempts to move him and my mother to Rwanda. My brother, Noah, has never been found but is presumed dead.

One of my two younger brothers, Bonfils, is still a traditional herdsman but most of my other siblings have left the region for security reasons. My other younger brother, Ngirabakunzi, now lives in the Netherlands. My older brother Samuel and young sister Benite live in Rwanda. My cousin Samson lives in Belgium. My cousin Petero (Anti-Choc) lives in Florida (USA). My cousin-brother Ndoli, against all odds, has survived 22 years of conflict and he continues his fight for justice in DRC as an army colonel. I am convinced that, for the good of the region and its communities, all children should have an education. However, schooling is still seen as a privilege and is costly for ordinary people, who still live mainly by subsistence farming, the present annual fees for Primary being the equivalent of £60 and for Secondary about £100. It is difficult for villagers to find this money, especially for children orphaned by the on-going violence.

Recently, while preparing this book, I asked a friend to get certain details from my father about the horrific experiences he has endured. My father was surprised. "There is no point in going over all of that!" he said. In this I disagree with him: the world should know and this book is my testament to some of the suffering of my community.

Further reading

Dallaire, R. (2005). *Shake Hands With The Devil: The Failure of Humanity in Rwanda*, Arrow

Dallaire, R. (2011). *They Fight Like Soldiers, They Die Like Children*, Arrow

Dowdens, R. (2008). Africa, *Altered States, Ordinary Miracles*, Portabello books

Gashumba. U.F. (2007). *Chosen to Die: Destined to Live*, Sovereign World

Gasinzira, Muzuri, (1983). *Evolution des Conflits Ethniques dans l'Itombwe (Sud-Kivu)*, Memoire d'obtention du Licence en Histoire, Universite de Lubumbashi

Howard A. and Suhrke. A. (2000). *The Path of a Genocide: The Rwanda Crisis from Uganda to Zaire*, Transaction Publishers.

Hochschild, Adam. (1998). *King Leopold's Ghost*, London

Kingsolver, B. (1998). *The Poisonwood Bible*, Faber and Faber

London. C. (2007). *One Day the Soldiers Came, Voice of Children in War*, HarperCollins

Meredith, M. (2004). *The State of Africa: A history of fifty years of independence*. Free press

Melvern, L (2000). *A People Betrayed, The Role of the West in Rwanda' Genocide*, Zed Books

Mutambo, J. J., (1997). *Les Banyamulenge*, Imprimerie Saint Paul, Kinshasa

Ntung. A. (2007). *The influence of beliefs in witchcraft and prophecy on modern political processes in the conflicts in the Democratic*

Republic of Congo (DRC): Case studies from South Kivu,
MA Thesis, University of Sussex

Rukundwa, L. (2006). *Justice and righteousness in Matthean Theology and its relevance to the Banyamulenge community: a post-colonial reading*. Doctoral thesis, University of Pretoria

Ruhimbika. M. (2001). *Les Banyamulenge entre deux guerres*, Congo-Zaire, l'Harmattan (Paris)

Willame, J (1997). *Banyarwanda et Banyamulenge, Violences ethniques et gestion de l'identitaire au Kivu*, l'Harmattan (Paris)

Vlassenroot, K. "Identity and Insecurity: The Building of Ethnic Agendas in South Kivu", in Doom, R. & Gorus, J. (eds) (2000). *Politics of Identity and Economics of Conflicts in the Great Lakes Region*, VUB University Press, Brussels

Timeline

OF KEY POLITICAL EVENTS IN THE GREAT LAKES AREA

The huge country now known as the Democratic Republic of Congo (DRC) previously had other names and was Zaire during a large part of this autobiographical account. To avoid confusion, in this book it is usually referred to simply as the "Congo" and its people as "Congolese".

It is extremely difficult to simplify the history of this large area but the following notes provide a summary of key issues affecting this autobiography. For more in-depth analysis, see the recommended reading list.

Historical times: The Great Lakes is one of the areas most affected by artificial borders imposed by the colonial power. Previous to the "partition", Tutsi and Hutu were spread over a large area of central Africa, mostly in those places now known as Rwanda, Burundi, the south-west of Uganda and Eastern Congo. Probably about three hundred years ago, a group of Tutsi people moved mainly from what is now called Rwanda to the area now called South Kivu, DRC. As cattle herders, they were nomadic, moving when conditions made it necessary to move for the health of their families and cattle. Having this historical relationship and being trans-border communities, the descendants of these people speak related languages: Kirundi in Burundi, Kifumbira and Gikiga in Uganda, Kinyarwanda in Rwanda, Kinyamulenge in South Kivu, Kigogwe/Kinyejomba in North Kivu (Congo). The Tutsi of South Kivu are now known as Banyamulenge, meaning "people who live in hamlets in the hills"; this is a name that became popular in the 1970s.

1884:	**Partition of Africa** by the colonial powers: King Leopold of Belgium, who had funded the explorer Stanley, claimed a huge area, naming it The Belgian Free State. Germany was given land that is now Burundi and Rwanda. The divisions did not take into account tribal groupings and the straight lines drawn on a map were later to cause great problems (e.g. see Katanga/Shaba).
1908:	The Belgian Congo: Leopold's administration was brutal and it is estimated that he was responsible for the atrocious deaths of ten million innocent people. Following these tragedies that caused embarrassment and shame to European leaders, the Belgian government took over what was the Free State, renaming it The Belgian Congo. However, it was still viewed largely as an area to be exploited and little was done to develop the country for its "indigenous" people. French was the official language but there were more than a hundred African languages.
1912:	During the First World War, the Germans surrendered their land to the Belgians and it was renamed Ruanda-Urundi. Like the Germans, the Belgians allowed the traditional rule by Tutsi kingship to continue.
1950s:	European scholars developed theories around Tutsi and Hutu divisions based on physical features. Theories suggest that Tutsi were from North Africa and form part of upper class system. Some "scientific" experiments were operated to measure the size of Tutsi and Hutu noses. This encouraged an ideology of hatred.
1959:	Burundi asked for independence and the dissolution of Ruanda-Urundi.

1960: Hutu overthrew the Kingdom in Rwanda and later a Tutsi King was killed. Many Tutsi were massacred and large numbers fled to Burundi and other places.

30 June 1960: The Congo was given Independence from Belgium. Development had not been encouraged, there were very few educated Congolese people and the country was plunged into unrest. The name changed to simply The Congo. The president was Joseph Kasavubu and Patrice Lumumba was the Prime Minister. Lumumba was not well received by Western powers. By December 1960 he had been arrested and he was murdered in February 1961, some believe with US and Belgian backing.

July 1960–63: Katanga (now Shaba) secessionist war with Tshombe as leader of this new state. The United Nations Security Council sent in peace-keeping troops. The final deal included Tshombe becoming Prime Minister of the Congo.

1961: UN Secretary General, Dag Hammarskjold, whilst travelling to the Congo, was killed in an air crash.

1962: Burundi became independent and separate from Rwanda. The government was largely Tutsi.

1964–67: Mulelist Rebellion in the Congo: Lumumba's political party colleagues, led by Paul Mulele, started a rebellion based in the Eastern part of the country. Lumumba's ideas were seen as a communist threat by USA who backed Mobutu, an army corporal who had become a general at the time of Independence. He hired mercenaries to fight the rebels. Large areas of the country (including Uvira and Fizi) became a battle zone with foreign backing. Che Guevara operated for some time, supporting the Mulelists. Banyamulenge initially supported the Mulelist rebels, more as a matter of survival than out of any political conviction, but, when hungry, defeated Mulelists stole cattle to eat, they switched their allegiance to the nationalists.

1965: Joseph Mobutu overthrew and arrested President Kasavubu and Prime Minister Tshombe. It was the start of a 22 year dictatorship.

1966: Rise of Mai Mai nationalists and increased attacks on Banyamulenge villages. Rusimbana organised a Banyamulenge defence but was defeated and several massacres ensued. The worst was on 19 February when all the men of two villages were beheaded, supposedly for not having taken part in the Mulelist rebellion. This was followed by a massacre of another Banyamulenge village, Gugatongo.

1970s: The name "Munyamulenge" became widely used to distinguish the Tutsi of Congo (Zaire). The name means "people living in hamlets in the mountains". By the late 1970s, the Banyumalenge could no longer continue with their traditional nomadic lifestyle but continued a semi-nomadic way of living.

1971: Mobutu changed the name of the country to Zaire. Katanga became Shaba.

1972: Thousands of Hutu were massacred in Burundi following a revolt against the Tutsi-dominated government.

1973: Mobutu introduced the philosophy of "Zairianisation", calling it the "return to authenticity". He banned westernised names, including Christian names. Foreign-owned firms were nationalised and foreign investors forced out of the country. He seized lands and fortunes belonging to "white" investors.

1978:	Increased insurgency with the Congolese National Liberation Front trying to overthrow Mobutu. USA airlifted French and Belgian forces into the area to protect the white population but they effectively stopped the insurgence.
1979–85:	Mai Mai nationalist militias continued to target Banyamulenge cattle and herders in the area of Lulenge and Nganja.
1981–85:	The 1964 Mulelist rebellion was transformed into a racist identity ideology to discriminate and exterminate Congolese Tutsi specifically. The Law on Citizenship was re-written to reinforce this, making Banyamulenge and North Kivu Tutsi people foreigners (Rwandese). This ideology was soon exploited by extremist national leaders such as Anzuluni Bembe.
1990:	Mobutu repealed the authenticity law in Zaire (Congo) so people could again have "Christian" names etc.
1990:	The Rwandan Patriotic Front (RPF) was started by General Fred Rwigema and later taken over by Paul Kagame, exiled in Uganda, to fight for the rights of Rwandan people scattered around and in Rwanda. Many Congolese Tutsi (Banyamulenge and others) joined the movement because they perceived the exclusion of Rwandan Tutsi as similar to the persecution of all Rwandophone people in the region.
1991:	Destruction of the urns: Excluded from electoral rights, Banyamulenge destroyed electoral polling stations in the Fizi area.
1993:	Coup in Burundi leading to the assassination of the first democratically (Hutu) elected president. This led to the genocide of more than 300,000 Tutsi in Burundi.

April 6 1994: A plane carrying many important Hutu public figures (including the presidents of both Rwanda and Burundi) was shot down. At the time it was assumed that the Rwandan Patriotic Front (RPF) was responsible so retaliation against Tutsi began immediately. Between 800,000 and 1,000,000 people, mostly Tutsi but also Hutu moderates, were massacred in Rwanda. The truth of who shot down the plane is still under contention but it could have been the RPF, the former Rwandan Presidential Guard or even French troops.

1994: RPF won the war and formed a transitional government.

1993–94: Increased violence in the Congo against Banyamulenge as a result of the genocide in Burundi and Rwanda.

1994: The Banyamulenge were finally noticed internationally as one of the groups most severely affected by the genocide and general upheaval.

1994–95: The new Rwandan government, aware that the violent groups who had perpetrated the genocide had now found a base in the DRC, warned the International Community that they should address this issue. Rwanda insisted that, the world having failed to stop the 1994 genocide, the RPF (now the official Rwandan army) would take responsibility for dealing with these murderers.

March 1996: The Congolese (Zairian) national and regional leaders such as Anzuli Bembe, Kyembwe wa Lumona and Shekwa Mutabazi systematically planned and organised a massacre of Banyamulenge people in South Kivu. The main sites of the massacres became Baraka, Mboko, Abela, Ngandja, Kamanyola, Bukavu, Sange, Mutalule and Bwegera.

Sept 1996: Thousands of Tutsi of South Kuvu and North Kivu were forcibly and cruelly deported from Congo (Zaire) to Rwanda.

Oct 1996: Banyamulenge and other anti-Mobutu rebels, supported by Rwanda, asked Laurent Kabila to be their leader because, as he was not Tutsi, this would avoid the rebellion being seen as a Tutsi insurgency rather than an attempt to get rid of the dictator Mobutu.

March 1996: The Congolese (Zairean) government declared that all Tutsi in the country were foreigners.

1997: The Alliance of Democratic Forces for the Liberation of the Congo (AFDL) captured much of Eastern Zaire while Mobutu was away for medical treatment. This became known as the First War.

May 1997: Kinshasa fell to the AFDL rebels and Kabila was installed as the new president, the country was renamed the Democratic Republic of Congo(DRC).

July 1998: Kabila turned against the Banyamulenge and Banyamulenge people experienced hideous atrocities. Tutsi people were hunted and murdered everywhere in Congolese territory.

1998–2003: The Second War in DRC. Following peace talks, a transition government was set up in 2009.

1999: Massacre in Makobola village by member of the 'Rassemblement Congolais Pour la Democratie' rebel group.

1999–present: The United Nations establish a Peace Keeping Mission in Congo following the resolutions 1279 (1999) and 1291 (2000) of the United Nations Security Council to monitor the peace process of the Second Congo War. This became the largest UN peace keeping forces in history.

2000–2013:	More than 10 'nationalists' militia groups continue to operate in eastern DRC with a mission to exterminate Tutsi or Rwandophone people.
2001:	Laurent Kabila was assassinated by his body guard. His son Joseph Kabila became president.
2004:	A selective massacre of Banyamulenge people in the Gatumba (Burundi) refugee camp.
2006:	The first democratic national election in DRC.
2006–2009:	Another rebellion was led by a Tutsi from North Kivu called General Laurent Nkunda. It ended with his arrest by the Rwandan army in 2009.
2012–present:	A rebellion called M23 is going on. M23 claims that it will fight for the rights of Congolese people; they want to address internal governance issues and to provide protection of Rwandophone communities (Tutsi and Hutu) who continue to experience persecution.

About the author

 **Alex Mvuka Ntung** has a background in international development with a particular focus on conflict transformation, peacebuilding and sustainable development. With an MA in Anthropology of Conflict, Violence and Conciliation from Sussex University, he has conducted a wide range of research on the Great Lakes Region of Africa. In the UK, he has occupied various responsibilities in voluntary and public organisations in areas of inclusion, equality and social cohesion. He is an independent researcher on matters relating to human rights and political violence, and is an expert on the DRC. He is a regular international speaker on matters relating to asylum and migration, war and security, cultural sensitivity in conflict resolution. English is his fifth language.

"A compelling story of the triumph of humanity over ludicrous odds. This book gives a rich and unprecedented insight into the life of a community fighting for its very existence while a failing state falls apart around them."

Richard Wilson, author of *Titanic Express* and *Don't Get Fooled Again*